"If there's only one book to read to understand how to become a champion for life, *Contenders* is that book. As expected from a skilled debater, he lays out a structured and compelling call for caring individuals to be a voice for the voiceless. Whether you sense a call to engage, or simply want to understand the arguments in play better, *Contenders* is the book to read now."

— **Jor-El Godsey**. President, Heartbeat International

"Marc is one of the most insightful and clear thinking communicators in the world today. His understanding of the Pro-life discussion in its varied and personal aspects is second to none and everyone we know would benefit from reading this book."

— **Bill and Pam Farrel**, directors of Love-Wise.com and authors of *Men Are Like Waffles, Women Are Like Spaghetti*

"In *Contenders*, Marc Newman — one of the most articulate and experienced communicators on life issues — delivers a wakeup call to the Christian church and provides a step-by-step roadmap to help us think more clearly, speak more persuasively, and act more compassionately. Read this book, become a *Contender*, and let God work through you to change hearts and minds, help expectant mothers, and save lives."

— **David Bereit**, Founder, 40 Days for Life

"Marc Newman has been training prolifers to communicate the truth more effectively for over three decades. From his experiences as a university speech professor and debate coach Marc brings a unique set of gifts, skills and know-how to his book *Contenders*. I happily recommend this book to everyone who wants to speak up more skillfully for those who cannot speak for themselves."

— **Randy Alcorn**, author of *ProLife Answers to ProChoice Arguments* and *Why ProLife?*

"Abortion only exists with the consent of a sleeping church. Thus, *Contenders* provides the body of Christ with a much needed wake up call. It also provides readers with the intellectual ammunition needed to rebut the arguments of those who would justify harming the weakest amongst us. This book is both brilliantly written and desperately needed. I cannot recommend it highly enough."
— **Dr. Mike S. Adams**, Professor of Criminology, University of North Carolina Wilmington and author of *Letters to A Young Progressive.*

"*Contenders* shows how any of us can play a unique and vital role in creating a seismic societal shift toward life. For every Christian, *Contenders* is the right read, at just the right time."
— **Kirk Walden**, Pro-Life Speaker and Host of The Faith Revolution Podcast, author of *The Wall*

"*Contenders* takes what you believe about human value and human rights, and grounds it firmly in the science and moral reasoning that explains why you stand for life, and then—and here is the payoff—shows you how to communicate it persuasively."
— **John Ensor**, President, PassionLife

"*Contenders* is a must-have manual for every believer. If you truly believe the Bible from cover to cover then we all have a civic duty to speak clearly and boldly against abortion. This book helps you do just that. Lives are depending on it. 3,000 lives a day to be exact. There is revival waiting when we finally speak out and unmask the abortion giant in our communities. What are you waiting for?"
— **Valerie Millsapps**, Executive Director, Pregnancy Resource Center, Maryville, TN

"Compelling and powerful, *Contenders* is both a clarion call and real-world toolkit to contend for the lives of the unborn. A must read for all church leaders!"
— **Barry Poudrier**, Discipleship Pastor, Grace Church, Reno, Nevada

"This is a powerful and practical book. *Contenders* should be in every pastor's, priest's, minister's, teacher's and layperson's hands not just their libraries. It is an operation manual and it needs to be used."
— **Rev. Dr. Thomas J. Carmody, PhD.**, Anglican priest, Professor of Communication Studies, Vanguard University

"Christians should desire to be confident in addressing this issue in defense of life, and Marc Newman's book will lay out a firm foundation for our ability to do just that. Get the book. Read the book. Church, it is time to armor up for LIFE."

— **Connie Wyatt-Coleman**, CEO, Wise Choices PRC

"The new must-read book of the pro-life movement, those interested in advocating for the life of the human being in the womb should not miss it."

— **Andrew J. Harris**, Associate Professor of Communication, Cedarville University

"*Contenders* creates a great marriage between philosophy, church application and practicality for those who want to begin or readjust their strategy to further the pro-life cause."

— **Christopher Hilken**, Apologist, Teaching Pastor and Young Adult Pastor, North Coast Church, Vista, California

"Marc provides straightforward, compelling, and persuasive arguments. His writing is well-researched, so the academic pastor will appreciate the wealth of background material referenced, but it is very accessible to the average person in the pew. Marc gives you the tools to vigorously and passionately contend for the pro-life position."

— **Stephen Wheeler**, President, White Fields Ministry

"*Contenders* equips women and men, young and old, to make a comprehensive case for life with timeless reasoning and up to date research. Dr. Newman does not write behind a wall of cultural separation, but with countless interactions with real people and real worldviews. If you are anything like me, you will read this with a pen and highlighter in hand because you will find yourself referring back to it over and over again as you seek to contend for life."

— **Dr. Jason Salyer**, Student Teaching Pastor, Carmel Baptist Church, Matthews, NC

CONTENDERS

CONTENDERS

A Church-Wide
Strategy
to Unmask Abortion,
Defeat Its Advocates,
Empower Christians, and
Change the World

MARC NEWMAN

FOREWORD BY SCOTT KLUSENDORF

Refocus
PRESS
Sevierville, Tennessee

Contenders
Copyright © 2020 by Marc Newman
Published by Refocus Press, Sevierville, TN 37862

For bulk purchases, contact Refocus Press at *www.refocuspress.com*

All rights reserved. No part of this publication may be reproduced, stored in a retrieval system or transmitted in any form by any means, electronic, mechanical, photocopy, recording or otherwise, without the prior permission of the publisher, except for brief quotations for use in critical reviews or articles.

Cover Design: Daniel O. Ojedokun
Book Design: Bruce DeRoos

Scripture quotations taken from the New American Standard Bible® (NASB), Copyright © 1960, 1962, 1963, 1968, 1971, 1972, 1973, 1975, 1977, 1995 by The Lockman Foundation. Used by permission. www.Lockman.org

Printed in the United States of America

ISBN: 978-1-7351962-0-6 (*paperback*)
ISBN: 978-1-7351962-1-3 (*hardback*)
ISBN: 978-1-7351962-2-0 (*e-book*)

Contents

Foreword

'veᅠtaught pro-life apologetics for thirty years, but Marc Newman said something in August 1995 that truly changed how I view pro-life advocacy and evangelism.

Marc had selected fifteen aspiring pro-life leaders to go through his one-day "Pro-Life Speaker Training Seminar" in the conference room at the La Quinta Inn of Vista, California. I jumped at the opportunity to learn from the best.

Besides moderating dozens of public exchanges on abortion and other hot topics, Marc taught competitive speech and debate at Palomar College, where his students routinely took top awards in national tournaments. As expected, in just six hours, I got a crash course in public speaking that equipped me to reach millions of lay Christians with compelling pro-life content through both media and public presentations.

Twenty-five years later, I'm still using the speaking tactics I learned from Marc that day.

But I got something more from Marc when he provided the missing link between abortion and evangelism that's stifled the pro-life movement for decades. For years, pro-lifers have heard, "The church is about saving souls, not saving babies. Don't distract us with political stuff." Marc buried that false dichotomy with a single sentence:

"One of the greatest obstacles to evangelism today is the body of a dead child."

That's more than 60 million bodies since 1973. Think of Yankee Stadium filled 1,200 times over—and that's just the beginning. For each woman who aborts, there's a boyfriend, parent, friend, or co-worker who also played a role in her decision. If we assume three people involved in each abortion (a conservative estimate), that's 180,000,000 Americans who've participated in abortion. Many of these people sit in our churches with unresolved abortion guilt.

How is that *not* a discipleship issue?

In the Great Commission (Matthew 28:18-20), Christ commands His church to make disciples. Making disciples means teaching them to obey all that Christ commands. One of those commands forbids us from shedding innocent blood (Exodus 23:7; Proverbs 6:16-19; Matthew 5:21). Abortion sheds innocent blood. Thus, abortion connects directly to the disciple-making responsibilities of the local church. Why, then, do many church leaders prefer to let parishioners figure it out for themselves?

Tim Keller, perhaps the most popular pastor in evangelicalism today, calls abortion wrong and says unborn children deserve better treatment. He doesn't preach on the subject, however, because "pushing moral behaviors before we lift up Christ is religion," a thing Jesus warns against. The biblical approach to controversial sins, Keller says, is to preach the gospel and let people arrive at the right conclusion. He mentions an Ivy League graduate, a lawyer from Manhattan, who thanked him for not focusing on abortion from his pulpit. Her history included three abortions. Eventually, the woman converted to Christianity under Keller's influence. Later she approached him to ask, "Do you think abortion is wrong?" He said yes. She replied, "I am coming to see that maybe there is something wrong with it."[1]

I'm glad she eventually figured it out, but what are we to conclude? That pastoral silence in the face of child sacrifice is an acceptable means of evangelism? Marc argues that we don't have to choose between our Christian witness and pro-life advocacy. We can and should pursue both as biblically grounded Christians.

Step one is truth telling within our own churches. Marc has a clear and pointed thesis: Abortion is not *like* Molech worship, it *is* Molech worship—even if it doesn't go by that name. Both Molech worship and abortion promise people that they can solve their pressing problems outside the counsel of Scripture. When you pay a price to solve a pressing life problem, we often call that price a "sacrifice." Abortion is the practice of paying a price—a child's life—to solve a life problem. Thus, abortion is indeed child sacrifice, which means pastoral silence on the issue hurts our Christian witness.

Step two is knowing how we got here. How did we shift from an old ethic of treating every human being as equally valuable to a new one that treats human life as a mere commodity? And how does that new ethic impact our churches? We need insight to understand why people adopt a destructive new ethic. Marc provides it.

Step three is equipping Christians to engage ideas hostile to the knowledge of God (2 Cor. 10:5). That means learning how abortion-choice advocates argue; in particular, how they shift their responses when confronted with persuasive pro-life truths. If you recognize these shifts, you can direct critics back to your central pro-life argument and keep the main thing the main thing.

At this point, you might think, *Why bother? I just want to do evangelism, and everyone knows that you can't argue anyone into the kingdom.* That's a half-truth. You also can't love them into the kingdom or preach them into the kingdom. Without the Spirit of God moving on human hearts, nothing works to awaken dead souls to their need for a Savior. But with the Spirit, many tactics work to draw people to Christ—including truth telling, insight, and engagement at the idea level.

As Marc often says, pro-life presentations, either to large audiences or one-on-one, invite unbelievers to look deeper. They plant the premise that if Christianity is true on a key moral issue, then maybe it deserves another look beyond that moral issue. An email I received about my Wayne State debate with Nadine Strossen illustrates Marc's point:

> Because of your recent debate with Nadine, my sister-in-law (who is not a believer) moved from a radical pro-abortion stance to an abortion-only-in-cases-of-rape stance. A few weeks after that change, she was reading a pro-abortion article in a magazine, and as she read their arguments, your answers kept running through her head. She realized that their arguments were completely bankrupt in light of your answers. On that day, she became completely and totally against abortion for any reason. This has provided me with solid opportunities to share the gospel with her.

Pro-life Christians don't have to pick between defending unborn lives and being good ambassadors for Christ. We can and must do both. That's why you need the training Marc provides in this book.

Since August 1995, Marc's been my go-to guy for talk development, debate debriefing, pro-life strategy planning, and banquet speaking. When a brief illness grounded me in 2015, Marc took my place at a youth conference with only twenty-four hours' notice. He delivered my exact talk with such mastery that nobody knew the difference. I thought, *How on earth did he just pull that off?* Answer: He's that good.

And now it's your turn to learn from the best. Don't just read this book. Master it—for the sake of saving souls and lives!

—**Scott Klusendorf,** June 2020
President, Life Training Institute
Author, *The Case for Life: Equipping Christians to Engage the Culture*

Acknowledgments

Thanks must begin with fellow pro-life advocates Scott Klusendorf, president of Life Training Institute, John Ensor of PassionLife Ministry, and Kirk Walden, president of LifeTrends. Your friendship, writings, prayers, and perseverance for the cause of life inspire me.

Thanks also to Jor-El Godsey and Bill and Pam Farrel who provided invaluable feedback in the creation of this book.

Students in my Applied Bioethics classes (special shout out to the A-Team!) and every center director and pastors who responded to questionnaires—all experts in their own fields who willingly shared their ideas, stories, and best practices with me—thank you.

Thanks to Arthur Ellison and Rev. Bob Foust. Without Arthur, I wouldn't have found my way to this ministry, and without Bob's prayers and encouragement, I wouldn't have had the courage to retire early from academia to throw myself entirely into this work.

As always, thanks are due to Grace Hoxsey. If she wouldn't have come to lunch that day, looked over my materials, and said she'd send seven of her staff to my first open training, I don't know that this book would exist.

Melissa Jordan, my longsuffering assistant, who coordinates my pastor trainings, apologetics sessions, and cheerfully interacts with everyone while wrangling my schedule—I appreciate you.

Thank you to my editor, Steve Halliday, whose comments and critique made this a better and more useful read. Any mistakes or errors are my own.

And to my other editor, Sharon Newman, the professional proofreader who married me because she thought I "had potential." Thank you for your endless patience, your constant love and care, and your unflagging support and partnership. Nothing I do would be possible without you.

To Almighty God, the Author of Life, be all the glory.

Introduction

The Gauntlet

A pro-life sidewalk counselor named Mary regularly stands, prays, and counsels young women heading into a local abortion clinic. She hopes to talk with them as they walk from the parking lot to try to convince them that they have more options than abortion to deal with their untimely pregnancy. Mary's done this for a long time.

Over weeks, months, and years, she's not only spoken to many women, but she's even struck up conversations with the clinic's abortionist. Repeatedly, she'd call out to him, "Would you please just come to church?"

One day, after innumerable such requests, the doctor stopped, walked up to her, and said, "I'll tell you what, Mary. I *will* come to your church. I will start coming to your church the minute your church *stops coming to me.*"

He meant *for abortions.*

I first heard this true story in the introduction to a speech by Jon DeLange, one of my speech students in the Applied Bioethics program. The story simultaneously riveted and dismayed me—riveted by Mary's courage and perseverance, dismayed by the hubris in the doctor's reply.[2]

I need to make something clear from the outset: this doctor did not make a political claim. He did not make a moral claim. He made a metaphysical claim and in so doing threw down a spiritual gauntlet.

The abortion doctor clearly implied, "Mary, your church and your pastor say that in your Bible you have all of the answers to life's most pressing questions. But it's a lie. When your people find themselves pregnant and they really don't want to be, they don't come to you; they come to me. I have the answer for the most pressing questions in their lives, not you."

You can tell him all day long that he's wrong, but his experience tells him he's right.

Challenge Accepted

Abortion became legal throughout the United States in 1973, and in some states even before that. Over that time, it has exterminated the lives of more than 60 million unborn children and injured well over 180 million mothers, fathers, family members, friends, and abortion clinic staff members in this nation alone. Some Christians have been and are fighting mightily for the lives of such children, and for the protection of all the others. If that's you, you need to know that God sees, approves, and will continue to strengthen you in that quest.

Others have been impotent while most have remained silent, sidelined by a culture that tells them to keep quiet. Unequipped to respond, far too many Christians become little more than bystanders, watching helplessly as violence preys on the weakest and most defenseless of their brothers and sisters.

The persuasive power of abortion—the narrative that promises a quick, permanent solution to a temporary problem—can be stopped. Its ravaging effects can be reversed. And it must begin with us.

Since you're reading this book, I believe you also want to see individual Christians, and the church, wield that kind of world-changing influence in the lives of everyone experiencing an untimely pregnancy.

My Story

I had my first interaction with the pro-life movement when I served as the Director of Speech and Debate at the University of California at Irvine. The associate pastor of my church, Arthur Ellison, took a one-year leave of absence to take on the role of executive director of this thing called a "crisis pregnancy center." He called and asked if I would train his staff in public speaking.

Like any good consultant, I said, "sure."

Then I asked what his people did. He explained, but it soon became clear I knew nothing at all about abortion, about crisis pregnancy, about the law, or about anything remotely related to his work. But I was a pretty good speech coach, and as an academic, a solid researcher. So I asked him to send me some seed articles and books that I'd use to retrofit training material I already had for corporate executives.

What started as a one-off seminar for a small center exploded into a nationwide training schedule—The Pro-Life Speaker Seminar—involving not only pregnancy help centers, but other pro-life direct-action and educational organizations. Along the way, a pregnancy help center director asked me, "Do you keynote banquets?" Again, like a good consultant, I said, "Sure." That first dessert banquet in Minnesota led to hundreds more, working with incredible directors and their staffs and raising tens of millions of dollars for these invaluable, life-saving organizations.

I continued as an academic, and while presenting at the National Communication Association's national conference, I happened to sit in on a session where scholars tore into Bernard Nathanson's film *The Silent Scream.* During the Q and A following, I stood up and engaged the panelists in what, in Washington D.C., would have been called "a frank and open discussion." Afterward, out in the hall, a man who sat two rows behind me stepped up and introduced himself.

David Mall was one of the great academic voices of the pro-life movement, serving as Executive Director of Americans United for Life and Illinois Right to Life. But on this day he didn't share his bio with me; he simply asked, "How would you like to speak at the National Right to Life convention?" Like a good consultant once more, I said, "Sure." A year or two later, David Mall and I co-taught a workshop. Dave spoke for fifteen minutes and graciously handed over to me the rest of the program. Next thing I knew, I began training statewide National Right to Life affiliates in Michigan and Wisconsin, with members of affiliates regularly present at my seminars.

I planned none of this. But I also don't believe it "just happened."

I took the assignments as they came and said "yes" to opportunities I believe God orchestrated. My wonderful wife, Sharon, was and is extremely supportive, despite the long extra hours and the time away from home and from our sons. Over the years, I have met incredible pro-life colleagues, speakers, and debaters; worked with directors of leading-edge centers and clinics; and continued to hone pro-life messaging strategies. I have been blessed.

Contenders comes out of that mix of time, people, and an unquenchable desire to see strategic messaging on abortion—one of the most significant spiritual issues of our day—make its way out of professional and volunteer pro-life organizations. I wanted this strategy in the hands of every Christian with a voice and a will to do right.

What This Book Is and Who It's For

I designed *Contenders* as a church-wide messaging strategy about abortion.

Church-wide means that it's for everyone in the church. "Everyone" means pastors, small group leaders, youth pastors, Sunday School teachers, or anyone who influences others, whether in person or on social media. If you talk to people, you have a place in these pages.

It's for women.

It's also for men.

A bizarre, politically-driven misconception calls abortion "a women's issue," which means that if you don't have a uterus, you don't get an opinion. The claim is so obviously false that it embarrasses me to have to refute it. Abortion affects men, women, boys, and girls. It's also a public policy issue surrounded by a host of scientific, moral, political, and theological arguments, *none* of which is rendered true or untrue by the gender of the person making the claims.

Abortion-choice supporters like to make this "no men" argument while keeping their thumbs on the scales. They don't really mean that no men should have any voice. They don't mind when, for example, a "men's magazine" such as *Playboy* advocates for abortion choice and financially supports it (as it has for decades), or when men in the media or the political class argue for them as allies. Abortion-choice advocates raise objections only when *pro-life* men raise their voices.

Gentlemen, you have self-censored for too long.

Contenders aims to educate, motivate, and activate you, not only so you can vocally defend the rights of unborn children to live, but so you can champion those organizations—staffed almost exclusively by women—who make that possible. They have grown tired of fighting this battle with one arm tied behind their backs. They desperately need male reinforcements.

Strategy means an overall campaign plan supported by a series of tactics. Tactics are the actual means used to implement a strategy. The subtitle of *Contenders* explains the purpose of the strategy: to unmask abortion, defeat its advocates, empower Christians, and change the world. The tactics include:

- increasing information about the significance of the battle
- scouting the field occupied by the opponent
- understanding our own weaknesses and strengthening our approach
- protecting the vulnerable
- creating enduring alliances that call upon and deploy our various God-given abilities and resources in order to achieve our goals.

By knowing the truth, rightly assessing our resources and abilities, and engaging our will to do God's will, we can accomplish great things. Rescuing innocent and vulnerable unborn humans from the violence of abortion is among the most critical.

What This Book Is Not

Do not expect *Contenders* to provide a detailed philosophical analysis of every argument ever put forth by every professional academic philosopher on the subject of abortion. Many books already do an admirable job in this department; you will find them cited throughout the coming chapters. If you want to engage at that level, everything you need to know is right there, in the end notes.

But you probably don't need to discuss abortion at the level of a professional academic philosopher. Why not? The overwhelming majority of people who say they support an abortion-choice position continue to make the same, old, defeated arguments they always have. So far, however, no one's informed them of their faulty reasoning, or explained why the pro-life counter-evidence devastates abortion-choice arguments.

It's not entirely their fault. They may never have encountered those claims or that evidence. But you will, and those claims and evidence will prepare you to make careful, well-reasoned arguments in defense of the lives of unborn children.

In the unlikely event you encounter a professional academic philosopher who engages you with arguments you don't understand, write down the key terms, and if you know where to look for answers, do some research. In the meantime, for such rare occasions, you can memorize this pride-killing (that's a good thing), yet effective, sentence: "I don't know, but I'll find out."

Terms

No book dealing with abortion can avoid controversy over terms. Different people have different approaches to handling the names for the various positions people take, as well as the words they choose to use when labeling what they're discussing.

No choice

When Randy Alcorn wrote *ProLife Answers to ProChoice Arguments*,[3] he chose to refer to both sides according to their own preferred terms—a strategic choice. Alcorn had written a book designed as a resource and knew that people who self-identified as "pro-choice" might feel put off by being called, for example, "pro-abortion." Christopher Kaczor used the same terms in writing his scholarly work *The Ethics of Abortion*,[4] adding the term "defenders of abortion" and "critics of abortion" for variety.

Over the years, the terms have morphed for people who argue in favor of abortion. As a rhetorician, I am well aware of the influence of words, and "pro-choice" was a smart and powerful identifier. It combined the benefits of sounding positive with a word that evoked "freedom." Who doesn't want the freedom to choose?

For those arguing against that position, however, the term rang hollow. The pro-choice movement didn't *want* to identify what they were choosing; and once the truth came out, it became apparent that they didn't offer much in the way of choices. The term concealed, rather than revealed, the true purpose of the movement.

Other descriptors evolved. Many on both sides rejected "pro-abortion." Some thought it went too far, because, after all, who is really "in favor" of abortion? (As you will read, in some circles, the situation has radically changed.) They really want women to have the *right* to have an abortion, regardless of the personhood of the one aborted.

"Abortion-rights advocate," for quite a while, became a more acceptable designation. It identified those who advocated, not for abortion specifically, but for abortion rights. Then some pro-life advocates started thinking that the term assumed rather than proved that there existed such a thing as abortion rights. Francis Beckwith, in his book *Defending Life*, chose alternative terms: "abortion-choice defenders" or "advocates."[5]

In this book, I will use the term "abortion choice" and identify those believing in or using arguments for that position as "abortion-choice supporters" or "abortion-choice advocates."

I choose the term "pro-life supporter" and "pro-life advocate" primarily because, while I have no problem being called "anti-abortion," those who oppose abortion don't reject it in the abstract. They oppose abortion because it *kills human persons*, and they want to defend *lives* from its intended violence.

"Supporters," as used in reference to both abortion choice and pro-life, refer to people who "lean" toward one side or the other, even though many likely couldn't make a significant defense of their position. "Advocates," on the other hand, are key influencers well-versed, at minimum, in the rationale for the arguments on their own side; they often know well the arguments advanced by their opponents. While virtually all supporters can be persuaded, some advocates are so committed to their cause that they will not, under any circumstances, be moved.

Targets of abortion

Abortion-choice advocates bristle when pro-lifers use the word "baby" to refer to the being in a woman's body after conception. They argue that it's not medically accurate, as they say the term *baby* is reserved for offspring after they are born. Often, they substitute developmental terms such as "zygote," "embryo," and "fetus." But these medical terms create their own problem. The rhetoric of abortion-choice advocates works so hard to deny the humanity and personhood of unborn children that these medical developmental terms, while accurate, obscure the matter rather than clarify it.

And there are other problems. Organizations that once opposed abortion but now have become its most ardent supporters, at one time freely used the word "baby" to describe the being in the womb. In order to clear up any confusion, in this book, for the sake of variety, I will use the terms "baby," "offspring," "child," "unborn child," and similar words. Frequently, I will use the phrase "human being in the womb" to identify what is inside a woman's body from the moment of conception. No one can argue either the descriptor or the location. It's not my opinion; it's scientific fact.

Pregnancy help centers and clinics

The organizations that actively engage in the rescue of unborn children from abortion use diverse names. Some are volunteer entities; others are staffed entirely by paid professionals; and many fall in between. They are known variously as:

Crisis Pregnancy Centers (or CPCs)
Pregnancy Care Centers (or PCCs)
Pregnancy Help Organizations (or PHOs)
Pregnancy Resource Centers or (PRCs)
Pregnancy Help Centers/Clinics (or PHCs)

All of these groups also exist variously as medical clinics. For the sake of simplicity, unless I reference a particular location, I will refer to all of these organizations as PHCs. You can read that acronym contextually as Pregnancy Help Center or Pregnancy Help Clinic.

A Painful Read, A Hope-filled Promise

A few chapters in *Contenders* may feel painful for you to read. If you're unfamiliar with the abortion issue, you may find the information you encounter both shocking and distressing. The truth can be that way. If you've had or been involved with an abortion in your past, your reading may reawaken feelings you once suppressed or forgot. Abortion is a difficult subject.

While I have aimed this book at the church, I can't assume that everyone who picks it up and reads it is a believer in Jesus. And even if you are a believer, I know that many Christians have been victims of abortion. As you read, if uncomfortable feelings arise, don't ignore them. But neither allow those feelings about past sin to define you.

The shed blood of Jesus makes forgiveness and healing available to *all* for *all* sins. If you don't know Him, seek out a Christian who can introduce you to the Savior. If you do know Jesus and have never confessed the abortion in your past (or any other sin), now is the time. No transgression lies outside the reach of His love and mercy. Just ask.

God not only will forgive your sin, but He will redeem your past and empower you to join the millions of believers who have told others of His mercy and goodness.

You, too, can be a Contender.

All Clear? Let's Begin

My dad, Lt. Col. B.B. Newman, always taught us that the first key to solving a problem is understanding it. "You can't change anybody's mind on a topic," he insisted, "until you know why they believe what they believe."

In the course of reading this book, you'll come to know what abortion really is, what its supporters and advocates believe, and why. By the time you've finished, you'll have a strategy to unmask abortion, defeat its advocates, empower Christians, and change the world.

Let's get started.

Part One

What We're Up Against

"What're you doing?" A server at a local restaurant I frequent wanted to know why I was sitting at the table with a big stack of paper to my left and a smaller one on my right. I was trying to make sure my iced tea didn't sweat on my work.

"I'm doing revisions on the book I'm writing."

"Oh yeah? What's it about?"

I provided my standard answer when trying to get work done and don't want to be drawn into a conversation just then, much like I do when jammed in the middle seat on an airplane.

"Bioethics." That usually gets a look, followed by freedom to work. But she had questions.

"What's that?"

"Bioethics covers a wide range of topics, such as euthanasia, embryonic stem cell research, and abortion. I train and speak for pregnancy help centers and clinics like the one here in town. I'm pro-life."

One of her male co-workers, standing nearby, commented, "Pro-life? Is that the side that's for abortion? What are the sides called? I can't ever remember."

I lowered my red pen and launched into a brief lecture (an occupational hazard) about the common terms for both sides in the abortion controversy, why "pro-choice" is not a very descriptive term for abortion-choice supporters, and...

"What's your opinion?" The female server cut to the chase.

"I don't have an *opinion*," I told her. "I have a position backed by scientific evidence and moral reasoning. What's in a woman's body from the moment of conception is a separate, distinct human being, and abortion intentionally kills that human being. It's not my opinion, it's a medical fact. And intentionally killing innocent human beings is wrong."

I answered a few more questions, both of them appeared thoughtful, and then both they and I went back to work. You'll find out later in this book that exchanges like these happen a lot.

After years of advocacy on the issue of abortion, you'd think that most people would know more about it. But one of the reasons it's difficult to discuss the issue is that so many people know so little about the true nature of abortion.

The church is not immune.

The first section of this book starts by unmasking the true nature of abortion. It's worse than most people believe. Then I'll examine why so many in the church have heard so little about abortion—although they've heard plenty of advocacy from abortion-choice supporters—and the fatally-flawed reasons given by messengers in the church for why they don't speak about it. Even when we do raise our voices in support of human beings in the womb, we get cultural pushback. But getting around resistance and overcoming objections is precisely what we need to do if we intend to speak truth in the midst of a dark world.

So let's examine the field we're about to enter and get an inkling of what it takes to be a Contender.

Chapter 1

Just Imagine What's at Stake

magine that a vacant lot sits next to your church. One day a construction fence goes up, and you discover that the lot won't remain vacant much longer—another church will build right next to yours. Prospective members can view the construction plans posted online. When a large sign with the church's URL appears on the fence, you decide to have a look.

At first, you have nothing but mundane concerns. With a sparkling new church next door, you may have to spend some money on your long-neglected physical plant. But when you examine the building designs for this new church, the size of its foyer startles you, along with its expansive fellowship hall and the beautiful landscaping planned for its extensive grounds. Then you notice the tag on the bottom of the plans, indicating the occupants of the new facility: The Church of Jesus Christ of Latter-Day Saints.

You know of this religious organization's robust family programs and other social events. Sure enough, after the doors open, friendly, well-dressed couples, shepherding their energetic children, come streaming into the facility. Only a small strip of grass separates your parking lots. Your people start to chat with their people, and before long, acquaintances begin to form. And why wouldn't they? Much of what your congregants see seems very appealing.

The next thing you know, a few of your families decide to head next door to hear what these "other Christians" with a different "testimony" about Jesus have to say. Three weeks later, the number has grown to ten. And a couple of senior high school girls from your church begin to hang around the handsome, new Mormon "elders."

What do you do?

Most pastors to whom I have related this scenario tell me that they would alter their preaching—and they wouldn't save it for a less-attended Wednesday evening service. Recognizing the spiritual danger, they would begin a sermon series on topics such as the Deity of Christ, Biblical Eschatology, and a comparative analysis of orthodox Christian doctrine with that of the Mormon Church (and they might throw in the Jehovah's Witnesses for good measure).

When I ask if they already have preached such sermons, some pastors sheepishly look away. No, they haven't. Why not? The next door lot still remains "vacant" in their minds, and they have other things to talk about. Since they don't perceive an imminent threat, they don't feel a pressing need to act.

Let's shift the scenario a bit.

Now, instead of a Mormon church, let's suppose that a Middle Eastern religious organization has purchased the vacant lot next to your church. Mounds of foreign money enables the building to go up quickly. As before, the facility looks impressive, slick, and inviting. Once again, only a small strip of grass separates their parking lot from yours.

Not only do the worshipers next door appear well-dressed and friendly, they begin to trade on the interesting differences between their faith and that of your church, which, by comparison, might seem a bit too tame, mundane, dusty, and (truth be told) boring. The faith of these people seems exciting and appealing. Like yours, it has roots in an ancient religious tradition, but they present it as a modern path to freedom that comes with spectacular promises.

The folks at the new worship center get to know your parishioners and their problems. They tell your people that if they have financial difficulties, they need only come to the worship center, because they have answers that work. No matter the problem, the worship center has an easy fix. Conflict with a spouse or with a boyfriend or girlfriend? They can smooth it over. Trouble completing school? They have just the solution. Body image issues? They can help them go away. Not feeling desirable? These people promise to help you get your mojo back.

And they don't just make postcard promises; they have testimonials about how this new way of life has both liberated and empowered their followers. No more "slave religions," they say. The time has come to embrace real freedom.

To benefit from these seductive promises, they claim your people have only to commit to come to the worship center, bringing their children with them. If they will do just that, the most significant issues they face can quickly become things of the past.

Some of your people decide to worship at the center, and then begin reporting back to their friends, your other congregants. One family after another begins to visit next door. Pretty soon, ten, fifteen, maybe twenty percent of your congregation has visited.

What do you do?

When I've laid out this second scenario at pastoral training sessions, I often get the same responses as to the one for the new Mormon church next door. Pastors say they would start a series on the distinctions between orthodox Christian doctrine and Islam. They might spend some time discussing Islam's origins, distinctions between the Bible and the Koran, or create an apologetics and witnessing team to try to win over their neighbor and, at the same time, protect their parishioners.

I tell these pastors, "You have just one problem with your proposed response. The Middle Eastern worship center in my hypothetical scenario isn't Islam, and the god worshiped there is not Allah. The worship center I have in mind is dedicated to a different Middle Eastern deity, one of the Punic gods that once held sway over the entire region: Molech."

The church must look beyond mere appearances to the spiritual underpinnings of ideas if it expects to recognize opponents of the gospel. Those who champion evil often portray themselves as humanitarians, as seeking the good of those they intend to devour.

Such a worship center dedicated to a pagan god is very far from hypothetical. Don't get too comfortable with the thought that it hasn't set up shop next door to your church; in fact, it's poaching your parishioners *right now*. How is this possible?

Pagan deities in the modern era tend to prefer a more clandestine operation than in the distant past. As C.S. Lewis, a brilliant analyst on demonic strategy, noted in *The Screwtape Letters*, the best way for the demonic to develop maximum cultural influence these days relies on camouflaging. As the demon Screwtape explains:

> Our policy, for the moment, is to conceal ourselves.… I have great hopes that we shall learn in due time how to emotionalise and mythologise their science to such an extent that what is, in effect, a belief in us (though not under that name) will creep in while the human mind remains closed to belief in the Enemy. The "Life Force," the worship of sex, and some aspects of Psychoanalysis, may here prove useful. If once we can produce our perfect work—the Materialist Magician, the man, not using but veritably worshipping, what he vaguely calls "Forces," while denying the existence of spirits—then the end of the war will be in sight.[6]

The demonic often prefers to keep its movements hidden in plain sight. No Molech worship center exists next door because building such a center is entirely unnecessary. Why erect a temple when its advocates can infiltrate your congregation through other means? If dark forces can get human beings to engage in child sacrifice without having to go to the trouble of constructing an overt religion and a competing theology (which might set off alarms in the camp of their Christian opponents), then why not do it? If the real Enemy can simply encourage a culture of consequence-less sex, create unlabeled temples of Molech masquerading as medical clinics with the state's stamp of approval, leaving behind it a mountain of dead human beings and a massive population of co-conspirators ready to evangelize others in order to normalize their behavior, then why not choose the easier path?

Here's the claim I will make and defend in this chapter:

Molech worship already has taken root in America and throughout the west, and both Catholic and Evangelical churches already are keenly feeling its destructive influence.

Molech worship in our culture has existed in plain sight, largely unacknowledged, for decades. Its seductive promises have placed what seem like insurmountable obstacles between sinners and the cross of Christ. It has lured even Christians away from the faith; and then, in true demonic fashion, destroyed those souls for Kingdom service.

If you google "Punic Worship Centers near me," you will not find The First Church of Molech. Like any good marketer, this enemy knows how to brand. Instead of a monolithic church, this worship system flies under the radar. It so effectively hides the theological underpinnings of its doctrines that it not only has escaped government notice of its religious associations, but it has won government approval and funding. It infiltrates schools, the entertainment culture, civic organizations, parts of our medical establishment, and yes, even our churches. It goes by a lot of names: Women's Health Centers, Family Planning Clinics, but most famously, Planned Parenthood. Its key act of worship remains the same: Child Sacrifice.

And what means does it use to perform this rite? Abortion.

Founded on a Strategic Lie

You may be thinking, *Wait a minute! Abortion clinics are non-profit medical facilities that provide women's health care.* I can't blame anyone for having such a thought. The public relations machine of Planned Parenthood, using American tax dollars to fuel its demonic message, has built one of the world's most pervasive and trusted brands. It has all the hallmarks of a benign, non-profit enterprise. It's become extremely skilled at hiding its core purpose.

I do not merely assert that abortion providers hide what they really do. As early as 1970, three years before the *Roe v. Wade* decision legalizing abortion, the editors of *California Medicine,* the journal of the California Medical Association, were not at all shy about revealing their strategy:

> The process of eroding the old ethic and substituting the new has already begun. It may be seen most clearly in changing attitudes toward human abortion. In defiance of the long held Western ethic of intrinsic and equal value for every human life regardless of its stage, condition or status, abortion is becoming accepted by society as moral, right and even necessary. *It is worth noting that this shift in public attitude has affected the churches,* the laws and public

policy rather than the reverse. Since the old ethic has not yet been fully displaced it has been necessary to separate the idea of abortion from the idea of killing, which continues to be socially abhorrent. The result has been a curious avoidance of the scientific fact, which everyone really knows, that human life begins at conception and is continuous whether intra- or extra-uterine until death. The very considerable semantic gymnastics which are required to rationalize abortion as anything but the taking of a human life would be ludicrous if they were not often put forth under socially impeccable auspices. It is suggested that this schizophrenic sort of subterfuge is necessary because while a new ethic is being accepted the old one has not yet been rejected.[7] (emphasis added)

I'll take a closer look at this essay in a later chapter. For now, it's important to recognize that abortion-choice advocates, eager to establish a "new ethic," felt justified in engaging in "considerable semantic gymnastics," a twisting of the truth that they would "often put forth under socially impeccable auspices." In other words, they would strategically lie about the nature of the unborn child, and then propagate that lie by consistently repeating it through the agencies of government, schools, medicine, media, and the church. They went so far as to acknowledge that the lie constituted a "schizophrenic sort of subterfuge," but rationalized it as "necessary," because the goal of eradicating the old ethic and establishing the new ethic was more important than the means.

What Was the "Old Ethic"?

Note that the authors of this *California Medicine* editorial describe the "old ethic" as "the intrinsic worth and equal value of every human life regardless of its stage or condition."[8] They tie this ethic inextricably to "the Judeo-Christian heritage" and note that this ethic "has been the basis for most of our laws and much of our social policy."[9]

The old ethic holds that God created human beings in His own image, and therefore, they possess inestimable worth. They have human rights by virtue of that image-bearing, by virtue of their inclusion in a class called "human beings," from conception to a natural death. The old ethic insists that intentionally killing an innocent human being is wrong, even if (particularly if) that killing is intended to advance some generally accepted social value.

What Is the "New Ethic"?

The new ethic proposed by the authors, way back in 1970, holds that human beings do not possess an inalienable right to life. Humans do not bear the image of God, created with intrinsic, objective, absolute value in comparison to other things. Instead, the new ethic insists that human beings, at best, have only relative value. When the needs of society—needs, we discover, that the medical community will identify and champion—are deemed sufficiently great, then other human beings can and should be sacrificed.

The authors knew *exactly* what they were doing. They intended to upend millennia of western cultural ideals: "This is quite distinctly at variance with the Judeo-Christian ethic and carries serious philosophical, social, economic and political implications for Western society and perhaps for world society."[10]

I saw an illustration of this disastrous philosophical shift decades later on a sign that once hung on a wall between the host area and the kitchen area of a favorite restaurant. The sign read, "Employees only. No persons beyond this point." I know what management meant: no patrons could step foot in the back, only employees. But a literal reading of the sign suggested that once a human being stepped into the kitchen area, that individual ceased being a person (or alternatively, the act of stepping into the kitchen identified them as never having been a person). I frequently pointed out to management the implications of this sign before they finally took it down. We don't lose our personhood, our humanity, once we move from one place to another, or just because someone in authority claims that we do.

In the old ethic, you are a person, a human being created in the image of God. In the new ethic, you are nothing but a resource. Do you see the massive difference? We value persons; we use and manage resources. The authors of the essay clearly made this distinction. They noted that in a future world—one marked by a desperate shortage of medical resources—someone would need to make choices between who, for example, is and is not to be offered long-term renal dialysis. They left little doubt about who they saw as those decision-makers. In order for physicians to establish themselves in the godlike role of death selection and death control, they explained, they first had to establish themselves at the forefront of birth selection and birth control.

They did it. They told the lies, using every available cultural channel. They engaged in this "schizophrenic sort of subterfuge." And it worked.

The world we live in, they tell us, is filled with problems. The only answer to many of these problems is for some elite individuals and groups to manage the rest of the human population. After all, as these self-proclaimed betters explain, it's for the good of society. And by "manage," they mean "sacrifice." When people have pressing problems and they reject God's counsel (they choose options "at variance with the Judeo-Christian ethic"), they seek a second opinion. They move from God's assessment of human beings and their value, to someone else's.

Enter Molech worship.

Abortion and Molech Worship

In ancient Israel, from the time of the conquest of Canaan all through the Kingdom era, idolatry consistently plagued the people. Much of it came through their refusal to completely remove the sites of worship erected to the Punic gods of the region. Other forms of idolatry infected the nation as a result of intermarriage between Israelite men and pagan women. The new wives often brought their local gods with them. Even Solomon fell prey to this monstrous error. First Kings 11:6-8 records that Solomon built (the text implies that he allowed his foreign wives to build) idolatrous high places, some of which they reserved for the worship of Molech.

It wasn't as if the ancient Israelites had no access to God. First there came the tabernacle, and later the temple. Israelites could go there and inquire of God if they had questions or problems. But the Israelites also knew that this God, the God of Abraham, Isaac, and Jacob, was not the kind of god with whom you bargained; He was the God you obeyed. He had given His people the Law. So, if you had a question regarding some problem—your crops didn't produce as bountifully as you thought you deserved, or you wanted to ensure plentiful offspring—perhaps you went to the temple and prayed. Sometimes you did not get the answer you wanted or expected. Perhaps the advice you received from a priest of God disappointed you. If so, some people sought out a "second opinion."

Israelites could go to a high place, meet with a representative of Molech—perhaps an assistant to the priest—and pour out their hearts, laying bare their anxieties and problems. These supplicants would hear that, indeed, the great god Molech could take care of their problems. All they needed to do was to make their request of the priest and offer the life of their child. Many parents therefore took their child, sometimes their firstborn, to the priest. The mother and father had to stand by, shedding no tears, to demonstrate their freely chosen sacrifice. The priest would take the child to a bronze altar—an idol with the head of an ox and the body of a man, seated, with outstretched arms. The hollow altar blazed with fire. The priest placed the child on the searing-hot metal hands of the idol, drums beat loudly to drown out the child's screams, and then the living sacrifice rolled into the open "lap"—a hole into which the child fell. The flames incinerated the infant's flesh, sending up a pleasing aroma to the god Molech.[11]

Another image-bearer of the true God, eliminated.

Today, just as in ancient Israel, people have access to God. They pray to Him, seek counsel by reading His Word, and if they lack experience or expertise in handling Scripture, or if they want godly counsel from a more mature believer, they can seek out their local pastor. But what if the young woman, or couple, already has a pretty good idea what the pastor will say if they come with a problem such as, "We made a mistake. We had sex, and now I'm pregnant. We're not ready to be parents"? Perhaps she has a college athletic scholarship at stake, and the presence of another human being growing in her womb would prevent her from competing. She may need that scholarship to remain in school. Maybe a job promotion hangs in the balance, and a pregnancy will interrupt an otherwise carefully planned career. Sometimes, the woman's untimely pregnancy brings shame to the couple as evidence of sexual sin, and they'd like it to just go away. The woman, or the couple, think they already know what many pastors would tell them. So, just like some ancient Israelites, they seek a second opinion.

Today, of course, they don't need to trudge up to a high place. Women's medical clinics provide many options, and some of these clinics sit in the middle of residential neighborhoods. Anyone can drive there and walk into an air-conditioned office. There they will meet with a counselor, the counterpart to the priest's assistant. They will pour out their problems. Perhaps they won't even mention their religious affiliation. They have a plan, and pregnancy will get in the way. They just need help to not be pregnant.

The counselor has them fill out forms, takes their payment, verifies the woman's pregnancy, and then schedules the sacrifice. On the appointed day, the woman arrives. Staff directs her to a cool surgical table. "Lie down," they tell her. Unlike the ancient priests of Molech, so unsophisticated that they had to wait for children to be born before they could sacrifice them, this "new priesthood" has developed its own set of tools. They no longer need the mother or father to remain stoic, avoiding tears that would undermine the value of the sacrifice. They medically sedate the woman, and if a man accompanies her, he will have to bide his time in a waiting room.

Abortionists invade the body of the woman with instruments designed to grasp, tear, kill, and dismember. These modern priests require no beating drums to stifle the screams of a burning child; the killing takes place in the silence of the mother's womb. Abortionists remove the child piece by piece, reassembling the body parts to verify their thorough work, and then, in most cases, they place the body parts of the sacrificed child in a medical incinerator.

The bodies still burn. The smoke rises, a pleasing aroma to the god Molech.

Five Key Elements

Please don't misunderstand. I am not arguing that abortion is *similar* to Molech worship. I am arguing that abortion *is* Molech worship, even if it doesn't go by that name, and even if the object of that worship goes unidentified. In 1 Corinthians 10:20-21, the Apostle Paul argues that when pagans sacrifice to idols they actually present their offerings to demons, and warns Christians against participation in worship connected with the demonic. Both Molech worship and abortion involve five key elements:

- People trying to solve life's most pressing problems;
- Ignoring or rejecting the counsel of the Word of God or a godly pastor;
- Accepting the diabolical advice that the best solution to their problems is the death of their child;

- Having their child killed (and in the case of abortion, dismembered);
- Incinerating their child's body.

We often use the word "sacrifice" to describe paying a big price to solve a difficult problem. *The practice of abortion is the practice of child sacrifice.* Sacrificing children in order to solve problems, in direct violation of God's command against killing innocent human beings, is the very definition of idolatry.

Idolatry? Really?

Youth pastors sometimes like to define idolatry by comparing it to a teen's maniacal devotion to a sports team, or to fixing up a car, or to slavishly following the latest fashions. The pastor has to use *some* modern example, after all. I mean, it's not as though you can find anyone in the contemporary West bowing down in front of a stone idol.

Unfortunately, such youth pastors have confused misplaced priorities with idolatry. I have often heard people say that anything you prioritize before God is an idol. In one sense that is correct—Colossians 3:5 connects "evil desires" and "greed" with idolatry—but such a definition often gets used as a means of identifying and vilifying behaviors we don't much like. Maybe Billy spends a lot of time on baseball and looks up to the players on his favorite team. For all we know, however, Billy will grow up to play professional baseball. His interest and these players aren't idols; they are vocational desires and role models. We need to take care not to water down our conceptions of idolatry to such an extent that we fail to see the real thing when it appears.

Abortion is idolatry. It has all the features of idolatry. People strike a bargain to solve a problem, and the commission of a sin is the price for supposed relief. Experts tell those with the problem that the only way to clear a path to live a good lifestyle is to remove what they call the key obstacle, by sacrificing the literal lives of their children.

But why take my word for it? Contemporary writers understand very well the nature of this bargain.

Mary Elizabeth Williams, writing in *Salon,* asks "So what if abortion ends life?" She recounts, with approval, an opinion piece she read in the *Michigan Daily:*

Emma Maniere stated, quite perfectly, that "Some argue that abortion takes lives, but I know that abortion saves lives, too." She understands that it saves lives not just in the most medically literal way, but in the roads that women who have choice then get to go down, in the possibilities for them and for their families. And I would put the life of a mother over the life of a fetus every single time—even if I still need to acknowledge my conviction that the fetus is indeed a life. A life worth sacrificing.[12]

Williams here expertly uses the fallacy of equivocation, when someone uses a specific word or phrase with two different meanings in order to deceive the reader. In this instance, the word is "life." In the second-to-last sentence, Williams compares the "life of the mother" with "the life of a fetus." But the context of her claim does not primarily reference the physical life of the mother. Instead, she refers to the lifestyle choices that a mother, willing to kill her offspring, can then enjoy. So she's not really talking about one life over another. This is no battle for literal survival. Rather, she elevates the supposed right of a woman to lead whatever kind of life she would like over the actual right of a child to remain physically alive. Quite accurately, Williams identifies the object of choice she champions, as "a life worth sacrificing." In other words, child sacrifice.

All hail Molech.

The Apostle John warned young believers that, because "the whole world lies in the power of the evil one," to "keep yourselves from idols."[13] Based on what Scripture reveals as the hallmarks of idolatry, we have little option but to believe that the act of abortion clearly makes the list of idols from which we must keep ourselves. If abortion is idolatry, and if we are to keep ourselves from idols, then there must be a way, a program of thought and action, to make our obedience to that command possible. Such modes of thinking and programs do indeed exist, to be detailed in later chapters; but first we need to address the necessary initial step for the church.

If keeping congregants from idols is paramount, and abortion is idolatry, then the first hurdle we must overcome is the reticence of many Christians to address abortion.

Chapter 2

Why We Don't Speak Up: Eight Common Reasons

People in ministry probably receive more personal complaints and petty accusations than anyone in nearly any other profession. And these grievance grenades get lobbed at them by their own congregants!

Letters of appreciation, by contrast, come so rarely that many church leaders have confessed to keeping what some might call a "rainy-day file," a slim little folder containing a handful of encouraging letters, received over many years. Ministry people read them on days when they feel strongly tempted to quit. No one enjoys feeling hated by the people they want to serve. Everyone prefers to be loved and adored. Don't you?

At the same time, ministry leaders have the tough job of biblical discipleship: teaching and training to help mold their congregants, through the power of the Holy Spirit, into the image of Jesus. These two goals, being liked and being effective, sometimes conflict with one another. So many potential areas of contention arise and so many chances occur for political missteps (that rile congregants and lead to a flood of messages that do *not* go into the rainy-day file), that it's easy to understand why pastors, teachers, small groups, youth leaders, and the church in general might shy away from talking about potentially incendiary topics such as abortion.

Believers give many reasons for not wanting to talk about abortion, some based on their incomplete knowledge of the Bible, others grounded in mistaken ideas about what "science says," or a lack of practice in making good moral judgments. Small group leaders, youth pastors, and senior pastors may also prefer to concentrate on what they see as church-wide issues that affect more than individual believers.

Over many years of training communicators in the prolife movement, I've identified eight common reasons believers and church leaders give for not speaking about abortion, whether personally or from the pulpit. Let's take a look at each of them.

Reason One: Abortion's Not Really a Sin

Since you picked up this book, you probably reject the idea that abortion is not wrong or a sin. It's important to know, however, that many people who claim to be Christians, including those in leadership positions, consider abortion no big deal. Not only is abortion not a sin, they say, but it can be a positive good, even a blessing from God.

One of the most startling public proclamations of support for abortion by professional clergy came from The Rev. Katherine Hancock Ragsdale, then Dean of the Episcopal Divinity School in Cambridge, Massachusetts (and later its president), at an event in a park in Birmingham, Alabama, on July 21, 2007.[14] Ragsdale extolled what she called the "blessing" of abortion and referred to abortion clinic workers as "saints." At the end of her presentation, Ragsdale had her audience chant along with her that "Abortion is a blessing and our work is not done." In November 2019, Ragsdale was named president and CEO of the National Abortion Federation.[15]

Ragsdale is hardly alone. Back in 1966, the Rev. Martin Luther King, Jr., accepted Planned Parenthood's Margaret Sanger Award.[16] In his defense—and as his niece, Alveda C. King, notes—this occurred before the abortion agenda of Planned Parenthood became explicit.[17] Nevertheless, Planned Parenthood continues to tout its relationship with MLK in press releases and on its website.[18]

In a 2019 article in *The Atlantic*, Jes Kast, an ordained minister in the United Church of Christ, describes her transition from pro-life Christian to a champion of abortion-choice positions. Raised in a conservative Christian home, Kast was initially pro-life, but then attended a private Christian college in Michigan. She began viewing herself as a feminist, then went on to reconsider her stance on a variety of social justice issues. It occurred to her that God would never oppose bodily autonomy for women, and, after all, "Why is it that when it comes to this topic [abortion] it's always white, straight, Christian men who are the loudest?" When asked to name her theological position on abortion, Kast replied, "When people talk about 'Our body is a temple of God, and holy,' I see that as *I have the right to choices over my body, and the freedom to make the decisions that are right for me.*"[19] (emphasis in the original).

The Religious Coalition for Reproductive Choice affiliate in Ohio schedules "clinic blessings" where an array of local clergy visit abortion clinics to pray for God's favor. At its 2019 clinic blessing, the group's website praised the abortion clinic for "the hard, holy work that goes on there day after day. We bless abortion clinics, because they represent the sacred space of decision—the holy ground where pregnant people can make the best decision for their life without judgment, fear, or coercion."[20]

———————— • ————————

Paul tells Timothy in 1 Timothy 5:20 that elders in the church who continue to sin need to be publicly rebuked. All church leaders who support abortion need education first, but if they persist, public rebuke must follow.

———————— • ————————

The Religious Coalition for Reproductive Choice has thirteen state affiliates. On May 19, 2020, the Coalition staged a virtual clinic blessing to honor abortion clinics for continuing to provide abortions during the COVID-19 pandemic. Since 2016, the group has conducted clinic blessings in three states and the District of Columbia.[21]

Clergy blessed an Austin, Texas abortion clinic in July 2019. The Rev. Amelia Fulbright, founder of Labyrinth Progressive Student Ministry, told the Huffington Post that "one of the most meaningful moments of the ceremony was when her 4-month-old baby became hungry. She said being able to nurse her child in that setting, surrounded by people who understood the importance of being able to choose motherhood, illustrated to her that abortion clinics are a 'life-affirming space.'"[22] Fulbright said that her portrait of the abortion clinic as life-affirming "paints a different picture than what the anti-abortion movement would like you to think happens in abortion clinics."[23]

Planned Parenthood has its own Clergy Advocacy Board. While the board has few members, Planned Parenthood uses these individuals as cover, acting as if abortion-choice advocacy is common within the religious community. When chilling videos from the Center for Medical Progress emerged in 2015, showing with disturbing clarity both the horror of the abortion industry and its cavalier attitude toward the bodies of its victims, many in the Christian community felt justifiably outraged. In response, Planned Parenthood fired off a press release from its Clergy Advocacy Board. In the release, the board lumped the Center for Medical Progress with other organizations that have "harassed" Planned Parenthood over the years, and called the CMP's tactics "fraudulent" and "extreme" (a favorite word of an organization that literally and regularly dismembers defenseless human beings in the womb). By contrast, the Clergy Advocacy Board[24] declared, "People who work for Planned Parenthood give care and respect to those in need, doing God's work."[25]

From its inception, Planned Parenthood's Margaret Sanger wanted to use black doctors and clergy in order to advance her agenda. In fairness, that agenda in the beginning did not include abortion, although it did include controlling the size of the black population. In a letter dated December 10, 1939, to Dr. C.J. Gamble, Sanger described the need to raise up and train black doctors to carry out her work among the black population, because only in the presence of black doctors will "the colored Negroes...lay their cards out on the table, which means their ignorance, superstitions and doubts."[26] Sanger also outlined the importance of black clergy in forwarding Planned Parenthood Federation's objectives: "The minister's work is also important, and also he should be trained, perhaps by the Federation as to our ideals and the goal that we hope to reach. We do not want word to go out that we want to exterminate the Negro population and the minister is the man who can straighten out that idea if it ever occurs to any of their more rebellious members."[27]

Did Sanger really mean to exterminate the African-American population? The writers at the Margaret Sanger Project don't think so. They write that such an idea "gives Sanger unwarranted credit as a remarkably cunning manipulator, but also suggests that African-Americans were passive receptors of birth control reform, incapable of making their own decisions about family size; and that black leaders were ignorant and gullible."[28] And yet, in the very letter referenced, Sanger referred to African-Americans as both ignorant and superstitious.

Clearly, Sanger had little respect for African-Americans. And regardless of her initial intent, Planned Parenthood *is* responsible for the deaths of millions of African-Americans, killing them in the wombs of their mothers. According to the clergy who advocate on behalf of Planned Parenthood, however, aborting African-American children should be celebrated and praised as a positive blessing, not considered something wrong or sinful.

Other Christians offer a variant of "it's not sin." The argument goes, "Since any sin separates people from God, all sin is equal." Some truth exists in what they argue. Every single sin human beings commit represents an act of rebellion against God. Whether people lie, run after counterfeit deities, commit adultery, dishonor their parents, or any other violation of God's laws, such behaviors create a divide between the Holy God and profane people. As a result, such Christians argue, speaking out against the particular sin of abortion is unnecessary.

One reason why people who attend many mainline Protestant churches have no opinion or a positive opinion about abortion, is that the pulpits in their churches either remain silent about abortion or affirm it. While most evangelicals reject abortion as sinful, too many churches, even the theologically orthodox ones, fail to call abortion what it is or minimize its impacts. Neither do they equip its members to reject abortion advocacy or help them to discover, support, and send people toward life-affirming alternatives. In these cases, the reasons why are not inherently theological.

Reason Two: Abortion Is Too Political

Even when pastors and other church leaders see abortion as a serious sin, many leaders—even conservative pastors—still hesitate to speak about abortion because they fear the issue is "too political."[29] They base their reasons in ideas about the church's role generally and what pastors, in particular, perceive as a (not unfounded) fear of stepping across a line set for them by politicians. I regularly encounter two rationales when speaking with pastors:

- The church should remain separate from politics;
- Speaking on political issues or endorsing candidates would place the church's non-profit status at risk and expose it to legal liability.

A longstanding social maxim declares that people should avoid speaking about politics, sex, or religion. How funny that a quick glance at the news and entertainment media demonstrates that those three subjects dominate discussions. Unfortunately, on these topics in the church, we are only one for three.

Separation of the church from political topics

We all know that many pastors avoid speaking on what they perceive as political and social issues, and abortion and homosexuality now regularly get lumped into that group. Respected researcher George Barna reported in 2014 that while 90 percent of pastors believed that the Bible speaks to social issues, less than 10 percent of pastors actually preached on social issues from the pulpit.[30] A more specific study, conducted by the American Culture and Faith Institute, compared data from 2014 and 2016 and discovered that the number of specifically "theologically conservative" pastors who spoke on abortion had dropped from 48 percent in 2014, down to 26 percent in 2016.[31]

I attended a chapel service a few years ago at Biola University. The chapel speaker asked how many students there had *never* heard a sermon on abortion. I looked around. About half of the students at this conservative Christian university put up their hands.

While some of the blame for failing to speak about abortion falls on pressure groups constantly hammering home a misleading message about the "separation of church and state," at least part of the problem stems from church members themselves. Barna Research reports in its 2019 study, "Faith Leadership in a Divided Culture," that 18 percent of pastors felt limited by church members who wanted them to avoid speaking on abortion, while only 17 percent of church members encouraged their pastor to speak out.[32] Note that these numbers closely approximate a bell-shaped curve, showing that approximately 20 percent of people occupy either end of the curve, while 60 percent reside in the mushy middle. In other words, this result is "normal." But here's the question: If an equal number of church members want the pastor either to remain silent or to speak out, why should the congregants wishing to muzzle the pastor prevail?

Fear of legal entanglement

Church leaders also fear that speaking on issues deemed "political" can open them up to risking their church's non-profit status, or to other forms of litigation. Even after a 2017 executive order from President Donald Trump that lifted the ban on political speech from tax-exempt organizations, including endorsing individual political candidates, many churches remain wary.[33] Some of that concern stems from apprehension that rich political advocates will tie church giving to political promotion. Others fear IRS or partisan scrutiny.

It's happened in the past. One of the more famous, recent cases, involved the Mayor of Houston, Annise Parker. In October 2014, Parker subpoenaed sermons from pastors who openly opposed the Houston Equal Rights Ordinance to see if they violated the law by preaching in opposition to the transgender rights law.[34] Parker tweeted, "If the 5 pastors used pulpits for politics, their sermons are fair game."[35]

It happened again in 2016, when the Georgia Department of Public Health rescinded a job offer to Dr. Eric Walsh after discovering Walsh's traditional Christian views on marriage. DPH employees combed through hours of Walsh's recorded sermons after discovering that an LGBTQ group had protested when Walsh received an invitation to speak at commencement services for Pasadena City College. After Walsh, a Seventh-Day Adventist lay minister, filed a discrimination lawsuit, Georgia DPH demanded that he turn over his "sermon notes or transcripts."[36]

Even though the Houston subpoenas went nowhere and Georgia settled the lawsuit brought by Dr. Walsh (though without admitting any state wrongdoing), merely the threat of subpoenas or litigation may cause some pastors to remain silent.

Reason Three: Abortion Is Too Divisive

At a banquet for a pregnancy help center (PHC) in Southern California, I once heard a pastor comment that abortion would divide his church. "I seek greater unity," he declared. While the church did come alongside the PHC—in fact, it became a generous supporter—I looked through the church's sermon archive and could not find a single sermon dedicated to biblical teaching on abortion.

In a highly polarized political world, church leaders who speak about abortion feel the need to tread carefully. The larger the church, the greater the likelihood that the congregation includes Democrats, Republicans, Libertarians, Greens, and Independents. Attendees also represent a wide array of maturity levels, both in terms of actual age and spiritual development. From the pulpit to the youth room to the small group leader, all know that a solitary word, too stridently spoken, will prompt some people to stampede for the exits, perhaps never to return. With them, they will take children, volunteer hours, and giving dollars. Many pastors, teachers, and leaders refuse to take the risk.

George Barna sums up the motivations of silent church leaders regarding politics and division: "The corollary information in our studies indicates that theologically conservative pastors are refusing to teach biblical principles related to current issues because they are concerned about being seen as political, not wanting to risk the loss of numbers of people or donations, and concern about the status of the church's non-profit designation."[37]

The grounds offered for avoiding messages on abortion are not always so calculating. They don't always focus on protecting church image, viability, or privilege. Sometimes, discussion of abortion gets set aside for deeply personal reasons.

Reason Four: Abortion Talk Hurts Congregants

Pastors and church leaders can do the math. Depending on their church's location, from one in three, to one in four pregnancies end in abortion. The likelihood that some women in your small group, college/career fellowship, or congregation have had abortions is exceedingly high.

When you add to that the number of men responsible for impregnating women who they later persuaded (or coerced) to get an abortion, and the number of other friends and family who have participated in some way in an abortion, the problem becomes glaringly apparent: Raising the subject of abortion means a lot of people will feel great pain.

By avoiding the subject of abortion, pastors and other teachers sincerely believe that they do their congregants a kindness. After all, such teachers reason, most people who have had (or have helped someone obtain) an abortion know that they have done something wrong, feel bad about it, and would prefer to put it behind them and just get on with their lives. Talking about abortion feels uncomfortable for everyone, including the pastor, so preference goes to other important but less distressing topics.

Reason Five: Abortion Talk is Unnecessary

I once made an unscheduled call to the pastor of a church located across the freeway from both a PHC and an abortion clinic. I wanted to survey local pastors to find out how they messaged both on abortion and on the help available to women experiencing an untimely pregnancy. I asked the pastor whether he had material from the PHC, and if he did, whether the church openly displayed the material or only made it available on demand.

"We certainly have the center's brochures," he told me, "and they're available at the information desk by demand, not display." A big smile broke out on his face and he added, "But you know, no one's ever asked for any!"

His tone and his smile told me that he thought no one at his church needed such information. His upbeat demeanor implied that his preaching, teaching, and the youth messaging at his church were all so incredibly effective that the general culture's problems with untimely pregnancy simply didn't exist at that church. While I couldn't say anything, I knew that the PHC across the freeway had clients who attended that pastor's church. I also imagine that the abortion clinic had received some of his congregants.

Similarly, in preparation for a talk I planned to give on teen sex and abortion in the church, I called a number of local youth pastors to conduct a brief survey. One question asked, "What percentage of the high school and college-aged students in your youth and young adults groups do you think are sexually active?" The most common response? Around 15 percent.

Clearly, if pastors don't believe the students in their youth groups have a problem with sex, they don't need to talk about untimely pregnancies or abortion. Right?

Reason Six: "I've Already Spoken on Abortion"

Some church leaders avoid the admission that they don't talk about abortion by claiming that they *have* talked about abortion. While some pastors reliably speak about abortion, and others do so once a year, in January on the designated Sanctity of Human Life Sunday, too many pastors have spoken on abortion just once, two or more years ago.

Remember that chapel service at Biola University that I mentioned earlier? The one where half of the students had never heard a sermon on abortion? I wonder what kind of response would have come had the speaker asked, "How many of you have ever heard more than one sermon on abortion?" or "How many of you have heard a series of sermons on abortion?" It's no stretch to suppose that the number of students with raised hands would have dipped significantly.

Pastors and other church leaders have a lot on their plates. Every interest group in the area clamors for a shot at their pulpit. Non-profit groups vie for space in the church program, hoping for an official endorsement. Many church members need to be taught the basics of the Christian faith, to grow in moral knowledge and practical obedience, and to engage in evangelism and discipleship. Some churches commit to teach through the books of the Bible, with few or no topical sermons or teaching series.

When pastors and other leaders consider abortion, then, they see it as one more thing in an unrelenting parade of issues that need addressing. With abortion deemed too political, divisive, and harmful, it is easy to see why church leaders might refrain from discussing the topic. Why not rather teach other important but less-inflammatory lessons?

Reason Seven: Ministerial Ignorance

While ministry leaders have recounted for me every one of the reasons outlined above for why they neglect, or avoid altogether, preaching about abortion, I suspect that a couple of other reasons also figure into the decision. These pastors don't tend to voice these reasons, but I can infer them from conversations I've had with pastors in training sessions.

First, some pastors remain ignorant about abortion. They don't know much about the topic medically, feel ill-equipped to wrestle with what they perceive as thorny moral and philosophical arguments, and some lack the training to advocate a biblical theology regarding abortion.

I find it very easy to believe that some church leaders know little about abortion. The Christian universities that produce many of our ministers seem nearly as reticent to take on the issue as many skittish churches. My colleagues Scott Klusendorf (president of Life Training Institute), John Ensor (president of PassionLife Ministries), and I have offered to teach an Applied Bioethics certificate program on any campus willing to champion it. The academically rigorous courses offer transferable college credits. Both Care Net and Heartbeat International, the two largest PHC affiliate organizations, have recognized the value of this Applied Bioethics coursework, either by providing certification for graduates or issuing units toward their own certifications.

So far, we've had one taker.

To my knowledge, despite the fact that abortion hovers near the top of surgical procedures in the U.S. each year (and that figure does not take into account "medical" abortions, which elsewhere I refer to as chemical abortions), only *one* Christian college—Cedarville University—offers a course dealing with the subject of abortion.[38]

When I present a one-hour pastor training or a three-hour apologetics class at area churches, most people frantically take notes. The information presented is new to them, even though abortion has been legal in the United States since 1973.

Because of the highly politicized nature of abortion, professional advocacy in academia and vote chasing in politics churns out a cavalcade of arguments. Some believers see a book, such as David Boonin's *A Defense of Abortion*, skim what they perceive to be dense philosophical arguments, and throw up their hands. In other words, too many pastors, leaders, and church members simply abandon the field because they believe they could never master such a complex issue. Since teachers at all levels in the church are perceived as the "go-to" experts on the subjects they discuss, lack of confidence leads to silence.

Reason Eight: Abortion In the Background

Most pastors and other Christian leaders know they don't walk on water, despite what some of their church members might think. They are all human beings, born with a sin nature, with lives full of mistakes and regrets, just like everyone else. They weren't born church leaders and many of them came to know Jesus after a long, rebellious life.

Some were born into a church family and embraced the faith of their parents, but went through a period when they struggled or walked away from the teachings of Christ. Others became Christians in their youth, stuck to the faith and had aspirations to enter professional Christian ministry, only to feel overcome by sexual impulses with a girlfriend in high school or college, and the girl became pregnant (perhaps after a single, unguarded act of intercourse). Maybe her parents insisted on an abortion and he could do nothing about it. Maybe they both felt ashamed of their behavior and chose abortion, mistaking it as a way to cover up their guilt.

We can never know the number of church leaders affected by abortion in this way, as it would be impossible to obtain the required statistical evidence. But as you will see in the next chapter, more than 50 percent of those seeking abortions self-identify at least nominally as "Christians."[39] Pastors and other ministry leaders have confessed to me that they have abortion in their backgrounds. Some told me how they had confessed to their congregations or youth groups. But such experiences cause me to believe that a significant number of ministry leaders avoid discussing abortion, not only because of the pain they fear it will cause people in their congregations, but because they've yet to come to terms with their own involvement with abortion. In order to avoid hypocrisy, some simply side-step the topic altogether.

The Answers Do Exist

These, then, are the eight key reasons, both spoken and unspoken, behind the choice of many believers and ministry leaders not to speak about abortion. If these reasons were true—that is,

- if abortion really were not sinful;
- if speaking on issues related to politics were wrong;
- if talk of abortion really did negatively divide the Body of Christ;
- if speaking of abortion would damage hurting women and men already past their abortions;
- if pastors were so effective from the pulpit that multiple sermons about abortion were unnecessary;
- if a single-shot abortion sermon could effectively inoculate a congregation from abortion advocacy forever;

- if ministry leaders had no way to address their ignorance about abortion;
- or if ministry leaders with abortion in their personal backgrounds could not overcome their shame or guilt enough to talk effectively about abortion—

then I might be able to understand the reluctance. But are these ideas and arguments in fact justified? In the next chapter, we'll evaluate each of them and see.

Chapter 3

Why We Must Speak Up: Answers to the Eight Most Common Objections

When you know the truth, you have an obligation to speak it. While we should choose our words carefully, "seasoned with salt,"[40] people who know the truth have an obligation to warn, instruct, and correct. Otherwise, those who believe lies might continue to do wrong out of ignorance, the evil influence of others, or self-deception.

The eight reasons outlined in the previous chapter explain why many Christians fail to talk about abortion, not only from the pulpit, but in Sunday school, small group fellowships, youth group, and even among church members. It's important, therefore, to carefully examine each reason to see if it provides a valid rationale to remain silent.

Answer One: God's Word Demonstrates that Abortion Is Sin

Despite the insistence of some clergy who vocally support abortion (even calling it a "blessing"), it can be demonstrated persuasively that abortion is sin. While the word "abortion" does not appear in the Bible and no law in Scripture declares "Thou shalt not abort," a strong case can be built by examining what the Bible does plainly say:

- Human beings are to be fruitful and multiply
- God recognizes the value of human beings in the womb
- God forbids murder
- Child killing was categorized with abortion
- God punishes violent men who cause accidental miscarriage

Be fruitful

The very first commandment from God to humans, in the very first chapter of Genesis, is "be fruitful and multiply."[41] The Old Testament consistently pairs joy with parenthood, while great disappointment often accompanies the barren womb.[42] Children were both desired and valued. The emphasis on children as a "heritage," "a gift," and "a reward" demonstrate God's highly positive attitude toward childbearing.[43]

Human value starts in the womb

Scripture firmly establishes the value of human beings growing in the wombs of their mothers. God knows unborn children long before their birth and already has plans for them, including the length of their lives.[44] The Bible describes the process of human development in the womb as the work of a master craftsman, as we are "fearfully and wonderfully made."[45]

One of the most specific attributions of value for the pre-born human comes in what we often call the Visitation. Mary, pregnant with Jesus, goes to visit her cousin Elizabeth, who is also pregnant; her son, John, will become "the Baptist." When Elizabeth hears Mary's greeting, the Gospel of Luke offers two fascinating observations: first, the baby leaps in Elizabeth's womb.[46] The Greek word for "baby" in this verse is *brephos*, a term used equally for unborn as well as newborn children. Second, Luke tells us that Elizabeth speaks after being "filled with the Holy Spirit," and speaking by the Spirit she attributes her child's leaping to "joy."

In such an historical environment, where God commanded human beings to procreate, where children were highly valued and where their worth was recognized even while still in the womb, who would have desired abortion? God gave laws forbidding certain acts because fallen humans are liable to commit those acts. Neither the Old Testament nor the New Testament specifically outlaw abortion because God's ancient people had very little inclination to end the lives of children whom they both wanted and valued. Besides, knowing God's law and attitude toward human beings developing in the womb, as expressed in the Bible, made it clear to both ancient Jews and Christians that abortion was a sin.

Forbidding murder

The Ten Commandments forbids the intentional killing of innocent human beings.[47] Scripture consistently describes people who commit murder as bearing bloodguilt, and prescribes execution as the harsh penalty. Human life is invaluable, and to wantonly murder, to intentionally take an innocent life, required (according to Scripture) the forfeiture of one's own life.

Child murder categorized with abortion

Although the Bible does not explicitly mention abortion, scholars agree that, among Jews and early Christians, abortion, along with infanticide (including child exposure), were forbidden. All three activities were discussed together as if they belonged in a single category: intentionally putting innocent human beings to death.

Yifat Monnickendam explains, "Following early Jewish-Hellenistic literature, Christian sources discussed the exposure of children alongside abortion or infanticide, thus implying that the child would, in all likelihood, die. Philo claims that those who expose (ἐκτίθημι) children are murderers, thus tying the practice to infanticide and abortion."[48] Abortion was regarded as child murder.

The Law punishes violent men who cause accidental miscarriage

Exodus 21:22-23 declares, "If men struggle with each other and strike a woman with child so that she gives birth prematurely, yet there is no injury, he shall surely be fined as the woman's husband may demand of him, and he shall pay as the judges decide. But if there is any further injury, then you shall appoint as a penalty life for life."

This Old Testament passage uses the Hebrew term *yeled* to denote "child," a word used to refer to children both inside and outside the womb. The second word of interest is the term translated "birth prematurely," which in Hebrew is *yatsa*, which means "to come forth." Some apologists argue that the structure of this verse describes a man unintentionally striking a pregnant woman, who gives birth prematurely to a child who survives. If both mother and child survive, then the man will be fined; but if either the mother or the child dies, the penalty is death.

Others have argued that the death penalty applied only if the woman died as a result of the blow; the fine was levied for the death of the unborn child. Since ancient Israel had no neonatal intensive care units, most preemies died.

A distinction appears to exist in the passage between the *direct* cause of death and the *proximate* cause of death. If the man accidentally struck the woman and she died, he would have directly caused her death and therefore must forfeit his life. If the blow caused the early delivery of the child, however, the child's lack of development (and not the blow itself) actually caused the infant's death. This might explain the reason for the fine. In that case, the penalty has nothing to do with the inherent value of the mother or the child; they both are human beings with equal value. But in one case, the death is direct, while in the other, it's indirect.

Regardless of how one reads these verses, the Law clearly expresses great value for both the mother and child. Additionally, both the death sentence and the fine come in response to the *accidental* striking of a pregnant woman in the context of two men struggling. If this characterizes the Bible's response to the *unintentional* death of a child, how should we imagine God would respond to people who *intentionally* conspire together to kill a child in the womb? Especially in a culture in which abortion was considered child murder?

All sins result in separation from God, but have unequal impact

What about the claim that "sin is sin" so no need exists to call out particular sins? The book of Romans clearly teaches that all human beings violate God's Law and, therefore, fall short.[49] Only the sacrificial blood of Jesus Christ creates the way of salvation and reconciles sinful people to a Holy God. But all sin is not equal in other respects.

In the Old Testament, violations of different laws led to differing punishments. In Leviticus 19-20, some sins receive the death penalty, others result in childlessness, and still others require an animal sacrifice. In Luke 10:13-15, Jesus calls out the cities of Chorazin, Bethsaida, and Capernaum for not responding to the gospel, and says they will receive a more severe judgement than that given to the Old Testament cities of Tyre, Sidon, and Sodom. Jesus tells His followers to beware of hypocritical religious leaders, saying such people "will receive greater condemnation," indicating hierarchy in sin.[50] In Romans 6:19, why would the Apostle Paul express concern with some lawlessness leading to "further lawlessness," if sin were merely sin? The Apostle James references the specific sin of partiality because the people to whom he wrote struggled with this sin.[51] The Apostle John warns Christians to "guard yourselves from idols."[52]

Stealing is stealing, one might say, but surely robbing an elderly woman of her social security check has more significant impacts than stealing (perhaps unconsciously) paper clips from work. Similarly, abortion – the intentional killing of an innocent human being in the womb – results in far more serious consequences than many other sins, and so deserves to be named and guarded against.

Answer Two: Is Abortion Primarily a Political Issue?

Did you know that sinners have political advocacy groups? Just read through the list of reprobate activities in Romans 1 and you'll get a preview.

If you have biblical attitudes about disciplining your disobedient children, you need to look at the U.N. Convention on the Rights of the Child. I scanned an indexed list of organizations that exist to support rights for homosexuals and stopped counting at twenty-three—before I got to the end of those starting with the letter "C." Pedophiles have NAMBLA, the North American Man-Boy Love Association. And abortion groups have the National Organization for Women, the National Abortion Federation, the National Abortion Rights Action League (now NARAL Pro-Choice America), and many more such organizations dedicated to maintaining the status quo: where some human beings get to kill other weaker, defenseless human beings.

Without question, abortion has political ramifications, and those determined to keep it legal are both vocal and aggressive.

Abortion has political backers, but abortion is *not* primarily a political issue. Abortion is primarily a spiritual and moral issue, though often such issues have political implications. Abortion is *framed* as purely political by its supporters; and in so doing, they intend to make the church shut up.

Would you like to see how to play this game? Pick a spiritual or moral issue: same-sex marriage, euthanasia, abortion, debt, chastity, racism, or anything else (I would have included no-fault divorce, but the church lost that battle ages ago). It's completely within the purview of a pastor or any church leader to speak on these and other moral and spiritual issues. But then one day, these issues get politicized in ways many people could not have imagined even a few years ago. The major political parties camp out on one side or the other. Suddenly the moral issue that was always fair game becomes a political mine field. Church leaders sense the danger and decide to teach on other, less controversial topics.

It amazes me how well this tactic has succeeded. No one has threatened jail for pastors and teachers; no one has threatened to take away their churches (as actually happens in China). In fact, most of the fear remains inside pastors' heads: "If I speak out against abortion, congregants will think this is a Republican church," or more ominously, "If I speak about politics from the pulpit, we will risk our non-profit status." The latter claim remains so ludicrous (so far) that when failed 2020 Democratic presidential candidate Beto O'Rourke suggested that churches who don't toe the line on same-sex marriage would have their tax-exempt status revoked by his administration, even the mainstream press howled.[53]

Under the Johnson Amendment, passed in 1954, ministers in tax-exempt churches cannot represent the church in endorsing a particular political candidate. Nothing in that amendment, however, prohibits a pastor from preaching a sermon on abortion and warning the flock that voting for candidates who support the abortion of children in the womb constitutes a grave moral sin. Neither pastors nor other spiritual leaders have to check their first amendment rights at the door of their church.

Self-censorship, however, can be every bit as effective as official censorship, because it produces the same results. Church leaders often choose not to speak on the very topics on which their congregants most need to hear pastoral voices. In my pastor training sessions, I warn church leaders, "If you don't stand up now and speak out on abortion and other significant issues, eventually you'll find your teachings limited to agricultural metaphors."

One role of the church is to stand in judgment when a culture heads toward, or gets mired in, moral disaster. Few moral and spiritual issues are as fraught with peril as abortion. Children, fellow image-bearers of God, die by the millions. Mothers and fathers are scarred, often for life. Those who persuade women to have abortions, or who procure abortions, also damage themselves spiritually. Those who teach in the church, by proclaiming the truth about abortion, stand in the gap for all of these individuals. We cannot allow threats to silence us, and we dare not silence ourselves.

Answer Three: The Imperative of Divisiveness

This one is easy. Is preaching, teaching, or speaking about abortion divisive? Yes, it is. But division isn't always bad. Sometimes, in fact, God requires it.

I know, the New Testament overflows with verses on unity in the Body of Christ. In His high priestly prayer of John 17, Jesus frequently admonishes believers to be "one" even as the Son and the Father are One. God desires us to be parts of one body, operate as a single organism, and be of one mind. Unity in marriage is a mystery designed to illustrate the indivisible relationship between Christ and the Church.

But is unity to be sought at all costs? No.

Jesus declared: "Do not think that I came to bring peace on the earth; I did not come to bring peace, but a sword. For I came to SET A MAN AGAINST HIS FATHER, AND A DAUGHTER AGAINST HER MOTHER, AND A DAUGHTER-IN-LAW AGAINST HER MOTHER-IN-LAW; and A MAN'S ENEMIES WILL BE THE MEMBERS OF HIS HOUSEHOLD."[54]

What prompts the kind of division that Jesus describes? The truth. The sword Jesus has in mind separates the obedient from the disobedient. It divides those who would follow Him from those who would reject Him. When church leaders teach the truth to their parishioners, people will either embrace truth or recoil from it. Those in ministry must come alongside those who reject the teachings of Scripture and work to persuade them to follow, to become a disciple of Christ. But if people stubbornly refuse to respond, or worse, openly and vocally rebel against a justifiable warning over doctrine, and church discipline results in no change, then division must come.

At the same time, it's important to note that the goal of division in such cases is not to permanently separate the rebellious from those who faithfully follow Christ. Rather, it's to demonstrate the seriousness of opposing the revealed truth of the Scriptures, with the hope of eventual repentance and reconciliation. Compromise is impossible with truth on the line.

Everyone with ministry responsibilities will someday give an account for those souls entrusted to their care. We must remain diligent and cautious not to conflate personal or cultural preferences with the revealed will of God. But the Church must clearly and vocally oppose abortion, and should publicly advocate for and support women who seek life-affirming alternatives. We avoid speaking of abortion at our peril. The blood of the innocent cries out from the ground and will not be silenced by appeals to false unity.

Answer Four: Does Silence on Abortion Harm Congregants?

Church leaders correctly assume that speaking about abortion may cause pain to some of their congregants who have experienced or aided in an abortion. But is the risk of causing pain justified? And is it preferable to silence?

The argument that discomfort should disqualify a topic from discussion is fatally flawed. If followed, no one could speak about gluttony, fornication, divorce, lying, stealing, or any other sin (and often, unfortunately, many of these sins also go undiscussed). How can we pretend that people in the church never need rebuke or admonition, that they will "figure things out for themselves" and correct their own behavior? This way of thinking equates talking about the issues publicly with shaming, and in the contemporary American moral climate, shaming is always bad. In fact, God commands us to use His Word as a training tool to help mold people into the image of Jesus and equip them to do good.[55] Christians can talk about sin without doing lasting harm to other believers.

The Bible identifies behaviors people should avoid, precisely because many people do *not* avoid them. Proverbs 23:17 warns us, "Do not let your heart envy sinners, but live in the fear of the Lord always." We tend to emphasize the second half of that verse and neglect the first half. Why does God command us not to envy sinners? Precisely because we feel a strong temptation to envy sinners, and many of us fall into this sin.

We need to learn to explain *why* people feel tempted to envy sinners, *why* the perceived benefits of envying sinners never last, and *why* thinking rightly about the end-state of unrepentant sinners while fearing God provides a better path. Now, if Christians get in the habit of envying sinners—and I would argue that our media-obsessed culture makes this common—then pointing out such a destructive habit will irritate some people. But is it kinder to cause temporary distress in those who do precisely what the Scripture forbids, and so spare them lasting pain; or to comfort them in their sin, and by doing so contribute to their ruin? On this issue, most would agree that pointing out their sin and helping people to repent and forsake it is the only right, sane, and profitable way to go.

Why, then, when it comes to abortion, do we become so reticent? Maybe we grow silent because we see abortion as a singular sin: committed only once, regretted, and then best forgotten. Such a position is wrong in at least two ways.

First, this approach is factually incorrect. Approximately half of the women seeking abortion already have had at least one previous abortion.[56]

Second, even if the abortion were a singular ignored event, it does *not* go away on its own. In fact, it becomes a powerful tool in the hands of the Enemy to sideline believers.

When we remain silent about abortion, we send the message that abortion is unimportant to discuss, perhaps not even a sin. When faced with an untimely pregnancy, some men and women feel freer to think, *It must be no big deal. I mean, the pastor or my youth group leader never even talks about it.* All of the media messaging we hear denies the humanity or the personhood of the human being in the womb. So why not make life simpler, like the counselor at the family planning clinic (or the student's high school counselor) tells them?

While in the back of their mind some doubts may linger, the crushing fear of the unknown, the effect of having a baby now, or the shame of being found out for having premarital sexual relations overwhelms them. In the absence of good reasons to do otherwise, or in ignorance of available competent and compassionate support systems, many young couples choose to abort their child.

For some, regret immediately follows the abortion. For others, it may take weeks, months, or years. The Enemy speaks to them, telling them that deep down they knew they were sinning against God. The Accuser's voice says that they have ruined themselves for service; how could God use a person who kills their own child? Silence by church leadership on abortion, once seen as tacit approval, begins to look like the unforgiveable sin—a sin so horrible it mustn't be discussed because it can't be expunged. Some people despair, while others act out in unhealthy ways. And for too many, abortion becomes a barrier to the gospel. The lifeless body of their unborn child lies between them and the forgiveness Christ offers, and they can't find any way to remove it.

———————— • ————————

Even gentle confrontation over sin can bring sorrow. But Paul explains in 2 Corinthians 7:10 that godly sorrow "produces a repentance without regret, leading to salvation, but the sorrow of the world produces death." Don't fear to call sin, sin. Especially your own. Confront it, turn from it, and choose life.

———————— • ————————

Not everyone, of course, feels regret after an abortion, just as not everyone feels regret or shame after committing any number of sinful acts. But lack of regret doesn't prove some behavior is morally okay. Proverbs 30:20 speaks of the adulterous woman (a verse which would apply equally well to adulterous men): "She eats and wipes her mouth, and says, 'I have done no wrong.'"[57] Our culture has so normalized abortion that it encourages people to ignore *any* contrary voice that might speak of personal sin or guilt.

In either case, ignoring sin in the hope that it will somehow sort itself out simply doesn't work. It causes people to hide their sin, rather than deal with it. The force and influence of hidden sin continues to grow, eventually burying such people under an avalanche of shame and guilt. Unconfessed and unforgiven sin can rob people of a life of Kingdom service and keep some from ever seeking out the hope freely available to them in the gospel. Speaking about abortion as sin, conversely, can do the opposite.

Healing from sin involves a five-step process: confession, repentance, forgiveness, healing, and restoration. We can't skip any step. Without acknowledging our sin, we can't repent. Without repentance, we cannot receive forgiveness. Without forgiveness, we cannot heal; and without healing, no restoration can occur. Silence on abortion leads to people feeling alone and trapped in their sin. Speaking of abortion opens a door, providing a way of escape and reconciliation.

Does it hurt the hearts of people who have experienced abortion to hear abortion classed with child sacrifice and idolatry? Yes, it can. Many people, both within and without the church, get caught up in sin. Hiding gives no answer. Cleansing through the blood of Jesus, through confession and repentance, provides the only way forward. Christians must acknowledge their sinful pasts. No matter how deep our transgressions, the Apostle Paul declares freedom in Christ. Once we may have been numbered among "such" people, lost in our sins, but through faith in the redemption offered by Jesus, *we are no longer.* Redeemed people can share with others how Jesus has set them free.[58] Christ-followers such as these become uniquely positioned to lead similarly burdened people to Jesus. Such a journey begins with compassionate, but firm, messaging on abortion in the church.

Answer Five: Silence Creates Targets for Abortion Advocacy

We all want to look good in the eyes of others. In the church, as elsewhere, most of us have a great desire to portray Christians, particularly our Christians (the ones who attend our church, or *our* Christian school or college) as a bit more "squeaky clean" than other people. Lots of reasons exist for this kind of thinking. Pastors may feel ego-involved, sometimes in an unhealthy way, thinking that the quality of the moral life of their congregants always directly reflects on them. Therefore, their squeaky-clean lives give testimony to the effectiveness of the preaching from the pulpit (and in small groups, and in the youth room, etc.), so that we needn't talk about certain sins. After all, we don't have that problem *here.*

Some Christians move into denial when confronted by statistics indicating that more than 50 percent of women seeking abortion have some relationship to the church. They dislike hearing statistics that show teen sexual activity remains roughly the same for teens both inside and outside the church. They imagine that those "liberal" churches down the street must skew the statistics. But research shows that approximately 40 percent of students have had sexual intercourse by the time they graduate, and 66 percent of college students have had sexual intercourse in the last twelve months.[59] None of this counts the number of students engaging in other sexual activity just shy of intercourse, such as oral sex.[60]

Discussions with countless pregnancy help center directors tell me that an astonishing number of young pregnant women who come in for counseling self-identify as Christians. A LifeWay research survey reported that "More than 4 in 10 women who have had an abortion were churchgoers when they ended a pregnancy."[61]

The level of ignorance regarding abortion among young people astounds me. I surveyed nearly 1,000 college students and discovered that only 10 percent understood the enormity of the problem. When asked how many abortions occur in the United States each year, 90 percent responded with 100,000 or less. One student wrote, "13,000—too many ☹." Imagine if she had known that the number that year eclipsed 1 million surgical abortions. 83 percent of students believed that abortion was illegal at the end of the first trimester (thirteen weeks). The majority of these surveys took place in California, a state with no limitations on gestational age for abortion.

Finally, when asked "If a woman had an untimely pregnancy, to what local organization would you refer her?" among students attending public universities, 57 percent responded "Planned Parenthood." The question wasn't multiple choice; students had to come up with an answer out of their heads. 39 percent of students replied with some version of "I don't know." Less than 4 percent of students identified their local PHC, despite every college surveyed having such a center close to campus.

The real eye-opener for me happened when I repeated the study at a large, evangelical Christian university located on the West Coast. Despite having multiple pro-life pregnancy clinics in neighborhoods surrounding the campus, 42 percent of students said they would refer the woman to Planned Parenthood. 53 percent said they didn't know where to send her. And just over 6 percent said they would send her to the local PHC.[62]

Only a tiny number of students in these surveys ever mentioned a pastor or a church as a referral for the pregnant woman. A survey conducted by LifeWay Research echoes these results. Of churchgoers who have had an abortion, only 7 percent discussed it with anybody at church; just over half say "no one at the church knows it. Nearly half of women who have had an abortion (49 percent) say pastor's teachings on forgiveness don't seem to apply to terminated pregnancies."[63]

When Christians stay silent on abortion, a host of other messengers rush in to fill the gap. Most people in most churches know next to nothing about fetal development, about what abortion is and does, and what the

Bible has to say about it. When women find themselves in the midst of an untimely pregnancy, many panic and reach for the nearest way out. The one resource they know about is Planned Parenthood, a brand with deep market penetration.[64] Planned Parenthood has a "sexual health chatbot" for Teens called Roo (ironic, as Roo is a loveable character, the young kangaroo in his mother Kanga's pouch, in the *Winnie the Pooh* books)[65]. The abortion giant keeps going after younger and younger clients. The church cannot afford to sit on the sidelines while Planned Parenthood recruits—dare I say, evangelizes? Instead, the church must educate and inoculate believers against relentless abortion advocacy.

Answer Six: What If You Already Have Spoken About Abortion?

I have never been arrested. I never plan to get arrested. You can bet that if I ever am arrested, it will be an *unplanned* arrest.

Nevertheless, for the many years I lived in North San Diego County, I knew the name of my bail bondsman: King Stahlman. I knew about him because of the endless repetitions of his commercial on my local radio station, along with his jingle: "It's better to know me and not need me, than to need me and not know me."

It's better for Christians to know about abortion and never need to consider getting one, than to land in a desperate position and not know about abortion. It's better for Christians to know the name and location of their local PHC and not need it, than to encounter a woman facing an untimely pregnancy and not know where to send her. Clearly, the research shows that most people don't know, but need to.

To know, really *know*, about something, requires repetition. The Apostle Paul doesn't worry about repeating himself: "Finally, my brethren, rejoice in the Lord. To write the same things again is no trouble to me, and it is a safeguard for you."[66] Paul understood the power of a persuasive campaign; so did the Apostle Peter: "Therefore, I will always be ready to remind you of these things, even though you already know them, and have been established in the truth which is present with you. I consider it right, as long as I am in this earthly dwelling, to stir you up by way of reminder…And I will also be diligent that at any time after my departure you will be able to call these things to mind."[67]

Pastors and youth leaders should deliberately speak on abortion at least once a year, and again every time the text of their message suggests a close connection. If they plan to discuss murder, children, idolatry, fornication, adultery, family, mothers and fathers, or any related topic, abortion should figure in. All of us would like to believe that every time we tell someone something important it will stick, but it doesn't. Only by repetition, by creating a campaign of persuasion, can we hope to make the message sink in. Be like Paul and Peter.

Answer Seven: The Embarrassment of Ministerial Ignorance

Everyone wants to play to their strengths. Pastors and other church leaders know that congregants look to them for answers. Younger Christians expect older believers to know more about life in the faith. What do we do when we don't?

Abortion isn't a complicated issue, but it's made to appear so by abortion-choice advocates. It's easy to feel overwhelmed by the sheer glut of arguments. But if Christian leaders allow potential embarrassment over their own ignorance to impede important teaching, other believers will suffer. Natural shame comes from sin and leads to repentance; but the shame of ignorance is best remedied by education, not silence.

I don't mean to browbeat Christian leaders. I understand why many don't know about abortion and the arguments constructed to advocate for it.

Schools have done a scandalously poor job of teaching about abortion. As I've mentioned, I know of *no* Christian colleges with regular courses dedicated to pro-life bioethics or advocacy. Secular colleges treat every kind of sexual activity as the norm, and abortion merely as a necessary medical response to unwanted pregnancy. The University of California launched the first online abortion class in 2014.[68] Many Christian leaders graduate from these colleges, and if even Christian schools avoid the issue, where would they encounter the right responses? Having successfully completed training, they believe they're prepared for ministry. They are the ones supposed to know; and then they find they don't. And there's no googling a quick answer either; the issues appear complex.

Modern-day idolatry masquerades as medicine, even within our congregations. We *must* know the answers. If Christians are to learn about abortion and how to persuasively argue for life, either in public or in conversations, they must intentionally go out and get educated. No one will do this for them (although abortion advocates would love to indoctrinate them).

I wish there were some way I could grant immediate understanding on this issue. I wish I could wave a rhetorical wand over you so that instantly you could make persuasive arguments. I can't. But reading this book is a good first step.

In the following chapters, you will learn how abortion-choice supporters talk, how abortion-choice advocates advance their ideology, and how you can effectively and lovingly respond. You hold in your hand the very tool needed to liberate you—but I can't read it or study it for you. You must do that for yourself.

Answer Eight: Break Sin's Hold on Your Voice

Sometimes, the issue holding back Christian voices from speaking on abortion is not ignorance, but intimate familiarity. Christians aren't immune from the lure of the abortion industry, as we've seen. In fact, abortion has likely touched more people in your church, directly or indirectly, than you know.

If you have abortion in your background—either you've had an abortion or you've been involved in somebody else's abortion—it can seem hypocritical or frightening to talk about it. If this describes you, you need to get competent, compassionate, and confidential help. Call or go to a PHC and ask if it offers post-abortion Bible studies and counseling. Most do. These programs, such as *Forgiven and Set Free,* or *Surrendering the Secret*, have led thousands of people to healing and restoration. Many centers have programs for men. *Deeper Still* provides multi-day retreats for those wrestling with abortion in their past.[69]

The sin of abortion shackles believers and unbelievers alike. If you want to free your voice, healing is available. Don't assume that praying in private, seeking forgiveness, and getting reconciled will suffice. For many, the wounds of abortion go deep and the self-recrimination can paralyze. Give yourself the gift of freedom. Humble yourself and seek counsel. Once liberated, not only will you recover joy, but you will make yourself ready to free others who also struggle under the weight of a past abortion.

Without question, the topic of abortion can cause tremendous distress. In the next chapter, we will see how that distress can become our friend when we engage other people about abortion.

Chapter 4

What to Expect When You Speak Up

Everyone says they like novelty, change, new experiences and ideas. Usually they lie.

When you walk into a restaurant you visit frequently, do they see you coming from a mile away and know exactly what you'll order? Have you driven the same kind of car for years, maybe decades? I wore the same brand of tennis shoes for so long that they morphed into an "old guy" meme. Fact is, people like the familiar and don't especially enjoy change.

This universal drive to anchor our beliefs and resist change comes in very handy. When you select a spouse and say, "I do," you really ought to stop looking for alternatives. Political incumbency has great power; once people select leaders, they tend to keep sending them back. In our court system, defendants are presumed innocent until proven guilty. Even in academic debate, judges defer to the status quo, the way things are, unless a compelling case can be made for change. We like things to stay the same.

While resistance to change helps if we want to create and live in a stable society, it can make shifting people's perspectives and actions on abortion much more difficult.

Once someone commits to a viewpoint, especially a culturally popular one, they tend to stick with it. When attacked, those same people will attempt some level of defense, often poor, of their closely-held beliefs. Surprisingly, however, the views many people hold, even on significant moral topics, aren't even their own. Christian philosopher Francis Schaeffer explained, "Most people catch their presuppositions from their family and surrounding society, the way that a child catches the measles."[70] In other words, we do not engage in close research and careful analysis to selectively choose many of the mental underpinnings of the ideas we hold. We simply get them from others.

In *The Abolition of Man*, C.S. Lewis reveals the impact of these acquired, rather than deliberately determined, ideas. Lewis recognized that much of what passes as education does not teach pupils how to critically evaluate ideas, but instead conditions students to reflexively choose culturally-approved worldviews: "It is not a theory they have put into his mind, but an assumption, which, ten years hence, its origin forgotten and its presence unconscious, will condition him to take one side in a controversy which he has never recognized as a controversy at all."[71] The view Lewis addresses in this passage concerns a perspective that he saw coming way back in 1948, a seed that has found its full flourishing in contemporary American education, namely that objective moral values do not exist.

Such a perspective encourages people to feel free to believe whatever they want, and to resist all attempts to change their minds. The more comforting, affirming, and option-producing the ideas, the more strongly people will hold them. If you want to engage others in mind-changing ways, you must introduce them to an experience most people don't like: distress. Fortunately, when the subject is abortion, that's easy to accomplish.

I Should Have Paid More Attention in Psych Class

In all of the years I've trained people in persuasion, the best explanation I've found for the resistance that pro-life advocates almost universally encounter when they talk about abortion can be summed up in three words: Cognitive Dissonance Theory.[72]

Okay, don't close the book! You might have seen all the many parts of this theory in a high school or college psychology class, but your teacher probably never took the time to explain why you should understand it (you know, *after* the exam). Allow me.

People will likely continue to think and do what they have always thought and done unless stress gets introduced into their lives. Many people will avoid buying a new car until the pain of continuing to repair their old car exceeds the anticipated discomfort of dealing with a stereotypical car salesman. In the world of ideas, the same holds true. Until we can make the holding of incorrect or morally unsupportable ideas uncomfortable, people will have little motivation to change. That's where cognitive dissonance comes in.

Cognitive dissonance refers to the psychological stress that people experience when their strongly-held beliefs come into conflict with new information. An encounter I had a few years ago with a university student provides a good illustration.

I received an invitation to participate in one of the Center for Bioethical Reform's Genocide Awareness Projects (GAP), this one at California State University, San Marcos. GAP goes onto college campuses to engage students about abortion. The group places signs around campus, warning students that large, graphic posters depicting human atrocities lie ahead, and pointing them to ways around the images if they don't want to see them. Those who want to see the images approach them and interact with volunteers. I stood behind the barriers with other pro-life advocates to engage members of the student body.

One male student spoke with me for a long time. I laid out the pro-life position for him, both the scientific and moral evidence, to help him conclude that the human being growing in the womb was both fully human and as morally valuable as anyone else. I exposed the lies of abortion-choice advocates, using evidence gleaned from their own writings. When I finished answering all his questions, he said, "I want to thank you for sharing your perspective," and then he turned to walk away.

"Stop!" I said, probably more loudly than I intended, and I called him back. "I'm sorry, but I can't let you leave here believing that what you heard from me was merely 'my perspective.' I provided you with evidence from embryology texts and Planned Parenthood's own documents, showing that human life begins at conception and that abortion kills that life. I've shown you evidence and analysis that demonstrates that human rights extend to all human beings, not as a result of what they can do or where they are located, but as a result of the kind of things they are. Unless you have better evidence and analysis to demonstrate that what I told you is untrue, you are being intellectually inconsistent if you leave here without changing your stance. I always told my students that the pursuit of the academic life is to discover the truth and then follow it. You can walk away unchanged, but you have to know

now that what you believe is not true. It's hard to live with that inconsistency. What I've told you is objectively true; it's not merely 'my perspective.'"

I didn't "convert" that student during our encounter, but I did forcefully introduce uncertainty into what he thought about abortion. I made him uncomfortable. Right in the middle of an intense public discussion (a lot of students stood around that day), few people will just roll over and admit defeat; doing so feels too embarrassing. But it's less likely that this student will continue to make the claims he made to me before our discussion ended. Over time, his views can change (though as you will see below, that's never guaranteed).

For others, especially when we speak interpersonally or in a public speaking environment, the influence of dissonance can have more immediate results. Regardless of whether attitude shift occurs now or later, without the discomfort, long-held ideas probably will not change.

How People Respond to Psychological Distress

Most of us don't seek out distressing experiences. And once distressing experiences arrive, most of us seek relief. People who hold a positive attitude toward abortion will respond in six differing ways to the discomfort you cause them when you speak the truth about abortion:

- avoidance
- twisting your meaning until it fits with theirs
- strategic forgetfulness
- rationalization
- finding ways to make your arguments less persuasive
- finding ways to make their own arguments less persuasive

Let's look at each of these tactics and then see what pro-life messengers can do to turn this distress into an advantage for the truth.

Tactic one: Where'd they go?

The easiest way to keep one's ideas, opinions, and beliefs intact is to avoid exposure to new information. People do this all the time.

In the digital age, every conceivable political, economic, or spiritual persuasion has its own set of websites, radio stations, and television and cable channels that will cater to, reinforce, and champion even the narrowest of those views. If you want to live in a comfortable ideological bubble or echo chamber, you live in the right era.

The very places that used to be hotbeds of controversy—universities, where competing ideas got placed in the crucible of debate in hopes that the truth would emerge—now come equipped with an array of "safe spaces" (allotted by race, gender, and other divisions). Texts and professors provide "trigger warnings." Psychological stress has a hard time developing when students can keep themselves from encountering information that conflicts with their beliefs.

Unfortunately, the same sometimes happens in church.

When I receive an invitation to preach about abortion, I go out of my way to get the pastor not to reveal my topic to the congregation. I have a great title for that sermon: "A City Full of Idols." Why that title? Well, think about it. If a church advertises a message about idolatry, who thinks, *Well, I support idol worship. In fact, I'm involved in it right now?*

That's right. No one.

If everybody knew several days in advance that I would speak about abortion, however, it's likely some of the very people I most need to reach would not show up. People in the church who have abortion in their background, or who have a political bent toward a favorable view of abortion as a morally-permissible choice, don't want to be confronted or challenged. Few people think twice about avoiding a "guest speaker." By skipping confrontation, congregants never feel the distress of the new information, and so they can continue to remain at ease.

Tactic two: Twist 'till it fits

Sometimes you can't avoid distressing messages. When that happens, listeners often unconsciously twist words, phrases, or ideas to fit their own assumptions.

Consider the words, "abortion," "fetus" and "embryo." Terms like these, and the ideas they represent, can be psychologically manipulated to fit quite nicely with whatever view one holds.

When a pro-life person says the word "abortion," individuals who do not oppose abortion for themselves or for others may *hear* "pro-choice," "a medical procedure" or "termination of a pregnancy." When someone uses the medically-accurate developmental terms "embryo" or "fetus," others can *hear* "blob of tissue," "undifferentiated cell mass," or, more commonly, "that thing that, if you don't get an abortion, eventually turns into a baby."

In debate, the person who controls the terms of the argument usually wins. Undermining or altering the way words are received allows opposing ideas to seem weaker, or even as supporting the listener's views. Listeners may do this unconsciously, but when they selectively perceive key terms, they can evade the stress of new, conflicting ideas.

Tactic three: I don't recall

Politicians grilled about questionable or compromising behavior like to respond, "I don't recall," a catch-all sentence designed to deflect responsibility and shut down further interrogation. In other words, it lets them "move on."

People tend to suppress uncomfortable experiences—it's called "selective retention." When abortion-choice supporters discuss abortion with knowledgeable pro-life advocates, selective retention can be an unconscious ideological survival strategy. Some of the information and images used in presentations about abortion unsettle people who want to hold on to the idea that abortion is an acceptable response to untimely pregnancy. It should surprise no one that such people would prefer to suppress or forget their exposure to these unsettling images and arguments.

As the Director of Speech and Debate at the University of California, Irvine, I moderated a lot of academic debates in our "Great Debate" series. We would invite professional advocates from both sides of a controversial issue and let them go at it. Each year we held debates on the topic of abortion. One year, a student of mine had an interaction with a pro-life advocate in the parking lot before the debate. My student approached me after the debate and showed me the brochure the pro-life advocate had handed her, featuring photographs of aborted *babies*. She looked at me and said, "I've always been pro-choice, but...these are babies." Do you think the experience converted her?

Months later, the same student came to my office and, during our discussion, told me that she had driven her roommate to a clinic to get an abortion.

What happened?

She had just one exposure to pro-life images and some new ideas that deeply affected her. Clearly, that exposure distressed her. She quickly came to a correct conclusion about the nature of the victims of abortion: "these are *babies*." But in the absence of continued exposure to a pro-life message, and her immersion in abortion-choice ideology on campus, the power of those photographs and ideas waned, while her interpersonal connection to her roommate increased. When faced with a choice between "helping her roommate" and obedience to a fading, politically and socially unpopular stance, she suppressed the new information and took her roommate to an abortion clinic.

Tactic four: It'll never happen to me

Too many people consider abortion an extreme, yet necessary, response to an unlikely event. For good reason, people use the term "unplanned" pregnancies. Millions of people no doubt think, before they get pregnant, *It'll never happen to me.*

If you don't want to get pregnant, you probably view the possibility of pregnancy as remote. It's easy to see how the topics of pregnancy and abortion can get dismissed by those who reason, "Well, I'll never be in a position to grapple with abortion; I'm not going to get pregnant."

Everybody thinks they'll be the exception to the rule. It's an odd phenomenon, and not limited to individuals. Many churches or Christian schools never address abortion because they don't believe they need to: "That kind of thing—unplanned pregnancy—just doesn't happen *here*."

While your discussion, message, or sermon about abortion might sound interesting in some abstract, academic way, people who rationalize feel free to dismiss any call for change because, in their minds, it just doesn't apply to them. Untimely pregnancy and considerations about abortion? Well, that's the kind of thing that happens to *other* people.

Tactic five: Attack the source

If people can't avoid discussing abortion, can't twist your words to fit their worldview, have a hard time forgetting what they have heard, and find themselves in a demographic that makes what you have to say difficult to dismiss, one way out of the distress remains: devalue what you have to say.

One of the most frequent ways distressed people devalue your message is through *ad hominem* attack. If they can't defeat your argument, they go after you. The popularity of *ad hominem* attacks has increased in these "progressive" times. After all, if I can label you a "conservative," "patriarchal," "anti-woman," "anti-choice" "bigot," then why would I have to listen to anything else you might have to say?

Other times, people will attack the source of the arguments you make. When pro-life advocates support their arguments solely from material gleaned from the National Right to Life or other identifiable pro-life organizations, they leave themselves open to charges of bias, followed by dismissal. The person remains unconvinced, leaving with their previous ideas intact.

Tactic six: I've changed my mind

The final response people can have to your distress-inducing message is to devalue what they currently believe and instead accept the claims and arguments you have offered. In other words, they change their minds.

Changing their minds relieves the stress you've caused by introducing information in conflict with their previously-held beliefs. A new belief, consistent with the evidence and careful analysis, produces no conflict and, therefore, no stress.

So, what can we take away from our brief tour of cognitive dissonance, conversation, and messages about abortion?

Persuasion Is Hard

You might think that if you have the truth, if you've marshalled the evidence and crafted a solid case for life, people would fall all over themselves to join the pro-life side. But go back and count the ways people can respond to the stress you cause by speaking to them about abortion. In five out of the six methods people use to reduce their stress, their beliefs and opinions remain unchanged. Consequently, so do their actions.

Persuasion isn't easy; it's hard. But that doesn't make it impossible.

First, many of those you speak to will have no significant hostility toward the pro-life message, so whatever resistance they mount will be weak. They just want you to prove your case, often because they've never heard a real, tightly-reasoned case for life.

And second, even when your listeners express some or total hostility, you still have a way forward. Pro-life communicators need to learn how to make cognitive dissonance their friend, and then manage their communication to overcome barriers they know their listeners will put up.

Leverage the Distress

Knowing that speaking about abortion induces stress, and understanding in advance how your listeners will likely react, creates a real tactical advantage. Think of it like a chess player who, at the beginning of the game, already knows the next ten moves her opponent will make.

Your goal in the conversation, Sunday School lesson, or sermon is to help people see the truth about the nature and value of the human being developing in the womb. You want them to understand what abortion is and what it does to that innocent human being. You want to clearly communicate what believers and the public can do about abortion. And you want to help those with untimely pregnancies to make life-affirming decisions.

Once you start talking, some people may have negative reactions to the stress you cause. Consider, then, a few things you need to do.

Keep on talking

I know of only one way to counter message avoidance or the inclination of some people to suppress the message they've heard: a prolonged campaign of persuasion. It's hard to avoid a message that gets in front of you wherever you are, and it's hard to forget a message when you hear it regularly repeated.

If pro-life advocates are to change the church, and through it, the world, the process begins with recognizing that a portion of the congregation would rather *not* hear about abortion. Perhaps they have abortion in their past, or they have participated in someone else's abortion. When Sanctity of Human Life Sunday rolls around, the choice to sleep in that day can seem very appealing. Churches with pastors who speak about abortion only once a year, on Sanctity of Human Life Sunday, do their most needy members a great disservice. By confining teaching about abortion to a single day, they make it easy for the most wounded believers to avoid much-needed change.

To fix that situation, the message of life—whether discussion of human development in the womb or abortion—must comprise part of the overall worldview message of the church. Beginning in elementary school and regularly thereafter, young people should consistently hear their pastors and other adults and leaders integrate biblical, scientific, and moral pro-life evidence and arguments inside related messages about topics such as life, marriage, children, family, and church growth. When young people grow older and begin to hear more mature messages about sexual sin, such as fornication and adultery, idolatry, bloodguiltiness, or murder, abortion should be in that mix, as it's intimately tied to all of these other sins.

———————————— • ————————————

Remember, when you speak on sexuality, the most attractive message on human relationships in history is yours to proclaim. Don't be shy about proposing it: A man and woman vow before God that they'll act in a loving way toward each other every day for the rest of their lives. They mean it, and—though imperfectly—they do it. Who wouldn't want to strive for that?

———————————— • ————————————

From Sunday School to small groups, Bible Studies to Sunday sermons, the life message should show up in your church in unavoidable ways. The more often people encounter the life message, the less able or inclined they will feel to suppress it. Repetition of a message builds worldview, as we've seen already.

When you were a little kid and you got a paper cut, you ran toward your mom, bleeding and shouting, "Mommie, mommie, I need a......." what?

If you thought *Band-Aid*, why is that? Why didn't you ask for a Curad Ouchless Flex Fabric Bandage? Curad makes those, you know. I'll tell you why. *You're stuck on Band-Aid, 'cause Band-Aid's stuck on...*c'mon, you know the words! Band-Aid brand has spent a lot of money getting you to associate its brand name with the product itself.

Maybe you have little kids at home, whom you entertain with animated vegetables that tell Bible stories. If I start you out—"*If you like to talk with tomatoes....*"—you probably can keep on singing. Why? Did you consider the words of the song so meaningful that you just had to learn them? No. As with the Band-Aid campaign, you "learned" it because it you heard it repeated so often that it became part of your cultural consciousness.

Many people favor abortion reflexively, not because they've thought about it. The claims they make supporting abortion don't reflect clearly crafted arguments; they simply repeat bumper stickers or echo the talking heads they've heard in the media. The church can combat such unthinking, wrongheaded support not only by making better arguments with better evidence, but by often repeating those arguments, teaching them clearly, and challenging our church family to defend them. That's one important way to build a culture of life.

Say what you mean so they'll see what you say

Most of us tend to twist the words we hear to fit with our already-held assumptions. You can short-circuit this tendency by carefully choosing your words, and if a word can be used in a variety of ways, define precisely what you mean.

As we've seen, the terms "embryo" and "fetus" are perfectly fine terms, so long as people understand that they refer to arbitrarily identified stages in the development of a human being in the womb. Too often, abortion-choice supporters use the terms to blur the truth and get people to think of the child in the womb as a thing rather than a person. To counteract that idea, think of the words "newborn" or "toddler," which also reference stages of development rather than the nature of the developing person. Throughout this book, I'll use a host of terms to describe the person in the womb. Frequently, just for added clarity, I will refer to "the human being in the womb," but other times I will use the word "child," or "baby." If Planned Parenthood referred to the being in the womb as a "baby" in its pamphlet *Plan Your Children for Health and Happiness*, then abortion-choice supporters can hardly blame you if you use it, as well.

Even a word such as "abortion" gets loaded with differing meanings. Some people use the word to describe what they think of as a "medical procedure," so when I use it for the first time in front of people whose position I don't know, I follow it with some version of this definition (which I first heard from Gregg Cunningham): "abortion, an act of violence that intentionally kills an unborn child." Today, I'd probably choose a slightly different definition: "abortion is an act of violence that intentionally kills an innocent human being developing in his mother's womb." With a definition like that, everyone clearly understands the nature of the discussion.

I avoid the term "pro-choice" as much as possible when discussing abortion, because it carries a lot of associated (and undeserved) positive implications. "Choice" is a euphemism employed so that the person speaking will not have to say or defend "abortion." This lesson got driven home to me one year when a political survey researcher called my home to ask about my position on "choice." I asked, "What do you mean by 'choice'?" Flummoxed, the caller just repeated it, "you know, *choice!*" I replied, "Well, I'm in favor of all kinds of choices. I think that parents should be able to choose the schools their children attend. I think people should be able to choose their doctors. Choosy mothers can choose Jif peanut butter." When I heard nothing but stunned silence on the other end of the phone, I continued: "But I don't think that people should legally be allowed to choose to put to death an innocent child developing in his mother's womb, just because they want to. No."

"Click." The caller hung up. I guess he didn't get the response he expected.

In fairness, I feel more than happy to abandon the term "pro-life" when I talk to some people about the abortion issue. I'll use the term "anti-abortion," if they prefer. People should be "anti" about a lot of things: anti-rape, anti-slavery, anti-spousal abuse, etc. Anti-abortion is one of them.

Consider carefully how someone who disagrees with you might twist your language choices to maintain their current beliefs. The more concrete your word choices, the less likely people can modify them. They will hear you clearly, and you will put on the table one less means of avoiding the stress of new, conflicting information.

Tell me a story

When an example or an outcome feels unpleasant, especially when viewed as a singular and unlikely occurrence, people want to think that such things or outcomes cannot happen to individuals like them. It's your job to show them that it can happen to them, because it does happen to people just like them.

Sometimes pro-life people get into the heat of a disagreement over abortion and have a compelling desire to win . . . the argument. But the true goal, remember, is to win the person. And it really is possible to do both.

Advocates, whether speaking with an individual or talking to a group, should recognize that two aspects of arguments can have very powerful effects when crafted together. First, make a claim and then prove it with evidence and reasoning. Second, tell a story illustrating the claim. Arguments over abortion occasionally forget to be human.

If I speak at a middle-class church where many of the members have teenage kids or college students, I will pepper my presentation with stories—detailed, compelling stories—about kids just like theirs. Imagine if I told you, "Amber walked through our doors with a positive pregnancy test in her hands." If I asked you to draw a picture of Amber, what would she look like? A stick figure, perhaps?

But what if I said, "Amber walked through the doors of our pregnancy help center. You all know some high school girls like Amber: five-foot three, long, blonde hair, dressed a little preppy, make-up carefully applied. The kind of happy, nice girl who would get voted 'most likely to succeed' in her yearbook. But the day Amber walked through our doors, her make-up didn't look so great. Most of the mascara she had put on that morning had begun running down her cheeks. Her eyes were puffy from crying. In her hand she held a crumpled yellow slip of paper from her school clinic—the positive result from her pregnancy test."

If I asked everyone in my group to draw a picture of Amber *then*, they might each draw a slightly different picture, but they would all have a more full-fledged image of Amber, likely drawn from girls they know in real life. Amber has become more than a faceless client; she is a living, breathing girl, like many others they know. As a result, her story has both familiarity and emotional power. Both elements help to overcome the idea that such a scenario couldn't possibly happen to people like them.

Get hostile (or neutral)

If we know that people will look for bias in our arguments, let's not give them easy targets. Avoid supporting your claims with evidence exclusively from people or organizations that have an unmistakable pro-life bias. I don't mean that pro-life sources are bad; quite the opposite. I think their claims are far more defensible than those of abortion-choice advocates.

In attempting to convince people who disagree with us about abortion, however, we'll have more success by using hostile and neutral sources. "Hostile" sources make claims you wouldn't expect, because those claims undermine the source's stated position. In later chapters, I'll identify testimony and claims made by abortion-choice advocates and organizations, such as Planned Parenthood, that actually undermine their positions and support a pro-life position. I'll also reference sources that many people might call "neutral" (no one is really neutral, but some sources, such as news organizations, often get viewed as neutral).

There's nothing like discussing the sanctity of life with someone who leans toward abortion, and you unexpectedly produce a pro-life argument supported by evidence from Planned Parenthood. You'll hear them say, "Well that's because you're so biased …. oh, wait . . . that bit was from my side." It's fatal to a person's argument to reject your claims when your evidence comes from those who represent their side.

See How the Other Side Argues

In the first part of this book, we examined the key lie about abortion, revealing it as a form of child sacrifice, a kind of idolatry. You saw why people, and not just pastors, self-censor about abortion and why those reasons for not speaking up have serious flaws.

In this chapter, you got a first glimpse into how argument works in real life, not merely on a page. When you introduce new ideas and evidence that contradicts what people already think and believe, it causes stress. People will do a lot to get back to "normal," but if you craft your arguments while remaining aware of those dismissive tactics, you will more likely get a hearing. If people will simply listen to and consider arguments defending life, presented and supported well and winsomely, minds can change and little lives (and the moral and spiritual lives of each child's parents) can be saved.

What we have seen so far is part of the strategic way pro-life people should engage about abortion. But we have a sophisticated, adamant, well-funded adversary. The gauntlet has been thrown down. We make arguments, but abortion-choice supporters also make their own arguments.

In the next section, we'll look at a strategy used by abortion-choice supporters that I can only call "arguing in retreat." We'll see how pro-life advocates can expose their flaws every step of the way, until the mask finally comes off and the true nature of abortion advocacy is revealed.

Part Two

The Five Big Shifts

When people talk about distressing topics, they not only try to find ways to avoid, twist, forget, rationalize, or devalue the message they've heard, they also try to make their own arguments difficult to attack directly. If you can refute one part of a major claim, suddenly that part of the argument gets minimized or abandoned by the one making it, and a new, different argument takes its place. Four arguments later, they return to the previously abandoned argument and you have to start all over.

Having a discussion with someone who talks this way is like trying to nail Jell-O to the wall. Just when you think you have their position fixed and have pierced it with better evidence, analysis, and reasoning, it slips off, reconstitutes itself, and you must begin again.

In the first section of this book, I identified both the physical and spiritual stakes of the battle and tried to help the church wake up to the fact that those who champion abortion have thrown down a gauntlet. Unfortunately, many pastors, leaders, and lay Christians have let the challenge go unanswered for reasons that seemed good to them, but which, in fact, have caused tremendous harm in the church and the world. Even when we do speak up about abortion, those who would rather not listen or confront the issue guard themselves with an array of psychological devices to try to maintain balance, even after they get exposed to credible information that conflicts with what they thought they knew.

In this second section, I want to walk you through the Five Big Shifts that occur in the minds of abortion-choice supporters when you talk to them about abortion. These shifts take place whether you preach about abortion from the pulpit, teach a youth group or Sunday School class, have a debate in your college or high school social studies course, or engage in a casual conversation.

Once you see how abortion-choice supporters shift ground, you will know how to "spike" one part of the argument (securely hold it in place so they can't come back to it), and then move the discussion forward. Talking in this way helps both you and the person you are speaking with to come to better, more informed conclusions.

Even if you understand the nature of the arguments you need to make and then employ them, you won't succeed with everyone. But that's okay; do it anyway. You'll be in good company. You'll find that your conversations likely will end in precisely the same way that the Apostle Paul's did in Acts 17:32-34, when he spoke to the leaders of Athens on the Areopagus on another controversial subject, the resurrection of Jesus: "Now when they heard of the resurrection of the dead, some began to sneer, but others said, 'We shall hear you again concerning this.' So Paul went out of their midst. But some men joined him and believed, among whom also were Dionysius the Areopagite and a woman named Damaris and others with them."

Count on it. When you engage in the defense of human beings in the womb against those who argue that exterminating those human beings is moral and should remain legal, some will sneer, some will continue to think and engage with you, and others will change their minds. The time and effort required of you to prepare yourself for those times is worth it.

Chapter 5

The Starting Point

When planning to talk about, teach, or preach on any controversial subject, you should begin by identifying the controversy and establishing what you need to prove before you can expect anyone to agree with you. When I first began teaching the Pro-Life Speaker Seminar, I would tell my students, "When I talk about abortion, whether with a single person or in front of a classroom or a large audience, I simply ask, 'Can we all start by agreeing that it's never okay for one human being to arbitrarily take the life of another innocent human being?'" Then I'd joke, "If the person next to you says 'No,' slowly move away."

By asking such a question, I'm trying to establish some common ground between myself and the person or audience I'm addressing. I want us all to agree that killing innocent human beings is wrong.

Where to Begin: The Case for Life as a Syllogism

Sometime after I started teaching my seminars, Francis Beckwith published a more philosophically sophisticated, formalized version of the same argument.[73] Scott Klusendorf has translated these ideas into a straightforward, easy-to-articulate series of statements that, for shorthand, he refers to as "The Syllogism." If you remember logic class, you know that a syllogism is a form of argument in which, if the foundational statements (premises) are true, and the form of the argument (the way it is constructed) is valid, then the conclusion of the argument is sound. Here, in three simple lines, is the pro-life position:

Premise 1:   It is wrong to intentionally kill an innocent human being.
Premise 2:   Abortion intentionally kills an innocent human being.
Conclusion: Therefore, abortion is wrong.[74]

Most people readily agree with the first premise: "It is wrong to intentionally kill an innocent human being." Most abortion-choice supporters reject the second premise; they simply deny that "abortion kills an innocent human being," emphasizing that the living being in a woman's womb is *not* a human being, in the common sense of that term.

The Foundational Challenge

I can think of many more pleasant ways to spend my time than thinking, writing, and speaking about abortion. If abortion-choice supporters correctly assert that whatever is in a woman's body after conception is not a human being, then not only could I freely spend my time elsewhere, but I would have to admit that I've been part of a movement intent on rolling back the hard-won rights of women to control their own bodies. If we are to get people who support abortion choice to agree with us that abortion is wrong, we must start by proving two key elements of the second premise of our argument:

1. What is in a woman's body after conception is a separate, whole, distinct, living human being;
2. Abortion kills that innocent human being.

"It's Not Really a Human Being"

At some abortion clinics, as well as at the popular level, abortion-choice supporters continue to assert that whatever occupies a pregnant woman's womb, it's *not* a human being. Common terms abortion-choice supporters use to describe the being in a woman's Body after a positive pregnancy test include: "blob of tissue," "the products of conception," "uterine contents," "potential life," or "pregnancy tissue."

Abortion clinics, in particular, seem reluctant to discuss precisely what it is they want to abort. Planned Parenthood's own website, in discussing aspiration abortions, never refers to the target of the suction device and curette as a "child." Here's how they describe the abortion:

> The doctor or nurse will . . . use a small, hand-held suction device
> or suction machine to gently take the pregnancy tissue out of your

uterus. They may also use a small surgical tool called a curette to remove any tissue that's left in your uterus, or check to make sure your uterus is totally empty.[75]

Planned Parenthood is not alone. A PDF flyer from The University of Michigan's Von Voigtlander Women's Hospital calls the living being in a pregnant woman's uterus both "uterine contents" and "pregnancy tissue."[76] Nowhere does this flyer reference the human embryo, which this procedure kills and removes.

To demonstrate how deeply such use of language has penetrated American culture, U.S. District Judge Lee Yeakel referred to aspiration abortions—indeed, even dilation and evacuation (D&E) abortions—as "procedural abortions," when they are generally referred to as "surgical abortions."[77] Yeakel issued his ruling as he attempted to bypass Texas Governor Greg Abbott's order to ban non-urgent medical procedures during the 2020 coronavirus pandemic. Just to clarify, virtually everything a doctor does to you could be classified as a "procedure." But Yeakel goes further, describing aspiration abortions in language nearly identical to that used by Planned Parenthood: "Despite sometimes being referred to as 'surgical abortion,' procedural abortion is not what is commonly understood to be 'surgery'; it involves no incision, no need for general anesthesia, and no requirement of a sterile field. Early in pregnancy, procedural abortions are performed using a technique called aspiration, in which a clinician uses gentle suction from a narrow, flexible tube to empty the contents of the patient's uterus."[78] While aspiration abortions require no "incision" for the mother, that "flexible tube" offers anything but "gentle suction" for the human being in the womb that it tears to pieces.

Information sheets for second-trimester abortions also refuse to acknowledge any human life in the womb. The "Health Information" page of UW Health (associated with the University of Wisconsin) describes "dilation and evacuation," noting that the process will include "suction aspiration," "dilation and curettage" and "surgical instruments (such as forceps)." The page describes the procedure in significant detail, but every time it mentions contact between the instruments of the abortionist and the human being aborted, the word used instead is always "tissue" or "uterine contents." The "tissue" apparently is both tough and resistant. The page notes that the abortionist will:

> Pass a grasping instrument (forceps) into the uterus to grasp larger pieces of tissue. This is more likely in pregnancies of 16 weeks or more and is done before the uterine lining is scraped with a curette.[79]

Apparently, even live birth is insufficient to grant the status of "child" or "baby" to a human being emerging from the womb as a result of a failed abortion. Notorious abortionist Kermit Gosnell was convicted of first-degree murder in 2013 for intentionally murdering living children who had managed to survive his attempts to kill them in the womb. To demonstrate how the language of abortion-choice advocates has made its way even into the vocabularies of advocates for life, Mark L. Reinze, an associate professor of constitutional law at Catholic University of America, not once, but twice in a *USA Today* editorial refers to Gosnell's post-born victims as "fetuses," despite Reinze's clear purpose to call out the way abortion "dehumanizes" its victims.[80]

In 2020, the U.S. Congress again tried to pass legislation—The Born-Alive Abortion Survivors Protection Act—designed to require medical attention and support for those newborn human beings who survive abortion attempts. The legislation failed. Reporting on Senator Ben Sasse's bill, CNN reporter Caroline Kelly described it as requiring "abortion providers to work to 'preserve the life and health' of a *fetus that was born* following an attempted abortion as they would for a newborn baby, or face up to five years in prison"[81] (emphasis added). While CNN "updated" its report to "more precisely reflect the language used in Sasse's bill," the fact remains that reporters at CNN, at least initially, would not recognize that once human beings emerge from the womb, regardless of the circumstances of their birth, even the most callous observers would now call them *babies,* not "fetuses."[82]

Abortion clinics, university medical units, and print and television news sources supply the terms that many abortion-choice supporters use in describing the person in the womb of a pregnant mother. If they correctly judge that we are dealing with nothing but "tissue," even "pregnancy tissue," or "uterine contents," or some rights-less proto-human "fetus," then the argument is over. For abortion to be morally wrong, that which is aborted must be a human being.

Is it?

What Science Says About What's in a Pregnant Woman's Body

When I want to find out about the status of "tissues" in a person's body, I go to doctors and medical researchers. It makes sense that if you want to find out the nature of what is inside a woman's body after conception, you would go to medical doctors who specialize in that area: embryologists.

Keith L. Moore, T.V.N Persaud, and Mark G. Torchia, in the latest edition of their longstanding textbook *The Developing Human: Clinically Oriented Embryology*, in 2020 explain that:

> Human development begins at fertilization when a sperm fuses with an oocyte to form a single cell, the zygote. This highly specialized, totipotent cell (capable of giving rise to any cell type) marks the beginning of each of us as a unique individual.[83]

So, these embryologists declare that fertilization is the point at which every one of us started life as a particular, individual human being. A sperm cell belongs to the father. The oocyte (egg cell) belongs to the mother. But once these two cells fuse, the resulting cell is neither the father's cell, nor the mother's cell, nor some kind of nondescript "fertilized egg." The resulting cell is the first cell of an entirely new, whole, distinct human being.

The first cell—the beginning stage of any particular human being's development—is called a zygote. A "zygote" isn't some proto-human life form that somehow gives rise to a human being. Instead, it's merely the stage at which all human beings begin. Later, that same human being will pass through a stage where they will be termed an "embryo," later a "fetus," and when that human being moves through the birth canal and emerges, he or she will be called a "newborn." After about a year, that same human being will be termed a "toddler," then a "child," an "adolescent," a "teenager," a "young adult," "middle-aged," and finally "elderly." All of these terms denote stages that this same human being, beginning in the zygote stage, will pass through—if he or she has the good fortune to live long enough.

None of this is new information. As noted in chapter one, all the way back in 1970—three years before the *Roe v. Wade* decision legalizing abortion throughout the United States—the official journal of the California Medical Association described "the curious avoidance of the scientific fact, which everyone really knows, that human life begins at conception and is continuous, whether intra- or extra-uterine until death."[84] So fifty years ago, who knew when human life began? According to this *California Medicine* editorial, *everyone* knew. Human life begins at conception, and then continues, both inside the womb and outside the womb, until death.

If embryologists know that every individual human comes into being at fertilization, and if *California Medicine* insists that this is no arcane fact known only to medical professionals, but that everyone knows it, wouldn't it make sense that abortionists would know this as well?

In 1951, nearly seventy years before the latest edition of *The Developing Human*, Planned Parenthood Federation of America already had begun distributing a little sex education booklet titled *The Gift of Life,* a flip-chart book designed to help young people understand their maturing bodies. The booklet explains, "If one of the male sperm meets and unites with an egg cell, a new life begins."[85] It describes the growth of this new life as "human growth" and by eight weeks gestation, the booklet declares that human being a "baby" who is "fed through a cord connected to its mother." You might note how much of the language used in *The Gift of Life* sounds like that used in *The Developing Human*. Everyone really does know that each individual human life begins at conception. Even people in the abortion industry know it.

They just don't like to talk about it.

Does Abortion Kill a Human Being?

Ask anyone who's worked in a pregnancy help center or clinic and they will tell you stories about young women who first visited an abortion clinic before coming to the center. Staffers at the abortion clinic spoke of unborn children, and the procedure used to kill and remove them, in vague, clinical terms. Why do they use clinical or obscure language? Not to provide the patient with greater clarity. On the contrary, they want to hide the true nature of the human being in the womb. They want to represent a violent, lethal procedure as something gentle and benign.

This is why abortion clinics and other abortion-choice advocates refer to abortion as a medical procedure designed to "terminate the pregnancy" by "evacuating the uterine contents" and "gently removing pregnancy tissue."

Language matters. While it is true that abortion "terminates the pregnancy," so does live birth, approximately thirty-eight weeks after conception. *All* pregnancies terminate. Abortion terminates a pregnancy by violently killing a human being in the womb, thus interrupting his or her natural growth.

The living being "evacuated" is contained in the uterus. But abortion-choice advocates don't like to explain what, precisely, is inside the uterus at the time of an abortion. Some abortion clinics like to use the wide-ranging term "pregnancy tissue." The term includes such tissues as the placenta and amniotic sac, but also the developing human being attached to that placenta and surrounded by that sac. They use the term "pregnancy tissue" in order to dehumanize the human being in the womb.

"Pregnancy" is a condition, not a living being. We identify a woman as "pregnant" whose uterus contains a human being (along with a placenta and the amniotic sac, both of which are produced by the developing human being, though the placenta works in concert with the mother's body). Human beings have "tissues," and the human tissues comprising a complete, whole, distinct living human body are precisely the target for removal in an abortion. Whenever you read "pregnancy tissue" in the discussion of abortion, you should think "human body parts."

Planned Parenthood certainly once did know that abortion kills a human baby. Its brochure, *Plan Your Children for Health and Happiness*, provides a tutorial on birth control, written in a question-and-answer format. A question regarding birth control, "Is it an abortion?" receives this firm answer from Planned Parenthood, "Definitely not." But then it continues: "An abortion requires an operation. It kills the life of a baby after it has begun. It is dangerous to your life and health. It may make you sterile so that when you want a child you cannot have it. Birth control merely postpones the beginning of life."[86]

What new information has come to light since 1951 that caused Planned Parenthood to shift its position on when human life begins or what abortion actually does? The organization used to argue that human life began at conception and that abortion "kills the life of a baby after it has begun." Whatever led to this shift in position and language, it certainly wasn't medical evidence.

———————— • ————————

Planned Parenthood likes to claim that abortion represents
only three percent of its services. They use pretty creative accounting
to arrive at that conclusion. And even if it were true, it wouldn't change
the fact that in 2019, Planned Parenthood, by its own account,
intentionally killed over 345,000 innocent human beings.

———————— • ————————

The writer of the *California Medicine* editorial gives the rationale behind the strategy: an old ethic needs to be replaced by a new ethic. In 1970, the old ethic held that human beings are created in the image of God and, therefore, are—each of them—of inestimable worth. The author calls this a foundational ethic in western culture. The suggested replacement ethic is entirely utilitarian. Those in the medical profession need to control the human population, both in terms of numbers and quality of care:

> Medicine's role with respect to changing attitudes toward abortion
> may well be a prototype of what is to occur. . . . Certainly this has
> required placing relative values on human lives and the impact of the
> physician to this decision process has been considerable. One may
> anticipate further development of these roles as the problems of birth
> control and birth selection are extended inevitably to death selection
> and death control whether by the individual or by society, and further
> public and professional determinations of when and when not to use
> scarce resources.[87]

In order to get to "death selection and death control," physicians first had to establish themselves at the forefront of birth control and birth selection. What persuasive strategies and tactics did they intend to employ to make that leap, in light of the biblical ethics held by their readers in 1970? First, they had to separate "the idea of abortion from the idea of killing" in the minds of the population.

Second, they engaged in "considerable semantic gymnastics"—in other words, they twisted the truth so that people would no longer consider abortion as "the taking of a human life." They recognized this as a tough sell to their 1970 audience. They knew that even trying to make the change would be considered "ludicrous," because people intuitively knew that the entity in a woman's body was a human baby, even from the moment of conception. Accomplishing such a goal required a campaign of disinformation that could take hold only if it were "often put forth under socially impeccable auspices." In other words, if the doctors would lead the way, if the government would go along, if the educational establishment could be induced to participate, the entertainment media willingly enlisted, and if they could even corral some clergy to agree with them, it might succeed.

The writer admitted that these cultural elites would have to engage in a "schizophrenic sort of subterfuge"—in other words, they would promote "subterfuge"; they would propagate a lie that was "schizophrenic"; they knew that lie had no basis in medical fact or experiential reality. But they had to do this, because the need for an accepted new ethic outweighed the biblical ethic currently held.

Abortion has become so widely accepted in our culture that some abortion-choice activists no longer feel compelled to hide the reality of abortion or the true nature of its victims. Camille Paglia, cultural critic and professor at the University of the Arts in Philadelphia, noted:

> Hence I have always frankly admitted that abortion is murder, the extermination of the powerless by the powerful. Liberals for the most part have shrunk from facing the ethical consequences of their embrace of abortion, which results in the annihilation of concrete individuals and not just clumps of insensate tissue.[88]

In the very next line in her essay she argues that the state has no right to regulate abortion—the act she just described as "murder, the extermination of the powerless by the powerful." Who is murdered? "concrete individuals and not just clumps of insensate tissue." Then, making a comparison to capital punishment, she identifies the human being in the womb as innocent, although she describes what is done to that human being as "extermination."

If that isn't schizophrenic, I'm not sure what is.

Even David Boonin, author of *A Defense of Abortion*, one of the most careful philosophical defenses for the position that abortion is morally permissible, gives away the game in his book's preface. After describing an array of photographs he has on his desk of his son, Eli, he continues:

> In the top drawer of my desk, I keep another picture of Eli. This picture was taken on September 7, 1993, 24 weeks before he was born. The sonogram image is murky, but it reveals clearly enough a small head tilted back slightly, and an arm raised up and bent, with the hand pointing back toward the face and the thumb extended out toward the mouth. There is no doubt in my mind that this picture, too, shows the same little boy at a very early stage in his physical development. And there is no question that the position I defend in this book entails that it would have been morally permissible to end his life at this point.[89]

The head, the arm, the hand, the thumb, the face—these are Eli's head, arm, hand, thumb and face. Boonin then spends 350 pages explaining why we should approve of killing children such as Eli, provided abortionists get at them early enough. Christopher Kaczor in *The Ethics of Abortion*[90] ably refuted Boonin's book, and should you like a deep understanding of the issues surrounding abortion as a philosophical exercise, I recommend that you read both.

For our purposes here, the second premise of our argument has been clearly established. What is growing in the body of a woman after the moment of conception is an innocent human being, and abortion intentionally kills that human being.

You Should Be Done, But You're Not

Continued agreement about your first premise means the argument is over. The clarity of your explanation and the mountain of evidence you produce about the nature of the being in the womb, combined with the intentional violence of abortion, should cause abortion-choice supporters to reject their support of abortion. They should line up to join pro-lifers in trying to end the scourge of abortion.

And some will.

Intellectually honest people whose support of abortion stemmed from the belief that the unborn child was not a human being should, and sometimes do, change their position, once they understand the truth about the human nature of the being in the womb. But in far too many cases, they don't. Instead, many of those you talk to will begin the first Big Shift. Abortion-choice supporters will retreat back to premise one—a statement most of them found entirely uncontroversial at the beginning of the discussion: "It is wrong to intentionally kill an innocent human being."

Chapter 6

The First Big Shift: Personhood

Carefully you explain the humanity of the unborn child. When you show them the Planned Parenthood brochure, proving they knew that abortion killed a baby, there's an audible gasp. But others, not wanting to let the abortion issue go, cast about for alternative rationales. At this point in the conversation, you need to expect the first major shift. Even if your conversation partner or members of your audience don't explicitly declare it, you should assume it's about to take place mentally.

Some abortion-choice supporters will agree that it's a human being in the womb, and that abortion ends that human being's life. But then they see a way out of their dilemma—a slight shift, but potent (at least in their minds). Why not simply change the words "human being" in the first and second premise to "person"? They will stridently agree that "It is wrong to intentionally kill an innocent *person*," but now they place upon you the burden of demonstrating that not only is the being inside a woman's body a human being (even from the moment of conception); they also want you to show that this human being qualifies as a "person."

The First Big Shift manufactures a division between human beings and persons. To address it, first I will identify the features of that divide, then confront the arguments directly, and finally examine the motivation for creating the division. In professional philosophical circles, the argument regarding personhood can become convoluted, so in this chapter I will focus on the key arguments that pastors, lay leaders, Christian college students, and other pro-life advocates likely will encounter.

Dividing Human Beings from Persons

In order for abortion-choice supporters to justify depriving innocent human beings of their right to life by intentionally killing them in the womb, they must do two things:

1. reject the idea that human rights extend to all human beings;
2. create a sub-class of human beings to whom such protections don't apply.

Defining terms in significant moral arguments calls for "bright-line" distinctions: clear, unambiguous guidelines. Unlike the bright-line distinction of DNA, which cleanly separates human beings from other creatures, abortion-choice supporters craft often ambiguous and ill-defined criteria for establishing personhood. Abortion-choice advocate Katha Pollitt dissembles, "What is a person? It's not easy to say."[91] She goes on to present a set of ad hoc criteria ranging from size, to development, to social interaction, and then finally claims, "If some combination of those qualities is what makes a person, it's hard to see how a fertilized egg qualifies as one."[92]

I don't want to misrepresent the abortion-choice advocates' side. Careful philosophers such as David Boonin have crafted well-organized arguments on personhood, worthy of engagement, trying to establish that abortion is morally permissible.[93] (Others also have done so.[94]) As I've experienced on many college campuses—and unfortunately, in some churches—abortion-choice supporters rarely plumb the philosophical depths of the abortion issue. Few have ever read any of the philosophical defenses of the abortion-choice position; still fewer have read a carefully thought-out explanation of the pro-life argument. Instead, they consistently rely on a well-worn set of claims that we will examine over this and the following two chapters.

To create a sub-class of human beings that have no inherent right to life, requires abortion-choice supporters to draw distinctions between human beings inside and those outside the womb. Pro-life philosopher Stephen Schwarz placed these apparent distinctions into four key categories, represented (for easy recall) by the acronym S.L.E.D.:[95]

*   Size
*   Level of Development
*   Environment
*   Degree of Dependency

Let's look at each, in turn, to see if these differences are morally significant.

Size

A human embryo is significantly smaller than a newborn baby; that's just a fact. And if you step back a bit to the zygote stage, abortion-choice supporters claim that one simply cannot make a single cell the moral equivalent of a post-born person. Katha Pollitt, in her litany of personhood-denying criteria, describes the zygote stage of human development: "It is the size of the period at the end of this sentence. Before it implants in the uterine wall, and usually for quite a while after that, the woman in whose body it exists does not even know it's there."[96]

Former abortion clinic counselor Amy Littlefield claims that because embryos and fetuses don't look like babies to her, they aren't persons. She notes that most of the children aborted at her clinic were "tiny. More than 90 percent of abortions occur at or before 13 weeks of pregnancy, when the embryo or fetus ranges from little more than a bundle of cells to no more than a few inches long."[97] In other words, the conclusion abortion-choice supporters want others to accept is that, at the very least, human beings at the zygote or embryonic stage of human development shouldn't count as persons because they are "too small" and go unnoticed even by the women carrying them.

Level of development

Not only are tiny humans too small to count as persons, abortion-choice supporters assert, but they also lack the characteristics of persons. David Boonin argues for a number of properties that human persons possess that pre-born humans do not, which justifies intentionally killing them in the womb. These properties include: consciousness, plans, desires, thoughts, feelings, perception, the ability to communicate, and relationships.[98] Boonin particularly identifies as a requirement for "personhood" that persons have a "present, dispositional, ideal desire" for a "future like ours."[99]

It doesn't take much to prove that embryonic or early fetal-stage human beings lack what adults would know as consciousness. Embryos cannot speak. Their cerebral cortex has not developed sufficiently to allow for simple thoughts or plans. They cannot desire a "future like ours" because as yet they have no experience of a future like ours. They do not "presently" possess these properties. By selecting criteria that supposedly indicate personhood, and by demonstrating that human beings in the womb (at least until very late in their development) have yet to acquire or demonstrate these properties, abortion-choice advocates claim that embryonic humans are sufficiently "other" than post-born humans as to permit their destruction. This otherness, according to abortion-choice supporters, makes intentionally killing human beings in the womb morally justified.

Environment

In order to express all of the properties identified above, a "person" must live outside of another person's body. Abortion-choice supporters argue that because humans at the embryonic and fetal development stage remain inside their mothers' bodies, they cannot be considered independent persons. As we will see under the next category, the concept of environment and dependency are closely linked as a means of suggesting that human beings in the womb are not persons in the same way as are human beings outside the womb.

Degree of dependency

The final characteristic offered by most abortion-choice supporters to distinguish human persons from human non-persons is the significant degree to which human beings in the womb depend on their mothers to sustain their lives. Some argue that in order to be deemed a person, a human must be able to live apart from his or her mother. Children who cannot do so are deemed not to be "viable."

It's true that children in the womb, for many months, completely depend on their mothers for their nutrition, hydration, oxygen, waste removal, and the safety provided by the uterus. An eighteen-week-old human fetus, at our current level of neonatal science, cannot survive outside the womb. Her lungs have not sufficiently developed. Before viability, a common argument goes, the "fetus is just part of the woman's body," not a separate person.

Responding to the SLED Challenge

Abortion-choice supporters claim that determining whether any given human being qualifies as a person presents all kinds of difficulties. Humans in the womb are smaller, undeveloped, hidden, and dependent—variables some say exclude them from the category of "persons."

Let's explore why these reasons offered for distinguishing persons from human non-persons not only fail, but have dangerous implications for everyone.

Size

Size does not indicate value. Every child learns that "good things come in small packages." When people try to determine human moral worth—and what is on the line is life and death itself—then choosing as a standard something as variable as size has no merit.

When individuals such as Pollitt and Littlefield essentially make the claim that the child in the womb is not a person because she is too tiny or doesn't "look like a person," the problem rests not with the size or appearance of the human being in question, but with the untutored eyes of abortion-choice supporters. All human beings, from the moment of conception forward, "look" like human beings. They can't look like anything else. On the first day of each of our individual lives, we humans look like a particular cell—a very dynamic, totipotent human cell. But each stage of human development differs in appearance from every other stage. Embryonic humans are not the same size as newborns. Newborns differ from both adolescents and adults in height, weight, shoe and hat size—in every conceivable dimension, just as adolescents and adults differ from one another. Yet at every stage, they remain the same human being. Human value does not depend on size.

Precisely how big must one grow to be deemed a person? I once wrote a study guide for the movie *Glory Road*, with former L.A. Lakers superstar A.C. Green. At six feet nine inches tall, Green towered over me. My hand, which I always thought of as fairly big, nearly disappeared inside his when we shook hands at the studio screening. Am I therefore less valuable than A.C. Green because I am shorter? On the basketball court, absolutely. But as human beings, as persons, we share the same human nature and are, therefore, of equal moral value.

Each of our lives began as a single cell, and through our various stages of development—embryo, fetus, newborn, toddler, teenager, young adult, middle-ager, and elderly—we each remain the same human being. That's why, when we showed our daughter-in-law photos of our son as a little boy, she could exclaim, "You were so cute!" Invoking size as a standard to determine who does and doesn't count as a person is both arbitrary and dangerous.

Level of Development

The lack of any clear, bright-line distinction makes categorizing humans as persons or non-persons a perilous business. Level of development fails as a category standard, just as "size" does, because of its imprecision. How much development is enough?

Consciousness, for example, does not provide a sufficiently precise standard for determining personhood. Consciousness comes and goes daily for most people (at minimum, when they wake and sleep); and even in healthy, awake adults, anesthesia can induce unconsciousness. Do adults cease to be persons when they slip into unconsciousness?

How about a developmental standard such as the ability to communicate? Newborns have virtually no ability to communicate—but they may have more of such an ability than a person lying in a coma. How about those with severely restricted communication abilities, such as those individuals with autism or Down Syndrome (who nevertheless are rightly protected as persons)? Eight-year-olds are less physically developed than twenty-one year olds; the latter generally are stronger, more capable of complex tasks, and have fully functional reproductive systems. But even twenty-six-year-old males are more developed than, say, twenty-two-year-old males, whose brains have not yet fully developed. Do human beings qualify as persons only when they can actively express the designated characteristic? How many properties are required, and to what degree must they be expressed, for a human being to be deemed a person with a right to live?

Like size, "level of development" is a bad standard to qualify for personhood, because it's entirely arbitrary and cannot be uniformly applied without placing many post-born people at risk.

——————————— • ———————————

For most unborn children to properly develop in their mothers'
bodies, they just need to be left alone. In the womb, provided with
nutrition, hydration, waste removal, and a safe place to live, self-directed
development happens because of the kinds of beings these children are.

——————————— • ———————————

David Boonin's developmental claim that personhood requires a human
being to exhibit a "present, dispositional, ideal desire" for a "future like
ours" would exclude newborns (who lack such concepts) and invites
infanticide. Christopher Kaczor provides a point-by-point, book-length
refutation of Boonin's claims; but Andrew Peach simply argues that Boonin
begins with a flawed premise stemming from a misunderstanding of a key
pro-life argument. Boonin keeps looking at which properties human beings
possess that would *confer* personhood, but neglects examining the kind of
beings humans *are*. Peach explains:

> To have a kind of nature is not to have a given property; it is to be a
> certain kind of being with certain kinds of powers ordered to certain
> kinds of activities and goods….one of the virtues of the argument
> against abortion based on a fetus's rational nature is that it maintains
> that all human beings deserve respect and should not be killed precisely
> because of what they are, not what they have done or can do.[100]

Whether a child in the womb exercises rationality cannot determine a right to
life; rather, the nature of the human to be a rational being should confer that
protection. Even in such instances where human expressions of rationality
are inhibited, or even if the individual never exhibits rationality—due to
genetic abnormalities, for instance—the nature of the being is still ordered
to be rational. The very existence of the concept of "abnormality" indicates
the recognition of a normal, rational nature for human beings. The inherent
capacity for rationality—the capacity, in fact, for all of the properties
Boonin and others require for personhood—exists in human beings from the
moment of their conception. They are ordered toward them by their nature.
Even Boonin's insistence that "persons" exhibit a "present, dispositional,
ideal desire" for a "future like ours" is met and even exceeded by Peach's

approach. Human beings, from the moment of conception, actually *possess* a future like ours, so long as that future does not get cut short by miscarriage, stillbirth, sudden infant death syndrome, or intentionally destroyed through abortion.

A human being's level of development, whether determined by identifiable properties or desires, fails the bright line test. It's difficult, if not impossible, to create a uniform, testable standard that would not put at risk many people currently recognized, universally, as persons. It also flies in the face of longstanding moral commands to defend the weak. As a culture, we provide extra protections to developmentally immature humans, *in every case,* other than when those human beings reside in the womb.

Environment

The separate, distinct humanity of beings in the womb has been firmly established by the scientific evidence cited in the previous chapter. The size and various abilities of those human beings are morally irrelevant. The smaller and weaker people are, the more they deserve, and need, protection.

But the environment standard posits location as an overriding determining factor for whether those separate, inherently rational human beings truly count as persons. When we look at the developmental similarities of human beings of the same gestational age, both inside and outside the womb, it becomes clear that environment is treated as a stand-alone standard.

In 2014, a baby in San Antonio, Texas, was born at twenty-one weeks gestation. The girl weighed less than a pound. She not only survived, but went on to preschool three years later and performed on par with her peers.[101] While children born this prematurely do not normally experience such an outcome, medical science is rapidly moving the boundaries that define "viability." On the other hand, the Boulder Abortion Clinic, founded and run by abortionist Warren Hern, advertises on its web page that it does first-, second-, and third-trimester abortions.[102] Hern specializes in late-term abortions, abortions on children identical in their developmental ages to many delivered preemie babies. The only real distinction between the premature children doctors heroically save, and the children Hern intentionally kills, is their location.

I write these words in my office. To take this manuscript to the post office, I will have to walk to my car, located in the garage at the other end of my house. To do this, I must travel orders of magnitude farther than a child must move from the interior to the exterior of her mother's womb. My value as a human being does not change even a little as I move from place to place. How ridiculous and depraved it is to assert that taking a seven-inch journey down the birth canal should magically convert a human non-person (that can be intentionally killed through abortion) into a human person (with a right to life).

Degree of Dependency

Like size and development, dependency is a moving target. How dependent is too dependent to count as a protected human person? All human beings, at various points in their lives, depend more or less on others for their survival. Human need, or its lack, doesn't indicate personhood. Not wanting someone to depend on us says nothing about the personhood of the dependent one. On the contrary. Refusing legitimate dependency claims—such as the claims for care that elderly, debilitated parents may make on their children—says more about the moral status of those who decline to meet those obligations. Refusing legitimate dependency claims, when it lies within one's power to help, is morally wrong.

Newborn babies depend entirely on others, primarily their mothers, in order to live. Left to their own devices, newborns would perish in very short order. Like children in the womb, they are not independently viable. Neglecting infants and children violates the law and can carry severe penalties. The dependency of newborns does not render them non-persons.

After my mother-in-law, Ginny, developed advanced Alzheimer's and became bedridden, my wife, Sharon, our son, Joel, and I moved her in with us, along with Sharon's sister, Susan Soesbe, and our niece, Deborah. Susan's subsequent book, *Bringing Mom Home,* chronicled the journey.[103] Ginny depended completely on our family and caregivers for everything: human touch and conversation, changing the television channel, medication, eating, drinking, toileting, clothing and linen changes, and getting turned in her bed so as not to develop bed sores. She lived with us in that state for two years. The human being she was as she lay helplessly dependent in that bed had no morally significant difference from the human being she was as a little girl, a young woman, a wife and mother, a middle-aged bowling competitor, and an elderly crossword puzzle wizard. Some abortion advocates might argue that Ginny still counted as a person with a right to life because she still possessed mental or relational abilities. But people familiar with the progression of Alzheimer's disease know that, eventually, even these properties disappear. Despite her utter dependency, Ginny never ceased to be a person—the *same* person. As such, we treated her with dignity, love, and respect until her final breath. Dependency was Ginny's circumstance, never her identity.

Significant dependency can strike anyone at any time. Imagine a healthy, energetic ten-year-old boy heading out to sled in the first snowfall of winter. After carefully looking both ways, he steps out into the street to cross to the park, slips on some black ice, and strikes his head on the concrete curb. Immediately, the boy goes from relative independence to complete dependence. A severe dependence could last for weeks, months, or many years. No one would argue that the boy's dependency had turned him into a non-person. No one would argue that the parents of this injured child should have the right to intentionally end his life.

Dependency is the natural circumstance of the very young and often the very old, not an identifying feature that denies a human being personhood. The dependency of a child in the womb doesn't erase the child's unique distinctiveness; she is her own person, not part of her mother's body. The absolute dependency of children—both inside and outside the womb— creates a moral obligation on mothers and fathers, not a lethal opportunity to achieve parental freedom. Schwarz clarifies: "To kill a normal child sleeping in his crib is a terrible evil. Killing a child in an incubator, dependent on that incubator, is no less evil. Abortion is killing a child in the incubator of his mother's womb. A more dependent child is a more fragile child. He deserves more care, not less."[104]

The Motivation for the Human Being/Person Distinction

The standards offered by abortion-choice supporters, specifically designed to separate persons from human non-persons, have been identified and refuted. While it may be true that not all persons are human beings (angels and God provide examples of non-human persons), all human beings are certainly persons. That said, it may shed some light to examine why the distinction between "human being" and "person" arises in the first place.

In popular usage, the words "human being" and "person" are interchangeable. From the *Oxford English Dictionary* to *Merriam-Webster*, "person" simply means an individual human being. The word "people" describes a group of more than one human being. When advocates define terms in unusual ways, the purpose often is not clarity, but to gain strategic advantage by obscuring facts or defining their opponents out of the debate. We already have seen how abortion-choice supporters use terms such as "pregnancy tissue" to hide the human nature of the targets of abortion. The goal of distinguishing between "human being" and "person" is to strip from some human beings the protections they would otherwise enjoy.

The broad term "human being" encompasses all of humanity, as does "person." But abortion-choice supporters know that even though "person" means a human individual, the term is not often used to describe human beings in the wombs of their mothers. They also reject words commonly used to more precisely describe that human being, such as "baby" or "child" (though recall that, in the past, even Planned Parenthood identified the target of abortion as a "baby").

"Person," when connected to words such as "personhood" or "personality," appears to describe something that humans attain, develop, or project, rather than something humans inherently are. As a result, abortion-choice supporters argue, personhood is something that human beings possess in varying degrees; or, in the case of human beings in the womb, not sufficiently to grant that human being a right to life.

Abortion-choice advocates desire to split human beings into two groups: human beings protected by rights and the law, and human beings morally permissible to kill. They accomplish this goal by creating two classes of human beings: human persons and human non-persons. By referring to the unborn as non-persons, abortion-choice advocates seek to deny such human beings 14th Amendment protections.

The tactic is not new. Such divisions of human beings into protected and unprotected classes have a long, unsavory and tragic history:

- slaves considered livestock in ancient Rome
- Native Americans dehumanized under European colonial powers
- Africans deemed as property during the time of chattel slavery in the United States
- the Jews (and Roma, and Slavs, and others) labeled sub-humans under the Third Reich

The list goes on and on.[105]

Our world has a dismal historical track record of the dehumanization of one group of people by another. Christopher Kaczor notes "in every other instance where personhood was denied to a class of human beings, we judge that a moral catastrophe took place. Since the human/person distinction has thus far had a 100% rate of failure, it's reasonable to adopt the inclusive view: every human being is a person."[106]

In each of the historical instances where one group of human beings dehumanizes, subjugates, and kills other human beings, the motivation never came by carefully examining scientific evidence and then concluding that these "others" were not actually human persons, and therefore open to exploitation, cruelty, and death.

Not once.

Instead, these targeted people were considered either a threat or a resource. They kept their abusers from getting something they wanted, or they had something their captors would do anything to possess. Therefore, justifications were created to dehumanize and then abuse or kill them. In the same way, no one suddenly discovered something new about unborn human beings that marked them as non-persons and so determined that it was morally permissible to kill them. Rather, abortion-choice advocates determined they could enjoy certain benefits by killing or exploiting unborn human beings, and then crafted justifications for doing so.

Not Done Yet?

Once more, you might think our discussion had ended. Chapter Five established the humanity of the being in the womb and that abortion intentionally kills that human being. The person (or audience) to whom we speak has agreed that it is wrong to intentionally kill an innocent human being. Since we demonstrated the truth of our premises, the conclusion is inevitable: Abortion is wrong.

But then the First Big Shift came, either directly in conversation or implied in the minds of resistant audience members. They wanted to do a little last-minute key term substitution. Changing the words in the Syllogism from "human being" to "person" appeared to give abortion-choice supporters a little more room to maneuver. While it might be wrong to kill a person, merely carrying some human DNA confers no right to life.

This chapter spiked that argument.

Here is a modified version of our Syllogism that shows our current place in the discussion:

Premise 1:   It is wrong to intentionally kill an innocent human being
Premise 2:   All human beings are persons
Premise 3:   Abortion intentionally kills an innocent human being who is a person
Conclusion: Therefore abortion is wrong.

What happens next is the Second Big Shift—a shift that takes these advocates completely outside the logic of the syllogism and into exception arguments.

Chapter 7

The Second Big Shift: Circumstances

Unable to refute the premises or conclusion of your pro-life argument, abortion-choice supporters move from the argument itself to the context in which the argument is created. In other words, they quit talking about the nature of the unborn, or the violent act that is abortion, and shift to claiming the circumstances of conception outweigh the right to live of the human being in the womb. They invariably offer the examples of rape and incest.

When people discuss "hard cases" regarding abortion, pro-life advocates typically talk about the small percentage of abortions performed as a result of rape or incest. The small numbers of such cases lead to the underlying notion that rape and incest do not provide appropriate test cases for the morality or legality of abortion.

Discussions of such hard case numbers nearly always use percentages. The Guttmacher Institute—a research organization with long ties to Planned Parenthood—reports that 862,320 surgical abortions were performed in 2017.[107] If we determined that only 1% of those abortions came as a result of a pregnancy resulting from rape or incest (sounds small, doesn't it?), that would still mean that 8,623 rape victims in the United States sought abortions, killing at least that many human beings. Those are *real, actual* lives.

As Christopher Kaczor explains: "It is not a comfort to someone dying from a lethal disease that the disease is extremely rare."[108] As contenders for life, we need to consider both the seriousness of the claims brought by those who consider rape and incest a reasonable compromise on the abortion issue, and the magnitude of the lives lost for this reason.

Why People Bring Up Rape and Incest Exceptions

Whether you speak about abortion to someone directly, or teach or preach to a large group, questions concerning rape and incest will unquestionably surface. The idea that a woman should be forced to carry the child of a man who violently raped her seems immensely unjust and unfair. People naturally, and rightly, have tremendous sympathy for rape victims. These people want to help. The reasons they offer for allowing abortion in the cases of rape and incest generally fall into two categories:

1. Rape and incest victims don't choose to become pregnant

Couples who voluntarily engage in sexual intercourse and who know that such activity sometimes results in the conception of a child, have at least some obligations toward the child they created. When a woman is sexually assaulted, however, no consent exists. The attacker forces the sexual intercourse, and certainly no woman wants to create a baby with an attacker. In fact, the violated woman may not want to have a baby at all. Because the conception happened involuntarily, abortion-choice supporters argue that the woman has no obligations toward the human being in her womb. They assert she has every right, morally, to abort that person.

2. Forced pregnancy compounds the violation

When a man violates a woman and she becomes pregnant, abortion-choice supporters argue that requiring the woman to carry the child to term compounds the violence of the rape. Every day that the woman contemplates her expanding abdomen, she remembers that the child growing in her womb is the unwanted result of a violent act. Once the child arrives, perhaps he or she resembles the attacker, and every time the woman sees the child, she relives the rape. Abortion-choice supporters argue that because the rapist forced her into sex, it would be immoral to force her to carry the child to term.

A more extreme form of this argument identifies the human being in the womb as a secondary aggressor. First, the woman gets attacked by the rapist, and then the presence of the growing child changes the woman's body and forecloses on opportunities she might otherwise have had. The first loss leads immediately to additional loss. The abortion-choice supporter therefore claims abortion is morally justified.

What to Say First When People Bring Up Rape and Incest Exceptions

If you have an apologetic mindset, or if you love debating, you already may have created counter arguments in your mind as you read the above scenarios.

Stop.

You likely have no way of knowing why the person speaking with you, or the brave soul who steps up to a microphone during a question and answer session or who talks with the pastor after a sermon on abortion, has asked about rape or incest. The person asking may have been a victim of sexual violence or knows someone so victimized. In asking the question, the person may not want to focus on whether conception took place after a rape; the questioner wants to know what such a conception would mean for the woman. Since we cannot know the motivation for questions about rape and incest, we simply must begin our response with compassion.

When you respond to questions regarding rape and incest in the context of talking about abortion, don't let the first words out of your mouth be an *argument.* Your first words must express concern and compassion, and you must mean them: "I appreciate how hard it must be even to bring up rape or incest. Rape and incest are horrible, terrible crimes and my heart goes out to any victims of violent aggressors. I believe that anyone who is arrested, tried, and convicted of rape or incest should be prosecuted and punished to the full extent of the law. All possible support should be made available to the victims. Now, since I want to make sure I understand what you are asking, can you tell me why a woman who has been raped, and who conceives a child as a result of that rape, would find it morally okay to abort that child?"

Almost certainly the person will offer up some version of the reasons already discussed. In the next section, we will explore responses to these claims. But before we get there, make sure you demonstrate that *the argument isn't everything.* When we talk about abortion, we never do so to score points in a debate. When we discuss abortion, we can't lose sight of our goal, to win over the person by showing them the truth. We strive to winsomely persuade others to see the human being in the womb as a fellow image-bearer of God, a fully human person, just like them.

When we speak and communicate in this way, we demonstrate that we understand the gravity of the issues raised. We empathize with the difficult circumstances in which rape and incest victims find themselves, particularly those who conceive as a result. We want to help.

But then we must turn to a particular action, abortion, that our culture regularly puts forth as the best way to help a woman who became pregnant as a result of rape or incest. And we ask: is abortion the right or the moral choice?

If people suggest abortion as a legitimate legal or moral exception only in the cases of rape and incest, then we have good answers to these questions that fair-minded people will consider. With unfortunate regularity, however, abortion-choice supporters use rape and incest exception claims as an emotional bludgeon to make pro-life advocates seem callous and cruel. Don't let that happen.

Separating the Sincere from the Sloganeer

If you've advocated for the pro-life position for a while, I know how easy it is to feel jaded by people you may come to view as "the enemy." You want to enter the arena with rhetorical guns blazing. This happens especially in a public forum, where debate (even a Q and A after a presentation) can feel like pitched battle. When you think someone wants to trick you into an embarrassing admission or make you appear uncaring, you may feel tempted to respond in a way that makes the person asking the question appear stupid or evil.

Don't do it. Don't be a jerk. It can undermine your argument, hurt the people you want to win over, and damage your witness.

Whenever questions about rape or incest come up in a conversation, or after a presentation, remember that you have a simple, winsome way to separate the person with a sincere desire to know, from a sloganeer looking to put you into what appears to be an impossible position. After you say the "first things" I just mentioned, ask a question:

"If, for the sake of argument, I were willing to allow for rape and incest exceptions, would you join me in speaking out against all other reasons for abortion, and campaign for those running for office who oppose abortion, except for reasons of rape or incest?"

The answer to that question will tell you all you need to know.

If the person truly feels concerned only about the plight of rape and incest victims and considers abortion in all other circumstances morally wrong, then they will say, "Yes." A discussion can then follow about why they find other reasons for abortion—economic reasons, or an unwanted baby, for example—insufficient to justify it. They might label those other reasons "bad." In other words, you'll discover in the answers they provide, at least the beginnings of the reason why abortion would be wrong in the case of rape or incest. The typical reasons given for abortion simply don't justify killing an innocent human being. Such a person will actually talk themselves out of the abortion-choice position. If not, the section below will give you specific answers to their likely objections.

If the person says "no" to your question, then ask: "I'm just curious, why would you use violent or debased examples as primary reasons to reject the pro-life case, when you wouldn't abandon your abortion-choice position even if they were granted? Does it seem right to you to leverage the pain of a rape victim to advance your own, primarily unrelated, agenda?" You'll often discover the real issue for that person is that they favor some version of abortion on demand. Their core concern has nothing to do with the rape and incest exception question; they merely want to see if they can make the pro-lifer publicly defend a position the abortion-choice supporter finds indefensible. If there's an audience, they want to make the pro-life speaker appear insensitive to the plight of women. The overall tactic is designed to make the audience reject all of the pro-life advocate's arguments. After all, who could trust the claims of a person so cruel?

In an interpersonal exchange, getting to the heart of the reasons why a person favors abortion allows you to choose the right place to begin your response. If hard cases genuinely trouble the individual, explain those cases. But if the person has a broader abortion agenda, start at the beginning, with the Syllogism, and then move forward.

In a public forum, you never engage only with the person asking the question; you have an audience listening to your answer. In chapter eleven I'll show you how to craft presentations that preempt these questions and so minimize their effect. Above all, avoid the temptation to respond with anything that looks like ridicule (I confess that I don't always succeed here). You may get applause from those who already agree with you, but you will fail to win over the person asking the question, or that person's friends (who might be more open to persuasion than the question asker). Your ridicule may only solidify their preconception that pro-life advocates care about arguments, but not about people. Always choose the more winsome way.

Responding to Exception Arguments for Rape and Incest

When people advance arguments or ask questions about rape and incest exceptions regarding the permissibility of abortion, the vast majority begin with a flawed premise. These people believe the being in the womb is not human, or at least is not yet a person.

"Now wait!" I hear you cry, "Didn't we already establish that the being in the womb is human and that human beings are indistinguishable from persons?"

Yes, we did. But the people arguing or questioning in this way have not sat down beforehand, crafting their response to you, with an outline in front of them of what you have discussed. They may not have considered *at all* the question of the status of the human being in the womb. The only part of this problem that concerns them at present is the horrible notion that a woman raped violently has become pregnant, and that forcing her to remain pregnant seems terribly wrong. Their moral judgment does not come from a careful analysis of your argument; it comes from a place of raw emotion, and (fortunately) some conception of justice. The question does not *argue* that the being in the womb is not human, it *assumes* it. Therefore, your answers will have to consistently circle back to the idea that abortion intentionally kills an innocent human being.

If you have established the humanity and personhood of the being in the womb, then any conception of justice that enters the discussion will help. Your questioner wants both compassion and justice for the female victim, and your response must show that you value innocent victims and that you insist on punishing the guilty.

1. Is abortion as a response to rape or incest compassionate?

First, fair-minded abortion-choice supporters feel that refusing an abortion to a woman who has become pregnant after suffering rape or incest demonstrates a lack of compassion for the victim. Stephen Schwarz disagrees:

> Refusal to allow abortion for rape cases is not a failure of compassion. On the contrary, allowing abortion is a lack of compassion for preborn children. It's approving their murder, the violation of their most fundamental right, the right to live. Saying no to the woman is not a lack of compassion for her, but simply calling attention to what abortion really is: murder. Refusal to sanction murder is not a lack of compassion.[109]

Understand that people often frame rape and incest exceptions as a conflict between the mother and the human being in her womb. In fact, the conflict is not really about whose rights should take precedence, as Schwarz says, but which rights: "the rights of the woman to try to alleviate her pain, or the right of the child to live? Clearly the latter. So it's not that one person is an adult and another is a child. It's that, in general, the right to alleviate the pain of one person cannot be exercised by denying the right of another person to live."[110]

If the choices appear too stark, the pro-life advocate can discuss the value of compassion and who needs it most in this case. The abortion-choice supporter argues that the woman deserves compassion as an innocent victim, for all innocent victims of the violent acts of others deserve compassion. To bring home this point, it sometimes helps to count people.

When a woman becomes pregnant after being victimized by an act of rape or incest, ask, "How many people are now in this scenario?" The answer, of course, is "three."

"The woman in this scenario, is she innocent or guilty?"

"Innocent."

"The rapist in this scenario, is he innocent or guilty?"

"Clearly guilty."

"Okay, the human being now present in the woman's womb, guilty or innocent?"

Any fair-minded person will recognize the innocence of the child in the womb; he or she did not come into existence until after the rape. The child bears no guilt.

"What should be done to the guilty rapist?" Some would recommend the death penalty, but most will suggest a very long prison sentence.

"What should be done to the innocent woman?"

"Done?" they might respond, dumbfounded. "*Nothing* should be done to the woman. She is innocent, she needs compassion and support!"

"Then what should be done to the innocent human being in her womb?"

Here things get difficult for abortion-choice supporters. If the innocent deserve compassion and support, and the guilty rapist gets a life sentence, then why does the innocent child deserve capital punishment? An abortion will not undo the rape—nothing can—but the abortion can further victimize the woman and kill the unborn child. The abortionist does to the child exactly what the rapist does to the woman. The abortionist violates the bodily integrity of an innocent human being precisely at a place and time where the child should expect safety.

Over time, the woman victimized by rape may find peace and healing. But an aborted child finds only violent death. If innocent women victimized by violent attackers deserve compassion and aid, then why should an innocent human being in the womb get handed over to a violent attacker in the form of an abortionist? The person in the womb also deserves compassion and aid.

2. Not choosing to become pregnant

While both innocent human beings in this scenario clearly deserve compassion and support, some abortion-choice supporters retreat to the idea that since the woman did not choose to have intercourse and didn't choose to create this child, therefore she bears no obligation toward him or her.

It's true that the victimized woman has no obligation to raise the child of her attacker (though many do). Both innocent human beings stand in the same condition: neither chose either the rape or the conception. But of the two, only one now has a choice remaining.

Unfortunately, the choices available to a rape victim who conceives an innocent child closely resemble many life circumstances that offer no morally neutral middle ground, as Christopher Kaczor points out. The choices following a pregnancy resulting from rape come down to two:

1. engage in a significant moral wrong (in some ways worse than the rape that precipitated the choice);
2. be morally heroic.

Kaczor uses this scenario: "If a dictator orders you to torture your mother to death or face a firing squad, you will be faced with the choice between the morally wrong and the morally heroic." One can choose to do the wrong thing, or one can choose to do the heroic thing. A third, less trying option, does not exist. The innocent child in the womb of a victim of rape or incest will either live or die, depending on the woman's choice.

Remember, the woman did not choose to become pregnant; neither did the human being in the womb choose to be conceived. But both the innocent woman and the innocent child exist, alive and whole, *now*. Like the person in Kaczor's dilemma, the woman can choose to intentionally cause the death of her child (recall that the child is also the product of her body), which is a great moral wrong. Or she can choose to be morally heroic and, at minimum, give the support that the innocent human being requires, at least until birth. At that time, she will have another choice: to raise the baby herself, or place the baby with a grateful adoptive couple.

3. Forced pregnancy and three thought experiments

Abortion-choice advocates argue that refusing to allow a woman to abort the human in her womb, conceived as a result of rape or incest, compounds the violence of her victimization by forcing her to carry her attacker's child. One way that pro-life advocates can shift the apparent conflict between the victimized woman and the human being in her womb is to flip the genders of the violator and victim. This allows listeners to keep the focus more keenly on the unborn child most at risk. Consider two thought experiments that propose to do just that.

First, a woman drugs a man at a bar, rendering him weak and incoherent. She and an accomplice take him to a room and tie him to the bed. When he regains consciousness, he finds himself in restraints, with his clothes removed.

The woman enters the room. She talks to him, tries to calm him down, and then begins to touch him intimately. He forcefully tells her to stop. She ignores his pleas and continues to work to arouse him. He tells her he has a wife and children and begs her to stop doing this. The woman forcibly gags him. Despite his unwillingness, his body responds and she initiates sex. In spite of his protestations, in spite of his claims that she is raping him, she continues and eventually his body has a normal physiological reaction. She becomes pregnant as a result of this forced encounter.

Unfortunately for her, the security camera at the bar captures an image of her and the accomplice taking the man to the room, and then leaving without him some hours later. A housekeeper finds the man gagged, naked and still in restraints. Once he puts on some clothes, he calls the police and reports the crime. The police investigate and twelve weeks later find the woman, who is three months pregnant. A blood test confirms that the child in her womb belongs to the victim. Does he have the right to legally require that his female rapist undergo an abortion to eliminate the unwanted child?

People generally recoil from the idea that any woman should be forced to abort a child. Most would reply that 1) the example is ludicrous because men can't be the victims of rape, or; 2) at least, the male victim should have no financial responsibility for the child conceived without his consent. Actual court cases have disproven both of these claims.

Robert Mueller, writing in *Psychology Today*, reports multiple instances where boys and men have been raped by females, and, despite being found victims of sexual assault by the courts, subsequently were court-ordered to provide child support when their attackers gave birth and wanted to keep their children.[111] While Mueller finds such forced child support a judicial travesty, nowhere in the essay does Mueller remotely suggest that the male victim should have the right to eliminate his unwanted offspring.

Now consider a second scenario:

A woman in a long-term relationship with a man shares an apartment with a female friend. One evening, after sex, she takes the man's condom from him and heads to the bathroom. The man doesn't know that her roommate desperately wants a child. Using the semen from the condom—a condom selected by the woman because it lacks spermicide—the first woman artificially inseminates her friend and she conceives. Four months later, in the middle of an angry spat, she openly admits what she did in an effort to wound her boyfriend. They break up, but he tracks down her old roommate and discovers that she is, indeed, four months pregnant. If a paternity test proves that this woman carries his child against his will, does he have the right to force that woman to abort the child?

If the woman—either as the victim or as the perpetrator of rape or any other form of non-consensual conception—has the right to decide whether the child lives or dies, then neither the concept of force nor the non-consensual nature of conception provides moral justification for abortion. In these scenarios, the only guideline at work is whether the woman wants to give birth. In the next section we will examine the issue of "wantedness," but astute readers already will have discerned that "wantedness" fails as a justification for abortion.

When discussing abortion as an option after a conception resulting from rape, we must always keep before us the target of that abortion: an innocent child whose conception was not her fault, but whose life now hangs in the balance. Both mother and child, innocent, deserve to live.

Finally, to examine the claim that women should have the right to abort a rapist's child because the child would remind them of the rape, consider a third scenario:

A woman marries a man and has five happy years with him. She and her husband have two sons together. In year six, police arrest her husband for a string of violent rapes. The arrest comes as a complete surprise to her, but at the trial, more than a half-dozen women recall in lurid detail her husband's crimes. At the end of the trial, the jury unanimously convicts him and the judge sentences him to twenty-five years to life. When she returns home after the trial, the woman looks at her sons, both the spitting image of her rapist husband. She never wants to see him again, but her kids constantly remind her of him. Every time she looks at them, she recalls the terrifying testimony of the rape victims. Why can't she kill these two children so that they will no longer remind her of the horror of sharing her life and her bed with a man she now knows as a violent monster?

Most people would recoil at the suggestion that any mother should have the right to kill her already-born children, even if their father is a serial rapist. The children of rapists have committed no rape. They are innocent human beings caught up in the backwash of the evil deeds of others.

Since we've already seen that the human being in the womb is morally indistinguishable from the child outside the womb, then it follows that the circumstances of a person's conception have no bearing on his or her value as a human being. Even children who may remind their parents of traumatic or painful events are still human beings with their own moral value.

4. Human in the womb as an aggressor

Some abortion-choice supporters see unwanted pregnancy as a kind of attack, with the human being in the womb considered the primary aggressor. To advance this idea, they do not rely on a rape scenario. Others frame conception following rape as a secondary aggression by the unborn child. They attempt to use the term "aggressor" to imply that the child somehow shares the guilt of the rapist. Don't forget that we have already established the innocence of the human being in the womb.

Aggressor arguments treat the unborn child as if she is doing something unnatural, but in fact, the unborn is doing the only natural thing she can do and live. The entire purpose of a uterus is to protect, house, and nurture a developing human. The woman's physiological response to the experience of pregnancy is also entirely natural. Yes, the woman's body will change and she may miss some opportunities because of it, but that is not the *fault* of the unborn child, who neither willed it nor caused it to happen. A woman who conceived through rape is a victim, and the developing human inside her is a biological consequence. Although the rapist is evil, seeing only the woman's instrumental value to him and not her proper worth, the woman should not aggress against the child by dehumanizing her, seeing her only as an obstacle. The child, too, is a human being deserving of life, just like the mother.

In rape or incest, the *only* aggressor is the perpetrator. The woman is an innocent victim who deserves compassion and support, as does the completely innocent human being developing in her womb. The circumstances of our conception do not define us.

Are We There Yet?

Thus far we have established the humanity and personhood of human beings in the womb and demonstrated that the circumstances by which humans are conceived do not define our moral worth. So, are we done?

Once again, if this were the last issue keeping an abortion-choice supporter from switching sides, that person should now have sufficient reasons to give serious consideration to becoming pro-life. Using reason and evidence, we have justified all of the premises of the case for life. Arguments concerning rape and incest, while brutal to consider, have no bearing on the moral value of human beings in the womb. Therefore, the number of those willing to continue trying to justify abortion should continue to dwindle with each refutation of their arguments.

Still, the remaining abortion-choice supporters haven't quite finished. It's time for the Third Big Shift.

Chapter 8

The Third Big Shift: Life Impacts

Cultural analyst Neil Postman, in his classic book *Amusing Ourselves to Death*, noted that the nature of television significantly diminishes our ability to pay attention. His aptly titled chapter "Now…This" illustrates the process:

> …there is no murder so brutal, no earthquake so devastating, no political blunder so costly—that it cannot be erased from our minds by a newscaster saying, 'Now…this.' The newscaster means that you have thought long enough on the previous matter (approximately fortyfive seconds), that you must not be morbidly preoccupied with it (let us say, for ninety seconds), and that you must now give your attention to another fragment of news or a commercial.[112]

The Internet now magnifies the effect Postman described, reducing people's ability to concentrate or to hold together the parts of a complex argument until its conclusion.

The pro-life argument, as demonstrated, is not particularly complex. As shown, you can state it in three sentences. Even the proofs for the claims in the basic argument are easy to understand.

But as abortion-choice supporters move to complicate the issue by introducing a host of arbitrary personhood arguments and hard-case apparent exceptions, clear concepts can become muddy. The sheer volume of exceptions can keep many people from ever getting to the core of the abortion issue: that abortion is wrong because it intentionally kills an innocent human being. And when some exceptions get cleared away, others quickly take their place.

In the Third Shift, abortion-choice advocates move away from hard cases to a long list of detrimental impacts of childbearing on women. These apparent harms, they argue, outweigh the right of human beings in the womb to live.

Convenient Amnesia

All of the arguments that this chapter explains and exposes, with a single exception, have one thing in common with the previous chapter: all of them assume that whatever is in the body of a woman after conception is *not* a human being.

Both the science of embryology and moral philosophy prove that the being in the womb is human and that all human beings are persons. The following arguments offered by abortion-choice supporters do nothing to undermine these facts; they simply ignore them and hope that you will, too.

The arguments have *no bearing* on the nature of the human being in the womb. They rely, for their impact, on two kinds of appeals: avoidance of threats, and people's desire to control their own bodies. This chapter will unpack both of these arguments and then evaluate them, in turn.

The Personal Impacts of Childbearing

A host of negative impacts can accompany childbearing. Abortion-choice supporters argue that the significance of these impacts makes "terminating pregnancies" permissible.

Threats to the mother

Abortion-choice supporters like to frame pregnancy as a condition rife with threats, including threats to the mother's life, health, psychological well-being, and economic stability. The first of these "threats," that a continued pregnancy could put the life of the mother in jeopardy. deserves serious and separate analysis.

Some conditions, such as ectopic pregnancies, can legitimately create life-threatening conditions for a woman continuing her pregnancy. Ectopic pregnancy occurs when, after conception, the newly-created child does not move into the uterus, but implants in her mother's fallopian tube and begins to develop there. While there exist vanishingly-rare cases of children born alive after ectopic pregnancies, odds of mother or child surviving an ectopic pregnancy are approximately 3 million to one.[113] Ectopic pregnancies, left untreated, virtually always result in the death of both mother and baby.

Treatment for an ectopic pregnancy involves either surgically removing the human embryo, or taking out the fallopian tube containing the embryo. The intent of such treatment is not to kill the unborn child, but to save the life of the mother. The death of the unborn child is both foreseen and inevitable, but that death is neither desired nor intended. The choice comes down to treating the ectopic pregnancy and saving the life of the woman, or leaving the ectopic pregnancy in place and losing both the woman and her child. The moral decision maximizes preservation of life. If abortion is the intentional killing of an innocent human being, then treating ectopic pregnancy does not qualify as abortion.

Abortion-choice supporters always fight to include exceptions to whatever new legislation might try to restrict abortion. They often claim that such legislation poses a threat to the woman's life or "health." Many readers assume that when they see "life" and "health" together in such a sentence, the words refer to the woman's physical life and physical health. Not so. While the concept of a threat to a woman's life is unambiguous, abortion-choice supporters rely on the ambiguity of the word "health" to gain allies and eviscerate any proposed restrictions on abortion. The Supreme Court ruled in a *Roe v. Wade* companion case, *Doe v. Bolton*, that "health" was a broad concept that could consider "the light of all factors—physical, emotional, psychological, familial, and the woman's age—relevant to the wellbeing of the patient."[114]

In fact, pregnancy sometimes does result in physical health complications. During pregnancy, some women develop serious conditions such as gestational diabetes, placenta previa (where the placenta covers all or part the cervix), or preeclampsia (high blood pressure, with its associated risks of organ damage). These health problems, however, don't require abortion as a solution. Gestational diabetes often can be managed or controlled through diet, exercise, and medication. Placenta previa sometimes resolves itself later in pregnancy, and when it doesn't, doctors can deliver the child via caesarean section. Physicians can monitor and treat preeclampsia, and, if necessary, deliver the baby early. When abortion-choice supporters smuggle in the word "health" as an exception to abortion restrictions, they typically mean much more than physical health.

People often argue for abortion because a woman cannot "afford" to have a baby (economic health). And no doubt, giving birth and raising children can carry significant financial expense. Some men also threaten to (or actually do) leave their pregnant girlfriends or wives.

Some family members threaten to disown or evict young women who become pregnant (relational or familial health). My wife and I hosted such women in our home after they were forced to leave—one rejected by her husband, the other kicked out by her parents—because they would not agree to abort their babies.

Some women suffer intense psychological distress at the thought of motherhood (emotional health).

But do any of these reasons justify the intentional killing of human beings in the wombs of their mothers? All of these arguments, at their root, involve appeals to pity, or if you prefer, sympathy. No one wants to watch another person suffer. When people get sick, we feel bad for them. We empathize with friends who struggle with difficult finances. It breaks our hearts to see relationships fall apart over a single issue between partners. We want to see healing. We want relief from distress. We want to find a way to solve the problems of our friends, loved ones and others in trouble.

When untimely pregnancy comes to a woman who subsequently suffers physical, financial, relational, or psychological problems, abortion-choice supporters step in and offer to kill the innocent human being in the womb through abortion. This they call "health care."

Human beings, whether inside or outside of the womb, have identical moral worth. All human beings are persons. So should we support the abortion of children for the "health" reasons that Doe v. Bolton allows? To answer the question, make a simple substitution. Since no significant moral difference exists between a six-month-old in the womb and a six-month-old outside the womb, replace the term "baby" with "toddler" or "adolescent."

Who would argue for killing toddlers because they might bring germs or infection into the house, potentially compromising a parent's health? Who would allow parents who just lost their jobs, and as a result suffered financial strain, to kill a few of their children in order to lighten their economic burden? No one would support destroying innocent family members because leaving them alive might result in a failed relationship between the parents, or because the kids might cause the parents distress. If you were to suggest such a lethal course of action, people would call you a monster.

If it's wrong (and illegal) to terminate the lives of troublesome or inconvenient toddlers or adolescents, then why should it be right (and legal) to terminate the lives of troublesome or inconvenient children still inside the womb? In fact, it's wrong to kill unborn children because they may cause inconvenience or trouble, just as it's wrong to kill toddlers or adolescents because they may cause inconvenience or trouble.

My Body, My Choice

"My body, my choice" has become the slogan for the so-called "bodily autonomy" argument. The simple form of this claim, the one used by the majority of abortion-choice supporters I have encountered on college campuses, insists that people should remain free to do whatever they want with their own bodies.

Many find this claim intuitively attractive—at least, on the surface. Which of us, after all, wants others to tell us what we can and cannot do with our own bodies? This claim appeals to our desire for freedom. But this claim, as stated, has at least two key problems.

First, we already have established the separate, distinct humanity of the human being in a woman's womb. The pregnant woman who wants an abortion is not really seeking the right to do what she wants with *her own* body; she assumes the right to do whatever she wants with *someone else's* body. In fact, she wants the right to use her body to transport someone else's body to a place where a third party will intentionally kill that unborn person, at her request.

Second, human beings clearly do *not* have the right to do whatever they want with their own bodies. Taking LSD, for example, or smoking crack cocaine, and otherwise ingesting any controlled substance violates the law. When I speak to groups, I often ask the women if they have had difficult pregnancies filled with "morning sickness," which many women experience as "all day" sickness. I tell them that I know of a drug that very effectively controls nausea during pregnancy and ask if they would like to know about it. Young women vigorously nod, but older women know where I am going and so they just look at me. "Unfortunately," I tell the young women, "no present-day physician will prescribe this miracle drug for you. It's called thalidomide, and even though it's effective, it causes significant birth defects." Doctors know that when pregnant women ingest drugs, those drugs don't affect the women's bodies only; they also affect the very separate bodies of the children nestled in their wombs.

Thomson's Violinist

The more sophisticated form of the bodily autonomy argument, which some people will reference but fewer can fully articulate, is called Thomson's Violinist, after the thought experiment offered in defense of abortion by Judith Jarvis Thomson. Note that Thomson, in making this argument, grants "that the fetus is a person from the moment of conception."[115]

Thomson proposes an analogy. Suppose you awaken to discover that you have been connected to a world-famous violinist. Music lovers had kidnapped you because they had determined that you alone had the right blood type to rescue the violinist, who suffers from an otherwise fatal kidney disorder. Because you share the same blood type, your kidneys can do double duty: filter poisons from the blood of the violinist while filtering your own. They have plugged the violinist, so to speak, into your circulatory system. When hospital administrators discover you, they apologize, but the deed has been done. If they unplug him from you now, it will kill the violinist. The good news? The situation will last only for nine months, after which the violinist will have recovered, can be safely unplugged, and you may go freely on your way. Thomson asks, "Would you be morally obligated to give up your body, to remain in the bed plugged into the violinist for nine months?" Then she extends the scenario. What if you had to remain plugged in for nine years, or for the rest of your life? Thomson concludes that a rational person would find the situation outrageous. The idea claims that one person has no right to use the body of another person, even if the first person's survival depends on remaining attached to the second person.

Thomson's analogy tries to establish that "you" represent a pregnant woman and the unborn child represents the violinist. As the violinist is "plugged into" you, so the child is "plugged into" (or attached to) the mother. Thomson wants her audience to conclude that exactly as it's unjust to expect one person to use his body to sustain the life of another person, even if that person depends on his body to live, so it's unjust to require a pregnant woman to use her body to nurture the life of an unborn child that she would prefer not to sustain.

While Thomson's argument has provoked a host of responses from fellow philosophers, this section will offer up just four, sufficient in most circumstances to refute her position.[116]

First, the relationship Thomson describes between the kidnapped individual and the dependent violinist fails to meet the requirements for a sound analogy. The kidnapped individual and the violinist are total strangers, unrelated biologically or in any other way. A third party, music lovers, has forged the link between them against the will of the kidnapped individual (and perhaps against the will of the violinist). A rape victim provides the nearest corollary, and we refuted those arguments in the previous chapter.

The pregnant woman and the child in her womb are not strangers. The little human being came from her body, and she (and the child's father) have obligations toward the child they have created. Kaczor notes the terrible repercussions that would follow from Thomson's assertion that biological relationships between mothers and their children carry no necessary obligations: "If mothers do not have a special responsibility for their children by virtue of a biological relationship, then the same lack of duty should hold true for fathers. Such a view would have profound moral and legal consequences."[117] If a man were to withhold child support, the law would treat him as a deadbeat dad. If a man used women solely for sexual pleasure, making it clear that he'd disappear if one of his conquests turned up pregnant, everyone would consider that man an immoral jerk.

The link that forms between mother and child is not artificial or forced upon them by a malicious third party. Nature links mother and child, not technology. The child implants and connects to his mother through the placenta and umbilical cord.

Second, Thomson's analogy uses the term "unplugging" to describe the separation of the kidnapped person from the violinist. While Thomson's scenario grants that the violinist will perish as a result of the unplugging, the process itself appears neat and clinical. Perhaps the kidnapped stranger could undo the coupling himself. One could almost see the violinist, kept comfortable on his separate bed, until he slowly slips away, a victim of his own impaired kidneys.

But imagine if, in Thomson's scenario, the kidnapped stranger instead had to employ a killer who used a chainsaw to cut the violinist in half. Would that change the emotional response to the story? Abortion is *not* unplugging. Planned Parenthood may describe aspiration abortions as "gentle suction," but that "gentle suction" provides enough tearing force to rip apart the tender bodies of developing human beings. Dilation and Evacuation abortions involve dismemberment, and, if the unborn child's head is too large, abortionists use forceps to crush her skull. For later abortions, the child in the womb is burned and poisoned to death using saline.

Because so many people discuss abortion as if it were just an abstract moral issue, they feel free to focus on "words" or "concepts" and end up ignoring or forgetting its inherent violence. If pregnant women were told the truth: that the abortionist will rip the limbs from her baby's body, I believe few would go through with it. Our job must be to help people to see the truth, and offer life and hope.

In the original violinist scenario, one could imagine that the violinist simply dies when nature takes its course. But abortion intrudes into nature by using surgical or chemical means. Abortions are violent acts that intentionally kill innocent unborn children, nothing like one person "unplugging" himself from another.

Third, Thomson's analogy overstates the burden of being "plugged in." In her own analysis, she notes that a lesser burden might be acceptable—for example, if the attachment time lasted ten minutes instead of nine months.[118] Her analogy portrays pregnancy as nine months of complete, stationary, miserable confinement.

Most pregnancies have little in common with Thomson's scenario. While the mother and child are indeed connected, for the first few weeks of that connection, the mother may not even know that she is pregnant. Even after she knows, most mothers remain free to continue their normal routines far into their pregnancies. Many women feel deep contentment during pregnancy. My "cold-blooded" wife, Sharon, confessed that the only time in her life she felt comfortably warm occurred during pregnancy.

Finally, Thomson's Violinist analogy provides a skewed ending. "Unplugging" from the Violinist supposedly relieves the kidnapped stranger from having to bear any burden associated with sustaining him. The story implies that, once relieved of the burden of keeping the violinist alive, the kidnapped stranger goes his merry way. As Kaczor points out, however, both continuing a pregnancy and aborting a child come with their own sets of burdens. Abortion does not relieve pregnant women of a burden; it instead substitutes one set of burdens for another. The significant difference is that choosing to accept the burdens of pregnancy results in the nurturing of an innocent human life, while choosing to accept the burdens of abortion requires that two people, at minimum, conspire to intentionally kill an innocent human being.

The key burden, then, is that abortion, unlike bringing a pregnancy to term and delivering a live baby, causes moral disfigurement. As Kaczor says, "To do anything morally wrong is to disfigure oneself in a moral sense, and the more serious the wrong chosen, the more serious the disfigurement. After the choice of abortion, many women bear a burden of guilt that is, for some, never terminated."[119] Kaczor's book analyzes the philosophical underpinnings of abortion arguments, and as such, doesn't talk about how women and men facing the guilt from a past abortion can learn to deal with it. Fortunately, most people in the U.S. live within close proximity to one of nearly 3,000 pregnancy help centers (and these centers continue to grow in number worldwide), many of which provide post-abortion counseling and Bible studies so that people can discover forgiveness, receive healing and find restoration.

Violations of My Expectations

Beyond the concept of childbearing as a threat or eclipsing a woman's personal bodily freedom, abortion-choice supporters also invoke arguments that try to justify abortion in order to make life experience meet expectations. Many of these arguments pretend to address the nature of the unborn child, but in reality, they merely cater to the desires of adults to avoid stigma, control the timing of childbearing, avoid the stress associated with disabled children, select gender, and have only the children one plans for and wants.

1. Avoiding social stigma

Abortion-choice supporters sometimes justify abortion as a necessary means to help teenage girls, pregnant outside of marriage, avoid social stigma. Elements of American culture seek to shame women who have "made a mistake," and because the men who impregnate them bear no visible evidence of their deeds, the women need abortions to level the playing field.

The social stigma that used to attach to unwed motherhood, however, has grown far less prevalent than in years past. Out-of-wedlock pregnancy, unfortunately, has become quite common. Our media-obsessed culture celebrates a host of unmarried movie, television, and internet stars when they reveal they're pregnant.

Whatever stigma still exists doesn't arise from the child, but from cultural attitudes toward the behavior of the mother and father. Fornication, a word hardly uttered anymore outside the church (or inside, for that matter), is still a sin, but that sin has nothing to do with the offspring that may result. (In the next section I will address church attitudes toward pregnant, unwed mothers.) The unborn child is innocent. We should encourage people who fall into sin to confess and repent. The powerful should not kill the powerless as a means of hiding guilt and shame.

2. Controlling the timing of childbirth

People often say, even in the church, that a teenage girl needs an abortion because "babies shouldn't be having babies." Alternately, older women may argue that they need abortion because they thought they had finished bearing children, or because of risks associated with having a baby later in life.

To be clear: babies don't have babies. Infantilizing young women as a way of making abortion appear more acceptable is wrong. While some young women may, in fact, lack the willingness, emotional maturity or financial strength to adequately care for the children they conceive, the appropriate answer to unwillingness, immaturity, or lack of resources is not to kill someone else.

Additionally, the young woman or the older woman isn't "going" to have a baby; she has a baby right now. A distinct human being, at this moment, is developing and growing in her womb. Abortion won't make that child magically disappear; abortion intentionally kills that child.

Parents who cannot raise the children they conceive have an appropriate course of action: adoption. Adoption respects the value of the child in the womb and allows birth parents to give a tremendous gift to another couple. Approximately 2 million couples in the United States are waiting to adopt, meaning that about thirty-six couples wait for each available baby.[120] Birth parents can now select the couple they want to parent their child, and in many cases can negotiate the level of contact they would like to have, varying from no contact up to substantial participation.

3. Avoiding the stress of disabled children

Challenges come with having a special needs child. Abortion is so routinely offered to parents who receive a prenatal diagnosis of Down syndrome or any other significant birth defect that it now seems normal. In the U.S., a prenatal Down syndrome diagnosis leads to abortion in about 75 percent of cases; in much of Europe, the figure reaches 90 percent or higher.[121]

Just because someone may present unexpected burdens gives no justification for intentionally killing them. Some parents, at various times in their lives, may find one or more of their children insufferable, emotionally draining, or difficult in a host of ways. Even parents with "perfect" children are just one significant accident away from having a special needs child.

The motivation to abort a child with Down syndrome, spina bifida, or other potentially demanding conditions does not reflect on the value of the child. But if parents find themselves unable or unwilling to raise a child with special needs, like the parents who deem themselves too old or too young, they can place their children for adoption. In 2007, in the Cincinnati area, a research study identified 199 prospective adoptive parents on a waiting list for a child with Down syndrome.[122] Let that sink in. Special needs children, at least those identified as such in the womb, often get labeled "unwanted," yet many families eagerly wait to welcome them. Unfortunately, developments in non-invasive prenatal diagnosis for Down syndrome has led to an increase the incidence of abortion, resulting in even fewer children available for adoption.

Children with special needs are human beings both inside and outside of the womb. They deserve a chance to live out their lives, even if their biological parents lack the resources or the will to support them.

4. Getting the gender right

The advent of ultrasound and other prenatal (and in the case of in-vitro fertilization, pre-implantation) diagnostic techniques created the ability for parents to "design" their children. Just as those technological advances enabled parents to use abortion to eliminate children with unwanted developmental problems, so they also allowed parents to abort children of an undesired sex. In other words, if diagnostics showed that a woman was pregnant with a girl, but she and her husband wanted to start building a family with a boy, they could abort the girl and try again. Research demonstrates that sex-selection abortion has become common. The Guttmacher Institute vigorously opposes sex-selection abortion bans because such bans "stigmatize pregnant people of color who seek abortions by questioning the motives for their abortion decision."[124]

Sex-selection abortions dehumanize human beings in the womb because they treat these people as accessories or commodities, valuable only because of a specific trait or ability. To determine that some should live while others should be put to death, solely on the basis of sex, is the worst form of discrimination. In some cultures, the strong preference for boys over girls is leading to what can only be called gendercide.

Such gender preferences can also be fleeting. Many a man eagerly awaited what he thought was the birth of his son. "I can't wait to meet my little man-cub! The adventures we'll have! I'll teach him to shoot a deer and field dress it, fish, and throw a football. We'll wrestle in the mud and I'll show him how to fight to defend those weaker than he is. It'll be AWESOME!" And then his wife delivers not little John, but little Julia. Often, in a remarkably short period of time (seconds, perhaps), this dad begins dreaming about making mud pies, attending his little girl's "tea party," going to his first daddy/

daughter dance, and escorting this radiant young woman down the aisle on her wedding day. People adapt.

What a terrible thing to declare another human being unfit to live because his or her existence disappoints what should be a temporary, malleable desire.

5. You're the one that I want

Planned Parenthood's perennial slogan is "Every child a wanted child." The idea identifies unwanted children as problems, and we should have only the children we want.

A child's being unwanted does not reflect on that child, but on the parents. Their inability or unwillingness to want and love their own children is a moral defect. Fortunately, like many other moral defects, it can be corrected.

In fact, every child is a wanted child. They just may not be wanted by their own biological parents. As noted, long waiting lists exist for all kinds of babies.

The "every child a wanted child" slogan also fails because it assumes that not wanting a child, especially at the moment parents discover they're pregnant, is an unalterable condition. It's not. Many children, conceived despite parental use of contraception, unfavorable economic circumstances, or other forms of "bad timing," nevertheless receive a welcome into their new families filled with love and gratitude.

Conversely, some parents want and even plan for a child, but when the child arrives, the parents feel disappointed, suddenly suffer a significant economic or relational downturn, or some other circumstance makes them question the wisdom of having a child. No one would argue that because the parents now do not want their baby, they should have a right to kill him. Innocent human beings inside or outside the womb deserve protection, regardless of the parental feelings (or lack thereof) toward that child.

It's Not Me, It's Everybody

One by one, the personal arguments fall concerning threats to health, bodily autonomy, and the disappointment of expectations people have on account of untimely pregnancies. Incredibly, these claims bear no relation to the Syllogism that began this part of our journey. *None* of them address the humanity of the unborn; in many cases, they simply *assume* unborn children are not human.

These categories of claims ignore the violence and death that abortion imposes on children in the womb. They rely for their power on the nature of human beings to place their own interests ahead of others, particularly if those others can remain unseen and unacknowledged.

Many abortion-choice supporters will, by this time, their reasons exhausted, abandon their support of abortion. But the remaining abortion-choice supporters advance to the Fourth Big Shift, the last set of developed objections. This class of arguments no longer relies on individual fears, but on group anxieties.

Chapter 9

The Fourth Big Shift: Policies

Recently, while speaking at the University of Memphis, a young man approached me during the break. He'd heard concerns expressed on campus that making abortion illegal would lead to more deaths and wanted to know what I thought. On its face, the argument is counterintuitive. How could the outlawing of a practice designed to kill a human being lead to more deaths? I'll answer his issue below (quick preview: it doesn't). Still, you can see that it employs a different angle of attack.

Not all abortion-choice supporters ground their arguments for abortion in the nature of the unborn or in pregnancy's effects on the individual. In the Fourth Big Shift, they cloak their arguments in concerns—not for women in particular, but for the planet, about supposed ineffectiveness and dangers of abortion restrictions, and about the legal plight of women caught in a world that criminalizes "choice."

Population Bomb

Ever since Thomas Malthus wrote his *Essay on Principles of Population* in the late 18th century, people in the west have obsessed over population control. Whether the variable is available food, enough clean water, or, lately, the impact of humans on the climate of the planet, the answer offered by population control experts is always *fewer people*. The promotion of birth control and abortion has become one method of obtaining that goal.

As a child in grade school in the 1960s, I remember seeing a fear-focused documentary about overpopulation. The film predicted that by now, Americans would live in apartments the size of egg crates, but stretching to the sky. China introduced its brutal "one child" policy in 1979, which led to forced abortions and child abandonment. The popular children's animated show *Captain Planet* had an episode in 1991 titled "Population Bomb" in which Gi, the water power Planeteer, explains a possible solution to her comrades: "In some countries, the government recommends a couple only has two children."[125] Groups such as Population Connection (formerly Zero Population Growth) and, not to be outdone, Negative Population Growth, continue to argue that the world either is or soon will be overpopulated. They insist we must take measures, even if draconian, to stop it.

Population control advocates have preached the death of the planet for centuries ... yet here we are. Humboldt State University economist Jacqueline Kasun provided a masterful examination of the unsavory underpinnings of population control organizations in *The War Against Population*.[126] She argued that human ingenuity and technology provide more than enough power to overcome population challenges.

When "experts" discuss population control, notice that they never want to volunteer to go first. Population control often focuses on which parts of the human populace must be controlled, and it should surprise no one to find that their targets often reside in developing countries. Significant evidence indicates that many nations in the west are "greying." After years of contraceptive and population control messaging, many countries now reproduce far below their replacement rates. Maintaining a stable population size requires a birthrate of 2.1 children per woman of childbearing age. The current birthrate in Europe is 1.6; in Japan it is 1.42; and in South Korea it is .98. Even in the United States, the birth rate is 1.72, below replacement rates.[127] In many nations, people are dying faster than others are being born.

But even if overpopulation presented a significant and urgent problem, it would have no bearing on the nature of the human being in the womb. While people might argue that using non-abortifacient contraceptives provides an appropriate response to their own fears of overpopulation, advocating killing human beings already in existence does not.

Abortion Restrictions Don't Work

One of the more unusual arguments recently advanced by abortion-choice supporters declares that abortion restrictions have no effect on abortion rates. If pro-life advocates truly want to reduce the number of deaths from abortions, this argument goes, then they should reject increased restrictions on abortion, because then at least legal abortions would be safer for the women who seek them. Research from the Guttmacher Institute and the medical journal Lancet supply the most frequently cited sources for this claim.[128]

You might respond by asking, "If I could show you counter-studies proving that increased restrictions on abortion, or making abortion illegal, would lead to a significant decrease in abortion, would you join me in trying to make it illegal?" After all, those who argue against abortion restriction on the ground that it will save more human lives—not by decreasing abortions, but by decreasing maternal deaths from illegal abortion—appear to claim that what matters is the balance of human lives. Since every abortion intentionally takes a human life, significantly decreasing abortion would significantly decrease human death. Wouldn't they support that?

Expect resistance, which reveals this claim as a ploy, not a position.

The claim that restrictions on abortion have no effect on the incidence of abortion rests on studies that for many reasons have serious problems. Michael New notes, "Most of the countries that restrict abortion are located in Africa, South America, Latin America and the Middle East. These countries have much higher poverty rates and cannot be compared to industrialized democracies in North America and Europe."[129] Additionally, these studies fail to account for alternate causes that might influence increases in abortion rates, such as political conditions or the age of the population.

Better studies exist, such as the one conducted by Phillip B. Levine and Douglas Staiger about the effect of abortion laws in Eastern Europe. Their study did control for many such variables and concluded that restrictions on abortion did not lead to an increase in maternal death. They found that "modest restrictions on abortion access have no significant effects on birth rates but do reduce abortion rates and, by implication, pregnancy rates by a substantial amount. Our estimates indicate that modest restrictions on abortion access reduced abortions by about 25 percent and pregnancies by about 10–25 percent."[130] In countries that limited abortion—allowed only to save the mother's life or to address specific medical conditions—the abortion rate was 95 percent lower than in countries with abortion on demand.[131] In other words, legal restrictions on abortion had virtually no impact on maternal death, and led to both a significant decrease in abortion as well as a decrease in pregnancy rates.

Other studies show that legalizing abortion in the United States led (unsurprisingly) to a surge in abortion, and laws restricting abortion effectively decrease abortion rates. In 1970, after fifteen states, including California, liberalized their abortion laws, approximately 200,000 abortions occurred in the U.S. In 1973, after *Roe v. Wade* eliminated restrictions on abortion nationwide, the number of abortions more than tripled. Abortion numbers peaked in 1990 at 1.6 million and have fallen slowly ever since. Would recriminalizing abortions lead to fewer abortions? Levine, Staiger, Kane, and Zimmerman's research concluded, "Based on the approximately 4 million births nationwide in 1993, we estimate that a complete recriminalization of abortion would result in perhaps as many as 320,000 additional births per year."[132] Even small, incremental restrictions have a significant impact. When Texas passed parental notification laws in 2000, it led to a 22 percent decrease in the abortion rate among seventeen-year-olds.[133]

Abortion restrictions do work to reduce abortions. These restrictions have no significant impact on maternal death. Fewer abortions mean fewer intentional deaths of innocent human beings in the womb. If someone's goal is a net life advantage, then restricting and eliminating abortion is the best way to achieve it.

Abortion Restrictions Punish or Kill Women

Finally, some abortion-choice supporters argue that misogyny—a hatred for women and a desire to punish them—motivates the drive to make abortion illegal. They say restrictions either directly punish women, or they punish women by forcing them into illegal, perilous, back-alley abortions.

The unspoken objective of claiming that abortion restrictions punish women is to prove pro-lifers don't really value the unborn as human persons because they refuse to charge with murder the woman who aborts her child. This claim attempts to create an unwinnable scenario. If the pro-life advocate says the law should hold women legally accountable for intentionally killing their children through abortion, the abortion-choice supporter calls the pro-life position "anti-woman." If the pro-lifer agrees that the law should not punish women—perhaps it should punish only abortionists—opponents then claim that pro-lifers don't really believe in the humanity of the child in the womb. If they *really* believed that abortion slaughtered human beings, the abortion-choice advocates claim, pro-lifers would act like it by pressing murder charges against the mother.

To respond to such an argument, first point out its unreasonable nature. You might reply: "If I say I will punish the woman, then you will say I am anti-woman. If I say I won't punish the woman, then you say I am inconsistent." In order to clarify the dilemma, ask a question: "Can different kinds of intentional killing result in different kinds of legal outcomes?" Then propose the following three scenarios.

1. The police arrest a professional hit man. They demonstrate in court that this man has killed ten people in the city and received $100,000 for every death. He shows no remorse; he held no personal ill will toward the people he killed. He sees killing people merely as a well-paying job.

2. A woman comes home early from work to find her husband having intercourse with one of his co-workers. Her feelings of betrayal quickly turn to rage and revenge. She pulls a shotgun from the closet and fires twice, killing her husband and the other woman. After many minutes of shock, she puts the shotgun down and calls the police to report the murders.

3. Late getting to their movie, a husband and wife take a shortcut through an alley. A man steps out of the shadows with a large knife. He tells the husband to hand over his wallet. The husband, unwilling to risk a confrontation over money, complies. Now emboldened, the robber tells the husband to get on his knees. The robber says he intends to kill the husband and then rape his wife. The husband holds a concealed carry permit. He reaches into his holster, pulls out his gun, the robber lunges at him, and the husband shoots and kills

the robber. The husband calls 9-1-1 and remains at the scene with his wife until the police arrive.

What should happen to the people who intentionally killed other people in each of these scenarios? Does the law treat them in the same way? Certainly not.

The hit man, if convicted, would receive the most severe penalty available. He has committed premeditated murder and with special circumstances. He would receive either the death penalty or life in prison without the possibility of parole.

The wife who killed her husband and the other woman also would be guilty of intentional killing, but since her "crime of passion" occurred without premeditation, a plea deal might reduce the charges to manslaughter. She probably would spend some time in jail.

The man who killed the robber/attempted murderer likely would face no charges at all. Many people would want to give him a medal. He still intentionally killed another person, but only in self-defense after a direct threat to his own life and that of his wife.

Not all forms of intentional killing carry the same legal penalties. When abortion is recriminalized, I can imagine a host of possibilities.

Abortionists who continue to intentionally kill human beings in the womb would certainly go to prison, and in some states, perhaps receive the death penalty. As doctors, they can't plead ignorance; they know what they're doing. Like the hit man, they get paid to kill people. The law against abortion would be fully and immediately enforced.

For women and men seeking abortions, the legal landscape, at least at first, might remain more murky. We have raised generations of people to believe that human beings in the womb have no value. It will take some time for education to overcome that cultural bias.

It would still violate the law to obtain abortions, or for people to seek abortion services on someone else's behalf, but it remains unclear how the penalty phase after conviction would play out. I would imagine that, just as in the crime of passion scenario above, the law would take into account both the knowledge and mental state of the accused.

The final argument in any abortion-choice supporter's arsenal claims that restricting abortions will lead to thousands of deaths each year from women seeking back-alley abortions. The abortion-choice supporter seeks to create the image of a woman so desperate to end her pregnancy that she will not only violate the law, but will seek out an old crone in an attic whose only surgical tool is a rusty coat hanger. Such imagery so fills the imagination of abortion-choice advocates that many wear a coat hanger lapel pin during marches.[134]

The governments of free people must advance policies grounded in moral truth. Human beings have value. That's the truth. Any policy that relies on rejection of moral truth to obtain its ends must be vigorously opposed.

But we must ask: did thousands of women die annually from back-alley abortions prior to *Roe v. Wade*? Pro-life advocate, Dr. Bernard Nathanson, a former abortionist and co-founder of the National Association for the Repeal of Abortion Laws (NARAL—which later became NARAL Pro-Choice America), admitted that the often-cited number of 5,000-10,000 deaths from illegal abortion annually was made up: "It was always '5,000 to 10,000 deaths a year.' I confess that I knew the figures were totally false, and I suppose the others did too if they stopped to think of it. But in the 'morality' of our revolution, it was a useful figure, widely accepted, so why go out of our way to correct it with honest statistics?"[135]

Nathanson, citing testimony at the Senate hearings for the Hatch Amendment in 1981, offered by Dr. Thomas Hilgers, associate professor of Obstetrics and Gynecology at the Creighton University School of Medicine, noted: "With his remorseless figures, he pointed out that far from the 5,000 to 10,000 deaths from illegal abortion annually which we in NARAL had fastened upon in our political campaign as a nice, round, shocking figure, the actual number in the twenty-five year period prior to *Roe-Doe* averaged 250 and the highest figure in any one year was 388 in 1948."[136] Hilgers claimed that with advances in the state of the medical arts by the early 1980s, the death rate among women seeking illegal abortions would be about seventy-five a year.[137]

Back-alley abortions are largely a myth. Mary Calderone, at the time the medical director of Planned Parenthood Federation of America, in discussing a medical conference held back in 1957, said it was "estimated that 90 per cent of all illegal abortions are presently being done by physicians. Call them what you will, abortionists or anything else, they are still physicians, trained as such; and many of them are in good standing in their communities. They must do a pretty good job if the death rate is as low as it is."[138] A lack of effective antibiotics had led to the higher death rates in earlier years.

Women still die from *legal* abortion. Studies show that 156 women died from legal abortions from 1972-1979, out of 7,298,000 abortions performed in the same period.[139] But while surgical abortion is very safe for women, 100 percent of their unborn children die.

The claim that if abortion became illegal women would seek dangerous back-alley abortions insults women. First, it assumes that women will not obey the law. Second, it assumes that women will foolishly procure abortions at the hands of an anonymous criminal. Such arguments infantilize women. Finally, it argues that the only way women won't break the law and won't risk their lives with unscrupulous abortionists is to make it legal for them to intentionally kill their unborn children.

A Word on Abortion as an Answer to Problems

Over the course of our lives we face a bewildering array of difficulties. Each of the problems explored in the last two chapters are real.

I reject the idea that most women abort their unborn children for reasons of "convenience." Too many pro-lifers use the term "convenience" as a catch-all for any rationale for abortion beyond the threat to a woman's life. But pro-life advocates must acknowledge the reality of the desperate circumstances faced by many women with untimely pregnancies. Fear drives the decision to abort for many of them. They fear a significant loss: losing a job, college prospects, the respect of parents (some of them, church members), or the love of romantic partners (even husbands). Others get pushed into abortions by boyfriends, parents, or husbands motivated by fears of their own. Many politically minded abortion-choice supporters genuinely fear that wrong-headed public policies will lead us toward disaster.

But killing someone else should never be the answer to economic and social problems, even when such problems appear hopeless. Fortunately, thousands of PHCs throughout the United States (and, increasingly, throughout the globe) reach out to women experiencing untimely pregnancies. These centers and clinics offer the physical, emotional, and spiritual support that women and their partners desperately need—from her first pregnancy test and ultrasound examination to aid throughout the pregnancy and beyond. They provide childbirth and parenting classes for women or couples who choose to keep their child, and adoption referrals so that birth moms wishing to place their children can evaluate and choose the right couple. For women and men scarred by abortion, they offer post-abortion counseling and recovery. And to help to prevent untimely pregnancies from occurring in the first place, many offer abstinence education for area schools.

Abortion is not the answer. Abortion compounds the problem. People experiencing an untimely pregnancy need hope—and hope comes only from life.

Game Over?

Human life begins at conception. All human beings are persons. It is wrong to intentionally kill innocent human beings. Abortion kills innocent human beings; therefore, abortion is wrong. It is wrong regardless of the circumstances of conception. It is wrong regardless of the impact of childbearing or of restrictive abortion laws.

Are we done?

Hardly.

After presenting evidenced-based and reasoned responses to all of these arguments from abortion-choice supporters, you might consider the issue settled. Clearly, it's not. But note the number of places in their arguments where you could ask, "If I demonstrated that your position is wrong, would you change your mind and join the fight to protect human beings from the moment of conception?" With unfortunate regularity, the answer will be "No."

So then, what have you accomplished by studying and understanding the opponent's position and learning how to respond with evidence and reasoning? You have accomplished two important goals.

First, a huge swath of the American public has formed its ideas about abortion solely through media representations and that "schizophrenic sort of subterfuge" described in the *California Medicine* essay. A majority of Americans have never encountered a reasoned explanation of the pro-life position. Slogans inform much of their thinking, rather than evidence or analysis. The majority of those inhabiting the mushy middle—especially Christians—can be persuaded to become pro-life in their ideology and actions. Later chapters will discuss messaging to effect that goal, in particular the kind that needs to begin in the church. You can voice these arguments and see real change among reasonable people willing to look at the evidence.

Second, peeling away abortion-choice arguments exposes people so committed to abortion that no amount of evidence, analysis, or reasoning will deter them. Such people simply want abortion. They believe that nothing should stand between them and what they want. I will unmask this group of people in the next chapter and demonstrate that if their vision of bioethics prevails, every human being, inside or outside the womb, is at risk.

Chapter 10

The Final Shift: "Okay, You Got Me"

C hapter after chapter, this section engaged the assertions and arguments that abortion-choice supporters use to try to justify abortion. Every turn reveals that science and moral philosophy show:

- what is in a woman's body from the moment of conception is a human being
- all human beings are persons
- neither the circumstances of conception nor the impact of childbearing change the nature of the human being in the womb
- arguments asserting negative cultural impacts of abortion restrictions are based on faulty analysis, and even if they were true, they would not alter the fact that it is wrong to intentionally kill innocent human beings; abortion intentionally kills innocent human beings; therefore, abortion is wrong.

As some people encounter the evidence and reasoning, they recognize that the only reason they had for approving abortion has disappeared. They once considered the object in the womb a valueless clump of cells. Now that they know the truth about conception and embryology, they change their minds.

Others bought into the idea that some human beings really weren't persons, and so aborting them had little significance (even if it seemed regrettable). Then they learned that the arguments that allowed for aborting so-called human non-persons actually placed post-born people, like themselves, equally at risk. Confronted by the appalling record of horror and abuse that historically has gone hand-in-hand with separating human beings from their personhood, they abandon their former view and begin to embrace a pro-life position.

At each step, reasons, rationales, circumstances, and positions fail to satisfy the moral demand that tells us we need to value and safeguard *all* innocent human beings, particularly the weakest and most defenseless. People who considered themselves "pro-choice" think again, honestly reflect, and decide that abortion isn't what they thought it was.

As we argue about the issue of abortion, our main goal should not be to convert our fully-committed opponents. In all my years as a debate coach or moderator, never once have I seen a true advocate for a cause concede during or immediately after a formal debate. Even despite a clear defeat, they never say, "Wow! I never thought of that! I was wrong. Thank you for pointing out my error so that I can consider this issue more clearly. This has really turned my life around!"

Not once.

But not everyone who claims allegiance to the morality of abortion is an *advocate*. That is why, throughout this book, I refer to them as "abortion-choice supporters." They support a woman's choice to have an abortion, but few have ever seriously researched the issue. Mostly they parrot talking points from like-minded friends, or which they've heard preached from media pulpits. Like the onlookers at a formal debate, these people are the true audience for pro-life advocacy. They live in the "mushy middle" of this issue, and remain open to being persuaded by evidence, analysis, and argument.

Who's Left?

What of those who remain steadfast in their devotion to abortion, despite the evidence? The Final Shift focuses on these abortion-choice extremists and advocates. They simply refuse to be persuaded.

Once upon a time, the rhetoric of abortion-choice advocates implied willingness to compromise, but the movement's voice today gives no quarter and viciously opposes any attempt to place restrictions on even the most horrific abortion procedures. Pro-life advocates face an emboldened abortion-choice movement in many states. Some people just want a culture that supports abortion—but the arguments these extremists use put everyone in peril.

Safe, Legal, but Rare

In 1993, newly-inaugurated President Bill Clinton intoned a theme that became the mantra for the abortion-choice movement at the time. In signing an executive order expanding fetal-tissue experimentation and rescinding the Mexico City Policy that had restricted the U.S. from exporting abortion, Clinton said, "As a nation, our goal should be to protect individual freedom, while fostering responsible decision-making, an approach that seeks to protect the right to choose, while reducing the number of abortions. Our vision should be of an America where abortion is safe and legal, but rare."[140]

Clinton appeared to be working hard to give both sides in the abortion debate something to cheer about. Abortion-choice supporters rallied around the idea that they now had a president who wanted to "keep abortion safe and legal." Signs bearing those words appeared in the hands of thousands of marchers at every major abortion-choice rally.

Clinton offered a sop to the pro-life crowd. While keeping abortion "safe and legal," Clinton said he also wanted it to become "rare." During the Clinton presidency, however, the U.S. averaged over 1 million surgical abortions each year. He expanded fetal tissue experimentation and allowed federal funds to flow to organizations championing abortion overseas.

Over time, the abortion-choice message shifted. "Safe and legal" remained, but the word "rare" got jettisoned. Continuing to say that abortion should be rare pointed up a weakness in the argument that pro-life advocates understood all too well: something must be deeply wrong with abortion if, as a nation, we should purposefully desire fewer of them. As a result, the Democratic Party removed the phrase from its 2012 platform, and it has disappeared from Planned Parenthood's lexicon of approved language regarding abortion.[141] Former Planned Parenthood president, Dr. Leana Wen, agreed with the choice of Rep. Tulsi Gabbard to use the "safe, legal, and rare" slogan during a televised debate between Gabbard and other 2020 Democratic presidential primary contenders. The media savaged Gabbard and Democratic primary voters soon sent her packing.[142] In agreeing with Gabbard, Dr. Wen gave a glimpse into why she is the *former* president of Planned Parenthood.[143]

Abortion: On Demand and Without Apology

You can still see the "safe and legal" part of the slogan at rallies supporting abortion, but it has rapidly give way to the more aggressive claim: "Abortion: On Demand and Without Apology."

The mask has come off.

Using *Roe v. Wade* and *Doe v. Bolton* as both legal shield and bludgeon, contemporary abortion-choice advocates want to maintain a country where abortion remains legal throughout all nine months of pregnancy, for any reason whatsoever, at taxpayers' expense, and—if the female involved is a minor—without parental knowledge or consent. Apocalyptic warnings about the erosion of the rights of women, along with hand-wringing over supposed threats to their health care, greet every attempt to pass even minimal restrictions on abortion.

Abortion-choice advocates do not want abortion to become "rare," as if it were something to be ashamed of. Today, they speak of abortion as something good and they want it to become common, almost like a rite of passage.

We live in the age of abortion pride. Actors used to thank God or their parents when accepting awards; now they thank abortion.

In her Golden Globes acceptance speech, actress Michelle Williams openly credited her abortion as pivotal in the success she has achieved. She stood, holding the golden emblem of her achievement in her hands, and told her audience, "I wouldn't have been able to do this without employing a woman's right to choose."[144]

Actress and talk show host Busy Philipps, yelling into a microphone at an abortion-choice rally, attributed the whole of her successful life to getting an abortion at the age of fifteen.[145] Williams and Philipps use euphemisms such as "a woman's right to choose" or "bodily autonomy." When testifying before Congress, Philipps used a more direct approach. Discussing her abortion experience, she noted that if a fifteen-year-old girl wanted an abortion in Arizona today, she would face obstacles. She laid out a list of what she considered abortion restrictions that cross the line: parental consent, an ultrasound exam, state-mandated counseling, a 24-hour waiting period, and giving a reason why she wanted the abortion. Note that *none* of these requirements prevent women from intentionally killing their unborn children. But to abortion-choice advocates, *any* inconvenience, *any* additional information, *any* second-guessing, *any* parental involvement represents an intolerable infringement on a woman's "bodily autonomy." In an attempt to defend her position, Phillips made all of the standard talking-point arguments addressed in previous chapters.[146]

Abortion-choice advocates encourage women to speak openly about their abortions to make it seem like just an everyday, normal part of a woman's health care. Shout Your Abortion describes its mission this way: "Shout Your Abortion is a decentralized network of individuals talking about abortion on our own terms and creating space for others to do the same, in art, media, and at community events all over the country. Abortion is normal. Our stories are ours to tell. This is not a debate."[147] Indeed, personal narratives are not up for debate; they simply describe an experience. The morality of actions, however, always must remain a fundamental area of debate. Just because someone has done something that fails to make them feel bad does not establish the moral rightness of that action. Shout Your Abortion doesn't want that debate; it simply assumes the moral superiority of its position.

When abortion counselor Emily Letts finally had an unplanned pregnancy, she saw it as a teaching opportunity. She explains, "Patients at the clinic always ask me if I can relate to them—have I had an abortion? Do I have kids? I was so used to saying, 'I've never had an abortion but...' While I was pregnant and waiting for my procedure, I thought, 'Wait a minute, I have to use this.'"[148] Letts was so early in her pregnancy that she admits she could have taken a pill, but instead she opted for an aspiration abortion so that she could film it and create "a positive abortion story." The film focuses exclusively on Letts' face. The viewer never sees the doctor and never sees the tiny human forcibly suctioned from Lett's womb. Her film won an award at the Abortion Care Network's Stigma Busting video competition. Looking back at the footage now, Letts says, "Still, every time I watch the video, I love it."[149]

But even abortion on demand and without apology doesn't take things far enough for some abortion-choice advocates. Feminist writer Jessica Valenti wants them to be free of cost as well. She wants all taxpayers to materially participate in the act of abortion.[150]

Mary Lou Singleton, midwife and founder of Personhood for Women, argues that the abortion issue isn't about "rights" (which she identifies with permission granted by "the patriarchy"). Instead, women should simply act with "reproductive sovereignty" over their bodies. In an interview with *Feminist Current*, Singleton excitedly discusses ways women can gain that sovereignty by using various methods of self-abortion.[151]

Some abortion-choice advocates feel deeply unsatisfied with merely reading about the issue or filming themselves while others do the work of killing. Abortionist Zoey Thill puts on abortion workshops where she provides average, everyday citizens with a chance to practice performing aspiration abortions, using a papaya as a stand-in for the baby.[152] She instructs participants not to punch a hole in the broad end of the papaya—a perforated uterus is one dangerous complication of abortion—but she reassures her students, "We're not going to shame perforators."[153] As each participant successfully completes their papaya abortions, they revel in their achievements. Thill tells them, "It's even more satisfying when it's a real abortion."[154] Thill says she holds her workshop to destigmatize the abortion procedure. Still, she admits her hope: "to eventually host an event for people providing underground abortions."[155]

———————— • ————————

Celebrating abortion requires a special kind of evil moral callousness. To get excited over the ability of the powerful to literally destroy a defenseless unborn baby is the ultimate perversion. These same people—who would scream "bullying" if a sixth-grader picked on a second-grader—now cheer over the thought of adults killing their own offspring.

———————— • ————————

Abortion pride is not limited to individuals. Entire states have recently celebrated the passage of state laws that expanded or reinforced abortion policies. When New York legislators passed and Governor Andrew Cuomo signed the Reproductive Health Act, they codified into state law the provisions of *Roe v. Wade* and *Doe v. Bolton*. The law legalized abortion throughout pregnancy, even deep into the third trimester, so long as the pregnancy was deemed a threat to the woman's "health." Insertion of that one little word essentially removes all restrictions. The governor openly declared his rationale. On his official webpage, Cuomo audaciously stated: "In the face of a federal government intent on rolling back *Roe v. Wade* and women's reproductive rights, I promised that we would enact this critical legislation within the first 30 days of the new session—and we got it done."[156]

Not satisfied with enshrining abortion for New Yorkers alone, Cuomo decided to turn the signing into a national spectacle: "I am directing that New York's landmarks be lit in pink to celebrate this achievement and shine a bright light forward for the rest of the nation to follow." So, in 2019, on January 22—the anniversary of the *Roe v. Wade* decision—the World Trade Center's spire lit up pink. How ironic that the landmark where millions come to mourn the deaths of nearly 3,000 innocent victims of terrorism on September 11, 2001, became a point of celebration for an act that, in the United States, takes the lives of nearly 2,500 innocent human beings in the womb *every single day*.

New York did not long remain alone.

Three months later, Virginia Governor Ralph Northam signed the Reproductive Health Protection Act, and with the stroke of a pen rolled back virtually all of the protections for unborn human beings that previous legislatures had put into place.[157] In 2017, Oregon Governor Kate Brown signed the Reproductive Health Equity Act, requiring all insurance companies to cover abortion without any co-pays.[158] Oregon already had positioned itself among the states most fiercely entrenching abortion. With religious allusion, Brown signed the legislation into law, "enshrining the right to abortion in Oregon even if *Roe v Wade* is overturned in the U.S. Supreme Court.[159]

All of these laws have a clear purpose. Abortion-choice advocates fear that the *Roe v. Wade* decision will soon be overturned. To pre-empt later challenges to the legality of abortion, they legislatively insert *Roe v. Wade* and *Doe v. Bolton* into their state law. I will address the implications of this move in the last chapter of this book, but the chest thumping and public civic celebrations over passing or extending laws that permit and even force taxpayers to subsidize the intentional killing of innocent human children, exposes their pride in a new church-state coalition. Except this time, the religious object of veneration for this church, and for these states, is Molech.

Abortion-choice extremists have emerged in the context of a pitched battle on the abortion issue. Emboldened by increasingly strident state governments and five decades of legalized abortion, they no longer see the need for *any* rationale regarding their positions. Unsurprisingly, some want to use their fundamental assumptions to press their case beyond the womb.

I Just Want

The first kind of hard-core abortion-choice extremist simply doesn't care that abortion kills innocent human beings. Remember the words of professor Camille Paglia, who has "always frankly admitted that abortion is murder, the extermination of the powerless by the powerful."[160] Despite that knowledge, she concludes, "The state in my view has no authority whatever to intervene in the biological processes of any woman's body, which nature has implanted there before birth and hence before that woman's entrance into society and citizenship."[161] The disconnect simply astounds. Paglia argues that the state has no authority to regulate what she admits is murder.

Recall the 1970 editorial in California Medicine,[162] whose authors recognized that "human life begins at conception," but were willing to engage in "considerable semantic gymnastics" and admit to foisting on a gullible public a "schizophrenic sort of subterfuge" designed to "separate the idea of abortion from the idea of killing."[163] They knew that abortion kills human beings, but saw as enlightened their propagandizing a nation to achieve their goal in the face of what they deemed to be scarce medical resources.

Author Mary Elizabeth Williams, also cited in the first chapter for her callously-titled essay "So What if Abortion Ends Life?" declared the lives of unborn children worth sacrificing. She placed lifestyle choices of women over the actual physical life of the unborn child. Why? Because she wants to preserve the ability of women to live whatever kinds of lives they want.[164]

Not only do many abortion-choice advocates not care that abortion kills innocent human beings in the womb, many would like to expand the killing to burdensome post-born human beings. Identifying the victims as human beings gives them not a single moment of pause. They coldly extend Camille Paglia's recognition of abortion as "the extermination of the powerless by the powerful" to a newly-created, additional class of human beings that the powerful may freely and morally kill whenever they wish.[165]

If I Could Kill You Then, I Can Kill You Now

The second group of abortion-choice advocates challenge the pro-life consistency claim. That claim argues that because you are the same human being you've always been, if it would be immoral to kill you now, it also should be immoral to kill you in the womb. Abortion-choice advocates don't *refute* the claim, they *invert* it. They argue that, since you are the same human being you've always been, and since it's plainly permissible to kill you in the womb, there should be no difficulty if they want to kill you now.

In his blog post, University of Chicago professor Jerry Coyne argues in favor of infanticide, using precisely these justifications:

> If you are allowed to abort a fetus that has a severe genetic defect, microcephaly, spina bifida, or so on, then why aren't you able to euthanize that same fetus just after it's born? I see no substantive difference that would make the former act moral and the latter immoral. After all, newborn babies aren't aware of death, aren't nearly as sentient as an older child or adult, and have no rational faculties to make judgments (and if there's severe mental disability, would never develop such faculties).[166]

While Coyne specifically references the killing of "deformed or doomed" newborns, the rationale he provides extends to all newborns. So what's to stop anyone from killing them as well?

The most stunning example undergirding this dark philosophical shift came in 2013, when Alberto Giubilini and Francesca Minerva published their essay, "After-birth abortion: why should the baby live?"[167] The authors create the term *after-birth abortion* in order to tie the rationale for killing newborns to the rationale for abortion. They see infanticide as always permissible, for virtually any reason: "when circumstances occur *after birth* such that they would have justified abortion, what we call *after-birth abortion* should be permissible."[168]

They give the example of a woman who discovers she is pregnant, but then her partner leaves or dies and she can't face raising a child alone. Since abortion is often justified for such reasons, they imply it should be permissible for a woman who has just given birth to kill her newborn if her partner afterwards abandons them.[169] Giubilini and Minerva ground their conclusion by including newborns in the unprotected class of human non-persons: "The moral status of an infant is equivalent to that of a fetus, that is, neither can be considered a 'person' in a morally relevant sense."[170] Infants gain moral status, the authors assert, only when the mother "projects" that value on them. If she withholds that projection, then newborns are not persons and can be permissibly killed.

To extend abortion to infanticide is bad enough, but the authors' final conclusion is particularly chilling. To quote them at length:

> Two considerations need to be added.
>
> First, we do not put forward any claim about the moment at which after-birth abortion would no longer be permissible, and we do not think that in fact more than a few days would be necessary for doctors to detect any abnormality in the child. In cases where the after-birth abortion were requested for nonmedical reasons, we do not suggest any threshold, as it depends on the neurological development of newborns, which is something neurologists and psychologists would be able to assess.
>
> Second, we do not claim that after-birth abortions are good alternatives to abortion. Abortions at an early stage are the best option, for both psychological and physical reasons. However, if a disease has not been detected during the pregnancy, if something went wrong during the delivery, or if economical, social or psychological circumstances change such that taking care of the offspring becomes an unbearable burden on someone, then people should be given the chance of not being forced to do something they cannot afford.[171]

In their conclusion, Giubilini and Minerva appear at first glance to argue only for infanticide in cases where newborns have significant birth defects. But on closer examination, time limits disappear and their rationale expands to encompass, potentially, *all* children. In the first consideration, they put no time limits on how long "after birth" a child can be killed. They imply it shouldn't take long, but they obliterate any limits at all. They also justify an open-ended time frame for "after-birth abortions" that extends *far* beyond disease or delivery complications. The authors contend that *any* reason might create "an unbearable burden on someone"—note that they do not limit the agent of action to the mother, just to "someone"—and since no one should be "forced to do something they can't afford," the right to intentionally kill one's offspring should be expanded to include post-born children, even those of indeterminate age.

Oppose Abortion in Self-Defense

While Giubilini and Minerva didn't publish their essay until 2012, way back in 1974, philosopher Gary M. Atkinson published a frank warning about the extended implications of the philosophical underpinnings of abortion-choice advocacy. In "The Morality of Abortion," Atkinson lists and explores virtually every reason offered to justify abortion on demand. He reflects, "It is worthwhile to note that abortion, viewed morally, is in practice an all-or-nothing affair. The person who accepts some reasons for justifying abortion will find it impossible to reject any reason, or at least his acceptance of abortion for certain reasons tends to have the effect of forcing acceptance of abortion for any reason."[172]

Atkinson argues that if the reasons offered by abortion-choice advocates in fact justify abortion on demand, then those arguments equally justify both infanticide and *involuntary* euthanasia. In an environment informed by justifying abortion for economic reasons, Atkinson contends that nothing prevents "senile or useless or burdensome individuals" from joining the ranks of unprotected human non-persons. He concludes that under such a moral cloud, "there is absolutely no reason to think that a future Supreme Court acting in such a climate could not interpret once again who is and who is not a person according to the Fourteenth Amendment."[173] Rational people, therefore, "will oppose abortion in self-defense."[174]

Many contemporary abortion-choice advocates neither like nor want infanticide or voluntary or involuntary euthanasia. No matter. They have laid the groundwork for it, and the outcomes of their philosophy in the form of public policy are inevitable, unless someone defeats their arguments justifying abortion, both philosophically and in the public arena. Atkinson makes this dark and dire prediction:

> It is believed that the line can be drawn at birth; but the line is arbitrary, and will be recognized as such by future generations precisely because it will be in their self-interest to do so and to justify infanticide and euthanasia. Those who desire infanticide and euthanasia have been given all the justification they need by the arguments supporting abortion; the only thing that remains to be done is to tear down the tissue of rationalizations that for the present acts as a barrier between abortion and euthanasia. Acceptance is first gained for abortion by emphasizing irrelevant or even imaginary distinctions between the fetus and the newborn child. For example, one speaks of "fetal tissue" or "developing human tissue" or "the products of pregnancy" while refusing to allow as linguistically proper any reference to the fetus as a child. Then, having justified killing the fetus, one proceeds to emphasize the similarities between the fetus and the infant so as to justify killing the born child and finally the adult.[175]

Atkinson spoke prophetically in his synopsis of the immoral progression of abortion-choice advocates and those they influence. Ideas do have consequences, and we are seeing them lived out today. If we fail to protect "the least of these"—the weak, defenseless human beings in the womb—we cannot expect anyone else to protect us.

Indeed, euthanasia already has become rampant in the west, and not always voluntary euthanasia. Jose Pereira already by 2011 had begun chronicling the slide down the slippery moral slope as practiced in some European countries:

> In 30 years, the Netherlands has moved from euthanasia of people who are terminally ill, to euthanasia of those who are chronically ill; from euthanasia for physical illness, to euthanasia for mental illness; from euthanasia for mental illness, to euthanasia for psychological

distress or mental suffering—and now to euthanasia simply if a person is over the age of 70 and "tired of living." Dutch euthanasia protocols have also moved from conscious patients providing explicit consent, to unconscious patients unable to provide consent.[176]

In 2015, *The Journal of Medical Ethics* examined the "deliberate" euthanasia of patients in Belgium without their explicit, voluntary consent, as required by law. The study's author, Raphael Cohen-Almagor, a professor of philosophy and ethics at the United Kingdom's Hull University, found that life-ending drugs were used "with the intention to shorten life and without explicit request" in 1.7 percent of *all deaths* in Belgium in 2013. In 52.7 percent of these cases, the patients were eighty years of age or older. Doctors did not discuss with the patient the decision to euthanize in 77.9 percent of the cases, because the patient was comatose, had dementia, or "because discussion would have been harmful to the patient's best interest," according to the study.[177] Doctors, apparently, know best who should live, who should die, and who should know.

Much of the United States already has joined several countries in Europe, as well as Canada, Columbia, and the state of Victoria in Australia, in permitting euthanasia—often by the euphemism "aid in dying." As of 2020, California, Colorado, Hawaii, Montana, Maine, New Jersey, Oregon, Vermont, Washington, and the District of Columbia all had legalized some form of assisted suicide.

Doctors in California diagnosed Stephanie Packer with scleroderma and gave her three years to live. After outliving their prediction, she wanted to continue treatment. But her insurance company refused to approve the new medication her doctors suggested. They would, however, offer her an assisted-suicide drug, though she had to cough up the co-pay: $1.20.[178] Packer ultimately triumphed over her insurance company. The evidence, however, points to a pro-death culture that places few, or ineffective, roadblocks to sick, depressed, or compromised people seeking death. In some cases, that culture actively encourages such death.

To visualize the kind of abuses that likely await, in 2019, a doctor in the Netherlands euthanized a dementia patient *over her objection*. She had signed the authorization earlier, but clearly had changed her mind. The woman so adamantly opposed her "good death" that she struggled with the doctor; her family members had to hold her down for the lethal injection.[179]

Atkinson correctly foresaw that the thinking leading to euthanasia and its abuses comes through the arguments for abortion on demand. If post-born people want to protect themselves, they must reject abortion.

"It Could Never Happen Here"

For as long as I can remember, abortion-choice advocates have dismissed pro-life warnings as mere "slippery slope" arguments. When pro-lifers pointed out that first-trimester abortions would lead to late-term abortions, abortion supporters minimized (but did not deny) the incidence of late term abortions. When pro-lifers claimed that abortion would lead to infanticide and euthanasia, abortion supporters accused them of fear-mongering. After all, this is America! It could never happen here.

The belief that infanticide, or even involuntary euthanasia, could "never happen here" demonstrates an appalling ignorance of history. If you grew up on *Hogan's Heroes* re-runs, you might be excused if you thought of Nazis as bumbling idiots—but they weren't. Germans in the 1940s were a literate, cultured, well-educated people. They possessed some of the finest continental universities in Europe. Still, they managed to generate the Third Reich and believed that the extermination of the Jews in killing centers—unfortunately known today by the euphemism "concentration camps" instead of "death camps"—served their best interest.

The existence of abortion in the United States demonstrates that it *can* happen here. It is happening. We simply have become so much better at exterminating unwanted human beings that we make the Nazis look like amateurs.

The Nazis had to build killing centers outside of the cities; we build abortion facilities in the middle of urban and suburban neighborhoods.

The Nazis had to round up Jews and force them into cattle cars to transport them to the killing centers; we have inculcated our youth so deeply in abortion culture that young women willingly drive themselves and their unborn children to abortion facilities. And, in nearly half of the cases of abortion today, if the woman is early enough in her pregnancy, abortionists can provide drugs so that she can chemically kill her child at home.

Between 1939 and 1945, the Nazis killed approximately six million Jews. In the United States alone, since *Roe v. Wade* in 1973, we have killed over 60 million innocent human beings through abortion.

If we expect to see actual Nazi hordes goose-stepping down Main Street before we recognize a holocaust, we will wait a long time. Evil rarely comes in the same guise twice, but it always comes bearing the same principles: find the weakest, most defenseless human beings; dehumanize them; then abuse, torture, and kill them.

As always, it's a wickedly diabolical plan. Doubly devastating, it intentionally kills someone created in the image of God while simultaneously scarring the perpetrator.

As the church, we must grasp the reality and enormity of the problem posed by abortion. We must learn how abortion-choice supporters think and argue, and know the responses we need to make in order to influence the persuadable. As noted in the first chapter, since abortion has infiltrated the church, our response must begin there.

In the following section, I will outline what the church must do if it wants to strengthen its people against the siren song of abortion advocacy. How can we raise up a generation ready to contend for a culture of life in order to overcome a culture of death?

Part Three

Speak Up, Rescue, and Change the World

Abortion is a form of idolatry that kills unborn children and scars parents. The church has shied away from in dealing with it, often for reasons it deemed good. But those reasons turn out to be not only unfounded, but damaging to the very people churches wanted to protect. We know people get stressed when we talk about abortion, but strategies exist to help overcome those objections and turn stress into a friend.

Abortion is no one-sided issue; the abortion-choice position has its own set of supporters and advocates. But their foundational argument about when life begins is fiction, rejected by science. Some supporters, undeterred, engage in a series of Big Shifts to obscure the issue, but through reasoning, evidence, and moral argument, we can bring clarity to the discussion.

Finally, most abortion-choice supporters, after discovering the truth, will fade back or adopt a pro-life world view. Those who remain are abortion-choice advocates, extremists who ignore the evidence because they believe that maintaining the choice to kill innocent human beings in the womb provides them with benefits and resources they consider more valuable than the lives they take.

This final section focuses on doing what is required to save the lives of vulnerable human beings in the womb—to speak up and to rescue. The next three chapters concentrate on speaking up; the final three are about rescue. If we will speak up and rescue, we can protect the church against abortion advocacy, empower Christians to do God's will toward our unborn neighbors, and change the world.

Chapter 11

Speak Up and Transform the Mind

As the number of COVID-19 infections continued to rise in 2020, governors placed their states on lockdown. Across the country, schools, restaurants, sports facilities—just about every public place—closed its doors, in some cases for months. In other cases, forever.

Churches also locked their doors.

The highly infectious virus put at high risk people with diabetes, hypertension, and other underlying health conditions. Elderly people were particularly susceptible. The "novel" virus meant we had scarce data on it, so closing the doors seemed the compassionate thing to do. Churches scrambled for alternatives. Leaders worked overtime and mastered new technologies to continue serving their people, but in ways that would keep them out of danger. No pastor wanted to do something that could risk the lives of his congregants.

If the church is willing to close its doors out of compassion to keep the vulnerable from infection, then why shouldn't it be willing to open its mouth out of compassion to keep the vulnerable from death? If the church could learn about the coronavirus problem, put a plan in place to deal with it, and execute it to keep COVID-19 from spreading among its congregants, it can do the same to keep a deadly ideology from destroying the lives of defenseless fellow image-bearers in the womb.

Knowledge Needs a Nudge

Walk down the street in any city in America and you will see people smoking cigarettes. They didn't purchase them one at a time out of a pencil cup on a street corner. They purchased a pack or a carton. Right there, on the side of every pack, appears the Surgeon General's Warning telling them that the product they are about to inhale will cause "lung cancer, heart disease, and emphysema, and may complicate pregnancy." Most smokers can read. The Surgeon General is a pretty credible source. But the smokers continue to deeply inhale, blow the smoke out of their noses, and go about their business, heedless.

Knowledge alone is never enough. If it were, you could hand the first ten chapters of this book to people at your church and walk away, secure in the assurance that "my work here is done." Have you ever wondered why God didn't drop Bibles into the laps of budding Christians and say, "This is all you need to know; now go figure it out on your own"? Consider the Apostle Paul. He went to synagogues, to the marketplace, to the Areopagus. When arrested, he stood before tribunals, governors and the emperor himself. What did he do in every case? He taught. He persuaded. He convinced.

He contended.

Like Paul, we can become Contenders. We can take the scientific knowledge we have learned about the human being in the womb, the moral knowledge that informs our values, the biblical knowledge that undergirds our faith, and the knowledge we have about the claims abortion-choice supporters make, and turn it all into persuasive messages designed to change minds and move hearers to action. In order to successfully contend, we need to create convincing arguments, the building blocks of persuasion.

Get into Arguments

Even people who say they hate to argue, nevertheless argue multiple times every day. Whenever you give a reason for something you want to do, or create an explanation for something you did, you are making an argument.

Arguments have two important features: claims and evidence. A *claim* is a statement you make that you want others to accept. *Evidence* refers to the information, testimony, or physical objects—anything you provide to support your claim.

Claims without evidence are mere assertions. Evidence without claims are only random facts.

As a teacher or any other person of influence in your church, people have a natural tendency to trust you. They believe what you say—so who needs evidence?

You do.

You still need to provide evidence for your claims when you speak. If you want your message to go out from the walls of the church and move effectively into the culture, you must prove your claims in ways acceptable to the people who hear them. Not everyone listens to Scripture, but you can still persuade them. In contending against abortion in a biblically illiterate world, this means using science, reasoning, and appeals to moral philosophy—just the way we did it in section two in responding to the arguments of abortion-choice supporters.

If I say that every human life begins at conception, I make an assertion. The person hearing me might think, *Well, you're certainly entitled to your opinion*. But if I follow up with evidence for my statement from a credible source, such as an embryologist who has written a longstanding textbook on the subject widely used in medical schools, then my statement ceases to be a mere assertion and instead becomes a claim backed with evidence: an argument, in other words. If I offer additional evidence in support of the same claim, my argument becomes stronger and, therefore, more persuasive.

Speaking on abortion requires Contenders to make and prove two initial claims, as our initial syllogism demonstrates:

  1. It is wrong to intentionally kill an innocent human being.

You'll recall that most people readily agree to this, until you prove your second claim. Then, they want to modify this one by turning "human being" into "person."

  2. Abortion intentionally kills an innocent human being.

Here you have two sub-claims to establish. A) what is in the woman's body from the moment of conception is a human being (innocence in the womb is virtually a given). B) abortion intentionally kills that human being.

If you can prove both claims, then you have established the conclusion that abortion is wrong. That's how arguments work.

But arguments don't exist in a vacuum. Abortion-choice advocates don't just sit on the sidelines, inert. They also make claims and they use a variety of support mechanisms to justify them. The writer of Proverbs recognized this conflict: "The first to state his case seems right, until another comes and examines him."[180] Examination can breed doubt.

Most adults have encountered abortion-choice advocacy. The claims that dehumanize human beings in the womb and justify abortion so thoroughly permeate all secular aspects of contemporary culture that they have become the default assumption, even among many in the church.

Teachers in the church have a two-fold task when it comes to abortion: to transform the thinking of people who have accepted the claims of abortion-choice advocates; and to protect those yet to be affected, by inoculating them against abortion-choice arguments. Fortunately, one persuasive model can accomplish both goals.

Inoculating Against Bad Ideas[181]

Most people are easy to influence because their ideas do not lodge in their brains through careful study and research. Rather, they pick up those ideas through association with others (friends, family members—people they like). As a result, their ideas rarely, or never, need to be defended. When someone finally does challenge their beliefs, people with inherited ideas quickly abandon them, often wrongly thinking that if *they* can't defend their ideas, *the ideas* themselves must be indefensible. Taught only to assert what they believe, but not to prove it, their weak responses when attacked lead them to jettison their beliefs.

On my shoulder I have a round scar from a smallpox vaccination I got as a kid. Back in the '50s and '60s, doctors in the U.S. eradicated the terrifying disease of smallpox. If you came along later, you might never have been vaccinated against it. But back then, everyone I knew had the same shoulder scar.

Doctors injected into us a weakened variant of smallpox. Our bodies then developed antibodies to the virus. That way, if we ever encountered the real thing, our bodies had the defenses to fight it off. Our inoculations granted us immunity through the Sabin/Salk vaccine.

Just as you can inoculate against disease, so you can inoculate against bad ideas. The process strongly resembles the way a vaccine works in the body. You give your audience your opponent's ideas, and then provide them with the means to fend them off. As a bonus, for people who already have encountered (and maybe even believed) bad ideas, such mental inoculation can help them to recognize error and replace it with truth.

Whether you teach in a church, speak to high school or college groups, or engage in debates, use this structure to format the body of your message. If you engage people in casual conversation or on social media, you'll also find value in this approach.

Four Fair, Winsome, and Effective Steps to Refute Abortion Advocacy

1. Respectfully explain your opponent's position.

Even if no actual opponents sit on the other side of the stage, the people in your congregation or audience have a wide array of abortion-choice arguments in their heads. If they've adopted any of these views as their own, they might think that the reason pro-lifers—as "closed-minded religious types"—don't join them is that they "just don't understand."

Disappoint them.

Always begin the body of your message by laying out the opposition's case. Do this respectfully, without ridicule. Don't get up and say, "Do you know what these foolish pro-aborts think?" Recognize that some of those listening to you *might be* one of those abortion-choice supporters you mock. Ridicule may get you cheers and applause from an audience full of supporters, but it won't prepare people to listen to what you have to say.

Instead, demonstrate respect for people who disagree with you by taking the time to understand their claims and the reasons they have for making them. Be sure that you don't misrepresent claims by abortion-choice advocates. One purpose of laying out the case of your opponent is to show your listeners that you know, understand, and have carefully considered these claims.

2. Respectfully demonstrate the flawed or false position of your opponent.

Do you notice a pattern? Be respectful, even when refuting. Respectful does not mean weak. You can make strong arguments without resorting to name-calling or mocking the other side.

Now that your listeners know that you understand the opposition's claims and the reasons for them, evaluate those claims and show your evidence and reasoning for declaring their claims and reasons either flawed or untrue. You can't merely *assert* this, otherwise both sides do nothing but state their own preferences. You must prove it using your own counter-evidence and reasoning.

3. Explain your own position.

Sometimes, all you need to do is show your opponent's error. Other times, you want to provide your own separate claims and prove them.

4. Demonstrate the impact of the argument.

Always end by explaining what all of this means. What makes it important?

In four steps, you show that you understand the other side of the issue and you ask your listeners to reject the false claims, both because the evidence doesn't support them and because reason rejects them. You provide a counter-claim with reasoning and evidence to support it, and then you ask your audience to agree with and act on an appropriate conclusion.

Different Time Limits, Different Formats

If you work with elementary school students or hyperactive middle-schoolers, you know these kids can't sit still through a three-hour pro-life apologetics class. If it makes you feel any better, I frequently teach a three-hour pro-life apologetics class to adults, and I can't cover everything, either. Fortunately, you don't have to.

You can format this inoculation model in two ways. The form you choose depends upon how much time you have.

1. Pro-Con, Pro-Con

If you have only ten to fifteen minutes or so, you may have time to cover only three to five issues. If so, structure each major point in your message using all four parts of the inoculation method. Since proving the humanity of the being in the womb is the foundational argument, always address it first.

Since our messaging needs to begin in the church, the following example includes evidence from Scripture. If you speak to people or groups who don't share your biblical worldview, stick to science and moral philosophy for your evidence and reasoning.

A. *Respectfully explain the opponent's position.*

"One reason people give for thinking abortion is okay is that there's no human being in a woman's womb; it's just a bunch of cells. No big deal. In fact, websites for Planned Parenthood and other abortion clinics don't even mention what's in a woman's womb when they describe what happens in an abortion. They just call it 'pregnancy tissue' or 'the products of conception.' If they're right, then getting an abortion wouldn't be much different than getting your tonsils out or having a wart removed."

B. *Respectfully demonstrate the flawed position of your opponent.*

"But the science of embryology—that part of science that studies how human beings develop in the womb—calls such claims false. Embryologists tell us that the moment of conception marks the beginning of each one of us as separate, distinct individuals." Here, I might insert the quotation from Moore, Persaud, and Torchia from *The Developing Human,* proving my point. "Not only do embryologists know this, but Planned Parenthood itself used to know it, too." Insert the material from Planned Parenthood's *The Gift of Life* pamphlet. "In fact, Planned Parenthood used to teach everybody that abortion was wrong because it killed a baby." As an example, insert material from the Planned Parenthood brochure *Plan Your Children for Health and Happiness.*

C. *Explain your own position.*

"From the moment of conception, each of us began our lives as separate, distinct, whole human beings. Embryologists know it; Planned Parenthood used to know and teach it. The Scriptures always have taught that human life begins in the womb." Here I insert Psalm 139:13-16, and maybe discuss John the Baptist leaping in his mother's womb when Mary came for a visit while pregnant with Jesus.

D. *Demonstrate the impact of the argument.*

"We can all agree that it's wrong to intentionally kill an innocent human being. The morality of abortion relies on the idea that abortion doesn't kill innocent human beings. But now we know that the being in a woman's body from the moment of conception is exactly that: an innocent human being, and abortion kills that innocent human being. The only conclusion we can draw, then, is that abortion is wrong."

If you have three major points in your message, walk each one through this format. Whether you move on to, "But they say it's not a person" or "but, doesn't a woman have the right to do what she wants with her own body?" simply explain the abortion-choice argument, give evidence and reasoning for why it's wrong, tell your audience the truth, and then show the impact of the pro-life argument. What should they believe, and/or how should they act differently in light of their new knowledge?

2. Set up and Destroy

My personal favorite.

When you have forty minutes or more, you have time to cover a lot of argumentative ground. Since you'll address more than five key abortion-choice arguments, you don't want to use Pro-Con-Pro-Con, because you never want to have more than five main points in any single message. Once you get beyond five, people have a harder time remembering.

Instead of organizing your message around individual issues you intend to refute, you organize your message around the inoculation structure.

I. The Case for Abortion Choice
    A. The fetus is not a human being
    B. The fetus is not a person
    C. Bodily autonomy
    D. Threat to the mother's life or health
    E. Too young/too old to have a baby
    F. Unwanted babies will be abused
    G. Justified for conceptions from rape or incest
    H. Thousands of women will die if abortion is made illegal
    I. Overpopulation

You will immediately notice two things. First, in the outline above, I identify only the claims. No, don't read these like a laundry list. Fill in your outline with sub-claims, evidence, and reasoning. You can get all of it from section two and from other sources as you become aware of them. Second, in the proposed outline I have not even remotely covered all of the arguments in section two of this book. In the time you have to speak, you could not read section two aloud to an audience (and please don't try). Time constraints always mean you have to make choices. You may not even make the same choices I have identified in this example. Consider your audience and select the arguments that would most interest your particular group.

While you can't present an exhaustive case within the time limits of most messages, most of the people in your congregation or youth group will fall into one of three categories: the nominally pro-life; those never before exposed to justifications for abortion; and those who either believe abortion is okay or are sympathetic to it, but who likely hold only a few of these claims as justification. Very few of these folks have ever encountered a well-thought-out, evidenced pro-life presentation. In this example, you cover nine abortion-choice claims. Any single audience member might know a few of the arguments you identify, but few, if any, could even list (much less defend) all nine claims.

You get up and cover the case, A-I (you can end this section, as I often do, with "And if I don't hit on your particular issue, be sure to ask me"). For those who have never heard the case, you preview it for them. For the others, not only do you cover all of the claims most of your audience might believe or have heard, you've covered a number of others besides. People will conclude that you've done your homework. By respectfully explaining these positions, you also show that you take the claims seriously.

Once you've finished laying out each of these claims—backing up the fact that these really do represent the abortion-choice position by providing proof and analysis—you can say something such as, "These are the main reasons abortion-choice advocates put forward to justify the choice to have an abortion. If they were true, they would have a pretty compelling case. So let's look at each claim to see if they all hold up."

II. Why the Case for Abortion Choice is False

    A. The fetus is not a human being

        1. The unborn child is a separate, distinct human being

    B. The fetus is not a person

        1. All human beings are persons

        2. Dangers associated with distinguishing human beings from persons

    C. Bodily autonomy

        1. The unborn child is not part of the woman's body

        2. No one has absolute bodily autonomy

    D. Threat to the mother's life or health

        1. Threat to physical life: maximize life—not an abortion

        2. Threat to health in its various forms—explain that since these reasons don't justify killing post-born humans, they also don't justify killing a human in the womb.

    E. Too young/too old to have a baby

        1. Already have a baby—just deciding whether she will live or die

        2. We don't kill people we can't care for

        3. Adoption

    F. Unwanted babies will be abused

        1. Abortion is the ultimate child abuse

        2. Abortion ideology leads to increased child abuse and infanticide

    G. Justified for rape or incest

        1. Rape is a horrible crime

        2. Circumstances of conception don't change the nature of the unborn

        3. Punish the guilty, protect the innocent—if needed, through adoption

    H. Women will die if abortion is made illegal

        1. Sad that anyone dies from abortion

        2. Their claim not supported by the evidence

        3. Every abortion kills at least one person

    I. Overpopulation
        1. Myth
        2. Even if true, we don't solve social problems by killing innocent people

In the second main point, you restate the claim and then your sub-points consist of claims, evidence, and analysis to prove the abortion-choice claims cannot stand up to scrutiny. Again, you have several ideas from which to choose. By now you know many of the alternatives.

———————— • ————————

Transforming the mind always precedes alterations of the will.
The way people think governs what they do.

———————— • ————————

For the members of your audience who've yet to hear some or all of the abortion-choice claims, you have begun the inoculation process. Now imagine that at school the next day, one of your listeners has lunch with another student who says, "Those pro-life people. Don't they get that a woman has a right to do what she wants with her own body?" The argument, once stated, triggers your student to reply, "You know, I was at a class the other day, and they showed that after conception, it's a whole separate body inside the woman's. If she should have the right to do what she wants with her own body, shouldn't the baby have the same right?" Stung, the other student replies, "What do you mean, baby? It's just a clump of cells!" Again, your student says, "You know, they talked about that, too. They had a book from a famous embryologist who wrote a medical textbook. It said that everybody's individual life begins at conception. I even got a Planned Parenthood brochure that shows they used to teach that abortion kills a baby. You wanna see it?"

Initially, your listeners will cite your message as a source. But once they've made the argument a few times, they will begin to own it. They may even dig deeper, discovering additional and better evidence. They've become invulnerable to those abortion-choice arguments.

For people who come to your message having already heard some or most of the abortion-choice claims, and perhaps even believed them, one of the great benefits of the "set up and destroy" approach is that it enables you to create what I call a "psychological vacuum." You fill the audience's mind with some or all of these abortion-choice arguments; then, one by one, you refute them all. You not only prove false all of the claims they may have held, but several more besides. Nothing's left. You need to imagine your listeners silently thinking: *Well, if what we believed all this time was false, then what should we think about human beings in the womb and what abortion does to them?* I'm glad you asked.

III. The Pro-Life Position
    A. The Syllogism
        1. It is wrong to intentionally kill an innocent human being
        2. Abortion intentionally kills an innocent human being
        3. Therefore, abortion is wrong
    B. The evidence proves that everyone begins their individual human life at conception
    C. The evidence proves that abortion kills that innocent human life
    D. The best case in favor of abortion is fatally flawed
    E. Abortion is wrong

The Syllogism stands out in stark relief to the case made for abortion. Abortion-choice positions are complicated and, in some cases, self-refuting (the bodily autonomy claim, for example). The pro-life case is uncomplicated and easy to understand and defend. But knowledge is not enough; you must drive your listeners to the implications of your argument.

IV. What Does All This Mean?
    A. If the reasons favoring abortion are wrong, then we live in the midst of a titanic holocaust—one abortion death is tragic, but we have killed over 60 million human beings in the United States alone.
    B. Abortion, if wrong, must be rejected
    C. Abortion, if wrong, must be opposed—explain how
    D. Life must be supported—explain how

I have given you just some examples of how you might put together your own message. Because audiences and contexts differ, sometimes you must modify your approach to the topic. If a parental consent law were being considered in your state, for example—in many states, a girl can obtain an abortion without her parents' knowledge or consent—and you were speaking to your "Seasoned Citizens" small group, you might talk about this issue as a way to spur them to action. You might say that if your granddaughter were to become pregnant, the law would permit her to get an abortion without her parents' knowledge or consent. The proposed law could be used not only to kill your first great-grandchild, but also to cover up sexual abuse.

If I were speaking to eighteen-to-twenty-four-year-olds about abortion during the time of that same political controversy, I would focus on other issues. Young adults have less interest in parental knowledge or consent laws. They likely aren't yet parents, and even if they are, their kids aren't close to the target age group for such a law.

Can't the Other Side Do This?

Over the years, some people I have trained have asked, "If inoculation is so effective, won't the other side do it to us?" Yes, they will try . . . sort of. When I encounter abortion-choice supporters, I routinely hear a kind of argument that I know they have designed to get their allies to dismiss me. "You're only pro-life because you are religious," they may say. "Pro-lifers will try to tell you it's all about science and natural law. In reality, many vocal pro-life advocates are Christians. That's the real basis for the pro-life argument."

Such arguments fail because they are they untrue, which is easy to demonstrate. And even if it were true that all pro-life advocates are Christians, how would it materially change the truth of their claims if the arguments pro-lifers make from science and moral philosophy were spoken instead by atheists?

To effectively inoculate an audience, it's essential that you honestly represent your opponents and their positions, and that the claims, reasoning, and evidence you use to refute them are, at the very least, superior to the opposing claims. For many pro-life claims—the humanity of the unborn child, for instance—the evidence is incontrovertible and overwhelming. It's much easier to inoculate when you're right.

The Next Step

Abortion-choice supporters and advocates audaciously broadcast their positions on abortion. Churches have long needed a strategy to protect their adults and children against abortion advocacy, and to empower them to respond with confidence. The inoculation method is just what the doctor ordered.

Thinking correctly, however, is just the first step. For knowledge to become action, you must engage the will.

Chapter 12

Speak Up and Engage the Will

In *The Screwtape Letters*, C.S. Lewis warns about the dangers of knowing truth without acting upon it. The demon Screwtape, instructing his junior tempter, Wormwood, says that if his "patient" were to be consumed by ideas—even ideas about things such as repentance and the feelings that go along with the knowledge of sin—all is not lost:

> Let him do anything but act. No amount of piety in his imagination and affections will harm us if we can keep it out of his will. As one of the humans has said, Active habits are strengthened by repetition, but passive ones are weakened. The more often he feels without acting, the less he will be able ever to act, and, in the long run, the less he will be able to feel.[182]

We don't teach people in our churches in order to create world-class Jeopardy contestants, as if we need only smart people who have all the answers. While we want well-informed believers—they *should* be able to give an answer to anyone who asks, as the Bible instructs—our task does not end there.[183]

We must not allow ourselves to merely "know things." Knowledge, by itself, tends to push us toward pride. True knowledge brings with it the authority to act. Teachers and influencers in the church have the obligation to help our congregants, students, and friends turn intellectual assent into definitive action. We need a different kind of organizational persuasion model to equip our listeners to take that step.

Shepherding Bystanders

Have you ever watched sheep in the field? They seem content to crop grass and just stand there. To get from where they are to where they need to be, they need a shepherd.

Even when it becomes clear that we must take action, many people, like sheep, just stand there. They do nothing. They remain bystanders. We all have heard horror stories of violent crimes that occur on the sidewalk right in front of apartment buildings full of people. Some look out the window, but few, if any, take action to aid the victim. We find it hard to believe, and even harder to imagine, that we could be among the onlookers.

Michael McKensie explains research by Bibb Latane and John Darley, who evaluated bystander behavior to explore the processes people go through to determine whether they will intervene. First, "the bystander must notice that something is wrong." Second, they must "define the event as an emergency." Third, they have to see "the emergency as his or her own personal *responsibility* to act." Finally, "he or she must still decide *how* to help."[184]

When it comes to abortion, too many in the church remain bystanders. They fail to notice the evil, even if an abortion clinic sets up shop in their neighborhood. Abortion has become so commonplace and has continued for so long that we hardly think of it as an "emergency." After all the years since 1973, some think, *what's another few, more or less?*

But, as a life-destroying action, every abortion invariably qualifies as an emergency. Women with untimely pregnancies often feel desperate for a way out. With so many problems calling for our attention, many of us find it easy to see abortion as someone else's issue. And even if people become convicted about their inaction, many believe they lack the information, resources, or ability to effectively do anything. And so crowds of us continue to stand on the sidelines—bystanders—while each day nearly 2,500 more unborn children lose their lives to abortion.

As teachers and influencers with a crucial message on abortion, we have the task of transforming the bystanders in our churches into Contenders. To do so, we need a sequence of steps of our own to counter each of the four steps that creates bystanders. Monroe's Motivated Sequence does this by mirroring the way people go about decision-making. When we use it in our presentations, we can shepherd people to make good decisions, followed by effective action.

The Motivated Sequence

Monroe's Motivated Sequence contains five steps.[185] The first step you accomplish in the introduction of your message, while the other four take place in the body. The five steps are: Attention, Need, Satisfaction, Visualization, and Action.

1. Attention

As you discovered in chapter four, people resist change. A student in one of my college classes, taught me a new expression (not an uncommon occurrence). When one of her friends asked about her current relationship, she described the young man as "my for-now boyfriend." What did that mean, I asked? "Well, he *is* my boyfriend," she replied, "you know, for now." I gleaned from that exchange that she was in a comfortable, quasi-committed relationship, but that if someone "better" came along, "for-now boyfriend" would quickly become "former boyfriend." Only no one else, as yet, had caught her eye.

Every week, sometimes two or three times a week, Christians take a seat in church and hear a message. Like my student who felt comfortable with her "for-now" boyfriend, they become comfortable with temporary, light confrontation. Pastors constantly tell them to do something they aren't doing, or to stop doing something they are. They get used to it.

In the media, we no longer have "problems;" everything has become a "crisis." People no longer have "concerns;" they feel only "outrage." When everything ramps up to the extreme, people start to tune out. They keep living as they always have. If we want to see change, we need to get their attention.

Too often, we mention abortion in the church only on Sanctity of Human Life Sunday or in a presentation by a local PHC director. What happens? The speaker mentions the problem of unplanned pregnancies. Someone else recites a laundry list of services offered by the center. The congregation sings a closing hymn. And then everyone bolts out the door.

But imagine if the message began something like my presentation a few years back at Truman State University:

> The incident occurred at 9 a.m. Thursday as Sherry West was walking home from the post office, pushing her son, Antonio, in a stroller. She said she saw two boys. "A boy approached me and told me he wanted my money, and I told him I didn't have any money. And he said, 'Give me your money or I'm going to kill you and I'm going to shoot your baby and kill your baby,' and I said, 'I don't have any money,' and 'Don't kill my baby.'" The boy tried to grab her purse and opened fire when she tried to tell him she had no money, West said, with the shot grazing her head. She said the boy then shot her in the leg... "And then, all of a sudden, he walked over and he shot my baby in the face."[186]
>
> This incident, reported by CNN online, occurred in Brunswick, Georgia, in March. Some of you probably heard about it. My guess is that all of you are horrified by it. Can we begin tonight by agreeing that: "It is wrong to intentionally kill an innocent human being"?

If we want to get our audience's attention, to wake them from their lethargy, we need to open our messages in such a way as to demand that they take their eyes off the next blank on their sermon outline and engage with us. I guarantee that when I finished telling the Sherry West story, the assembled students wanted to know what would come next.

In the next chapter, I'll describe various forms of attention-getting devices, but for the purpose of understanding this persuasion model, never forget that once you stand and take the platform, the first words out of your mouth *must* grab the attention of your audience.

2. Need

Once you complete the other obligations of a solid introduction, establish *Need* as the first major point in the body of your message. In the Need section, you define the problem you intend to address and also demonstrate the length, breadth, height, and depth of its impact.

When you speak on abortion, I recommend you first define abortion for what it really is, and then describe it and show what it does. While speakers may provide national or international statistics, they also should drill down to the city, county, or state where they speak. National statistics are numbers; local statistics are neighbors.

In the problem section, tell your congregation or group how Planned Parenthood obscures the reality of abortion by verbally eliminating the target of the act from its descriptions of the procedure. Define abortion as "an act of violence that takes the life of an unborn child." Describe the tools of the trade. Picture for your audience how suction machines rip away tiny body parts, or how forceps dismember older children. Some babies are poisoned, others burned. If you can get permission from the pastor or the person responsible for bringing you in to speak, I recommend showing a short video distributed by Abort73 called "This is abortion."

I understand the reluctance of people to show videos or images of aborted babies. I myself would argue that such videos are inappropriate at certain times and for certain age groups. Still, I use such videos and images (getting permission from church hosts) with audience members as young as thirteen. Does that seem too young to you? If so, recall "Roo," Planned Parenthood's chat bot. Planned Parenthood wants to lead teens into sex outside of marriage, keep the parents of these teens ignorant about their sexual activities, and kill their children when they get pregnant. This organization *already* has targeted your thirteen-year-olds. Planned Parenthood doesn't deal in images of abortion; it wants to make those abortions real. They see your teens as nothing more than future clients.

Shortly before World War II ended, Supreme Commander of the Allied Expeditionary Force, Dwight D. Eisenhower, toured Nazi concentration camps and had photos taken of himself standing next to men reenacting scenes of torture. Bob Greene reports that Eisenhower "wanted to bear witness, and in so doing send a message to every corner of the planet: Even in the most ghastly, unthinkable circumstances, compassionate and unblinking eyes must never turn away."[187] Eisenhower saw men nearly starved to death. He saw bodies stacked up like cord wood, others recently incinerated—horrific images assaulted him at every turn. "And so this soldier and future president from small-town Kansas, standing in the German concentration camp, made an almost instantaneous decision: As terrible as the sight of the torture and carnage was, it must be stared at straight on by the entire world. He ordered soldiers in the Army Signal Corps to begin photographing the camp."[188] Afterward, he arranged for members of Congress and newspaper editors to come to the camps to see the carnage for themselves, and challenged them to reveal the horror to the American people.

Bob Greene didn't write his article in the 1950s; he wrote it in 2020. While the Holocaust took place long ago, these photos remind us of the true depths of human depravity. These images compel us never to forget.

————————— • —————————

The people you speak with comprise the most messaged-to generation in history. They are bombarded daily by problems presented as crises of incalculable proportions. The issues are national or international in scope, fascinating, but beyond the influence of most audience members. You must find a way to break through that noise and confront them with the reality of abortion: a personal crisis affecting one person at a time. A problem they can solve today.

————————— • —————————

Although abortion has become one of the most common medical procedures in the U.S., comparatively few people have ever seen images of an abortion being performed, or its aftermath. Once you see it, you will never forget it. Using images to establish need creates the kind of long-lasting conviction that motivates people in ways that words alone cannot.

If your board of elders will not approve the use of graphic images, then pastors and teachers must rely on their ability to describe. Be specific. Provide details. You may have only words, but the mental pictures you create can help listeners to see what they have for too long ignored. Abortion kills real human babies.

Abortion also makes casualties out of many others. In your need section, if you have time, describe how the abortion industry preys on its own clients. Stories abound of women victimized by lies. Abortion clinic counselors cited in section two are in denial about the nature of the child in the womb. Post-abortion counselors at your local PHC, while not divulging names of clients or details, can tell you about the significant problems that many young men and women have after an abortion. Take a center tour and then ask to speak with the counselors—and take notes.

The difficulties faced by people who have had abortions extend beyond the physical and psychological. Many have a hard time finding forgiveness. They flounder, spiritually adrift, unconvinced that even a loving God would have room in His heart for them.

Women with untimely pregnancies face big problems of their own. People often look down on them and judge them. Many face enormous financial and familial obstacles to making a life-affirming decision.

When developing your presentation, don't allow your need section to take up more than one-third of your time. You may have to select which issues, beyond the actual abortion, you will tackle. But take care to obey one ground rule: *Never mention a problem in your message that you don't intend to solve.* Piling problem upon problem in the psyches of your congregation or small group, only to leave many of those issues unresolved, creates a sure path toward despair. We, however, must be messengers of hope.

3. Satisfaction

The second major point in the body of your message is the Satisfaction step. In it, you provide solutions for each of the problems you set up in the Need section.

You could take away the Need—the problem of abortion—by discussing how local PHCs offer abstinence education to help young people avoid untimely pregnancies in the first place. Teens learn to honor themselves and their bodies as gifts from God. If people experience untimely pregnancies, these centers also provide the medical, physical, emotional, and spiritual resources women and men need to make life-affirming decisions. PHCs also help those who've already had abortions find forgiveness, healing, and restoration, in part through confession and repentance. In describing the PHCs' services, it feels tempting to lay out a laundry list of everything they do. Better to tell stories of clients, with their permission, that describe how the services changed their lives.

You also can solve the problem by making abortion unthinkable. People need to hear the truth about abortion so that they can avoid it, which requires the creation of advocates who will speak in churches, civic groups and schools . . . and perhaps engage in debates. Testimonials can help. You can describe how you became a pro-life advocate, to show that it can be done.

Christians also can help create legislative answers by working with others who share their position on abortion. Even though *Roe v. Wade* and *Doe v. Bolton,* along with other Supreme Court cases, currently shield abortion from outright abolition, restrictions are increasingly being used to challenge the ability of abortion clinics to freely operate. As you will see in the final chapter, even hard-core abortion-choice advocates see the handwriting on the wall and have begun preparing for a post-*Roe* world.

By providing solutions, the Satisfaction step overcomes the anxiety you created in the Need step. Your listeners will get excited. When problems seem overwhelming, it can greatly encourage us to know that workable solutions exist.

4. Visualization

Your congregation doesn't merely want to know about solutions in the abstract; they want to see what those solutions look like in practice. While Visualization is the third main point in the body of your presentation, it often takes so little time that it melts into your action step.

Two things tend to motivate people: hope of gain and fear of loss.

Often, in my Visualization step, I try to get my audience to imagine a world with all the solutions already in play. "If we work together, imagine that in our city, out-of-wedlock pregnancies drop—not because children conceived have their lives ended through abortion, but because more of our teens make good decisions. A place where young couples who make a mistake, fall into sin, and conceive a child, can find a safe haven where they can go for counsel and support to make a better decision now. Where you walk past a playground and hear the laughter of more children playing because we did what we could to aid their parents. Imagine a world where you see *all* of your grandchildren."

Help them to envision it.

Conversely, sometimes I take a negative route. I describe what will happen if we *don't* act. "Planned Parenthood continues to grow in influence and deadly effectiveness. It infiltrates our schools and indoctrinates our children. It leaves a trail of dead babies and scarred adults. That's what will happen if we remain bystanders."

Sometimes, I offer both visions. What I do depends on what I know about my audience. If you know your group, if you are well-acquainted with your congregation, you will know which of these methods will provide the strongest motivation.

5. Action

The final section of the body of your message is the Action step. You might think, *Wait a minute. Didn't we already do that in the solution step?*

No.

If I have a pollution problem (Need), my solution (Satisfaction) might tell me to build a sewage treatment plant. But most local citizens lack the resources, ability, or time to build a sewage treatment plant. In the action step, I tell them the specific things they can do to bring the Satisfaction step to life. In this case, I might persuade them to make a donation, or write letters to public officials, or publish an op-ed in the local paper.

If you recommended working with PHCs and/or creating pro-life advocates, you now provide your congregation or group with concrete steps they can take in order to make that solution happen. People can donate money, join a prayer team, or volunteer to work at the PHC. Others may start a scholarship fund so that high school and college students can attend worldview summer camps, such as those put on by Summit Ministries, where seasoned advocates train participants to become new advocates. Many of these students become active on their respective campuses by coordinating with campus organizations such as Protect Life Michigan.

The key to a successful presentation is to make requests with great specificity. If you ask your church body for general, unspecified support, you'll almost certainly get a lukewarm response. To get people excited about supporting a PHC you must do your homework so you can ask with clarity and conviction. Visit that center or clinic long before your presentation. Maybe take the director and a staff member to lunch. Ask them about their needs. Do they require a skilled craftsman to do some work at the center?

Do they need more counselors or clerical help? Do they have any jobs with a specific start and stop date, such as painting the center or redoing the landscaping? Many people will happily volunteer if they know when the work will start and when it will end.

What kind of laptops do they use? Are they still running Windows XP? Ask for a tour of the center. Does any of the furniture need replacing? Is the roof or the HVAC unit going out? How much would each of these items cost to replace or fix? Perhaps the center is growing and requires additional staff. What positions do they need to fill and what would it take to fund them? Demonstrate that you care and that your church wants to provide. When you finally appear before your audience to make the ask, remember that the more specific your request, the more likely your success.

The same holds true for volunteers. A general ask for volunteers seldom works well. While a few people might step forward, when they go through training, they may discover that their talents don't align well with the PHC's needs.

I recently keynoted a banquet. As I interviewed the director, it came up that they needed more board members. "What kind of skills do you need on the board?" I asked. The director felt startled because no one had ever asked that question. They just figured they needed "more." So I pressed: "Do you need people with legal skills, an accountant, a pastor, someone who could provide medical oversight, someone with business or development skills?" Once we finished, the director and the board discussed their needs. At the banquet, I made a specific ask and the center received several notes of interest from *precisely* the people who had the kinds of skills they needed. These volunteer board members applied, of course, but application never guarantees a seat. And no one should sit on a board, anyway. Stand, run, swim or fly, maybe, but no one should just sit.

If at all possible, provide a dedicated envelope so that people can drop in a check or commit to become a monthly donor. If you ask for particular prayer or volunteer assignments, pass out cards that slip into the envelope, where people can put their contact information and the volunteer position they would like. If they support advocate development, collect donations and contact information. And if students from the congregation receive scholarships to a place like Summit Ministries, upon their return, have them present what they learned to their class or the congregation.

When your message ends and the people have responded, make a note to let the people know, once a quarter, what's happened as a result. Centers frequently report how many lives have been saved and how many men and women have received ministry services. Members who volunteer can tell about miraculous events they have seen through their work at the center. They also can encourage others to join them. Pro-life advocates also can serve small groups or Sunday school classes. If you want the action to continue, if you want to keep extending your ministry into the world, then understand that congregations need encouragement, opportunity, and recognition for jobs well done for the Kingdom.

The Rest of the Message

Whether your congregation or group needs to be convinced of the truth or challenged to engage their will, you now have two persuasive models to help you craft those messages. The next chapter will help you to pull together your message with other organizational pieces common to all presentations. These too-frequently-ignored pieces play a crucial role in the success of your message. Omit them at your own peril.

When you create a completely sound structure, people will remember what you had to say. And remembering will enable them to act.

Chapter 13

Pulling Messages Together

I see no basic difference between me and an NFL running back. Both of us possess the same physical components. We both have arms and hands, feet and legs, eyes to survey the field, and working brains. But you'll never see me on *Monday Night Football*. Though I have all these attributes, they lack the training and the, well, proper magnitude to secure me a spot on any player roster. My first encounter with a professional lineman would reduce me to a gelatinous heap.

I'm better off playing catch with my grandson.

Similarly, many people labor under the mistaken impression that if you can talk, you can speak in public. After all, conversationalists possess the same basic equipment as public speakers: mouths, lips, tongues, larynxes, gesturing hands, movable bodies, brains filled with thoughts. But I can't tell you how many times I have seen otherwise glib individuals completely implode on the platform. They had plenty of ideas, but they lacked training in how to effectively stitch them together to form a coherent, cohesive message.

As you try to convince abortion-choice supporters to change their minds during a casual conversation or on social media, you can see how the inoculation method works. They make a claim, you make sure you understand it by repeating it back to them, you demonstrate the falsity of the claim by providing evidence, you tell them what you know to be true, and finally you ask if they have any other objection to the pro-life position. You can do that on a single issue in less than a minute.

When speaking with Christians who identify as pro-life but who act like bystanders, you can take a page from the motivated sequence. Briefly explain the problem of abortion, suggest some solutions, and challenge them to act. You can accomplish that in a five-minute conversation.

While anyone can use features of these two persuasion models, you can make the most effective use of them in a prepared message. Speaking one-to-many has two clear advantages over sharing ideas one-on-one. First, it's faster. Imagine how long it would take to speak with 100 people individually. Second, people tend to pay attention to speakers and not interrupt. A message, talk, presentation, or sermon allows for more deeply-developed arguments and enables you to deliver a more comprehensive case for the pro-life position.

This chapter is for everyone who speaks to groups of any size. And if that doesn't describe you right now, read through it anyway. God may use this chapter, along with the preceding two, to magnify your ability to speak to others one-on-one. In no time, you might find yourself speaking to classes and groups. If you currently speak in public, this chapter will help your audience to follow along, make better sense of your message, and later, to remember what you said.

If you've used one of the persuasive models to create the body of your presentation, congratulations! You've nearly finished—but you don't have a cohesive message just yet. You need additional pieces. All effective presentations need introductions that move people into the topic and prepare them to listen, connective material that holds your ideas together, and concluding devices that reinforce the key arguments in your message. Without these additional structural elements, your presentation will lack unity, which will greatly diminish its power.

Make the First Few Minutes Count

I've seen seasoned speakers lose their audience mere moments after standing up in a classroom or taking the platform because they neglected to take the time to craft their intro. They greet people, make an off-handed comment about their kids or a fishing trip—neither of which has anything to do with the topic of their presentation—and blunder into their message. Teachers and leaders who speak to the same group each week regularly give in to this temptation.

The failure to prepare properly is a form of contempt. Don't allow your familiarity with your audience to breed it.

You have from four to six goals to complete in the few minutes it takes to deliver your introduction:

1. Draw in the audience
2. Reveal your topic
3. Convince your audience that the topic is important
4. Deal with feelings your audience might have about being judged
5. Demonstrate your expertise on this topic
6. Let audience members know where you will go in the message so they can follow along

I'll explain each of these in turn, and when we get to goals four and five, you'll see why one or both of these goals might not fit some presentations.

1. Earn their attention

Most people won't give you their attention willingly. Look around the church just before the beginning of a sermon. You might think that as the pastor takes the pulpit, preparing to deliver the *Word of Almighty God*, congregants would sit in hushed tones, eyes looking upward, bodies bent forward, pen and paper at the ready to take notes and advance their understanding, all eager in their anticipation.

Nope.

People look at their cell phones, maybe whisper or chat with a neighbor, some actually read the bulletin. They know it'll take a few minutes for the pastor to get to the meat of the message. Slowly, they slide into the sermon.

Things get no better in youth group, Sunday school, or small groups. People are easily distracted.

When you stand up or take the platform, the first thing you must do... *is absolutely nothing.* Stand there. Look across your audience. Silence has a powerful effect. Wait for noise to die down or for people to shift their attention from their phones to you.

And when you open your mouth, immediately say something that will grab your listeners by the scruff of the neck and drag them into the topic of your message. No greetings. No unrelated stories.

Countless speech books out there offer a host of attention-getting devices, but I will make it simple and suggest the few I think work best.

Startling statements or statistics are easy to devise and can pack a punch. "On September 11, 2001, three thousand people died in the World Trade Center disaster. The war in Syria has taken the lives of over 22,000 children. In 2011, a tsunami rocked Japan, killing more than 18,000 people. Over 11,000 people died in the last African ebola outbreak. These events all captured the world's attention. Many are commemorated annually. Yet here, in the United States alone, abortion claims more lives than the World Trade Center attack, children's deaths in the Syrian Civil War, the Japanese tsunami, and the African ebola outbreak *combined*—every three weeks." Claim upon claim, statistic upon statistic, you build to a crescendo, and when you finish, you wait. If anyone should drop a pin, you'll hear it.

**Focusing less on yourself and more on your topic gives you
the boldness you need to demand attention from your audience.
Never take yourself too seriously, but always care deeply about the
plight of your neighbor. Conviction on behalf of others creates courage.**

Quotations also work as an attention-getting device. Proverbs 24:11-12 has the advantage of connecting to your topic while also issuing both direction and a warning: "Deliver those who are being taken away to death, and those who are staggering to slaughter, Oh hold them back. If you say, 'See, we did not know this,' does He not consider it who weighs the hearts? And does He not know it who keeps your soul? And will He not render to man according to his work?"

Sometimes, using *historical quotations* provides a good way of making the familiar strange, since the language forces people to concentrate. In speaking of abortion, for example, you might feel tempted to use Edmund Burke's famous quotation, "The only thing necessary for the triumph of evil is for good men to do nothing." Two problems here. First, Burke never actually said it. Second, speakers use it so often that its power has waned. But you could use an actual Burke quotation instead: "When bad men combine, the good must associate; else they will fall one by one, an unpitied sacrifice in a contemptible struggle."[189] Imagine how you could unpack this quotation in your introduction, leading into a speech calling the uninvolved to action.

Stories, in my opinion, supply the best way to begin a message. Human beings have a natural affinity for stories. Well told stories, delivered with feeling, both draw us in and take us out. We forget for a moment where we are and place ourselves into the scene described by the speaker. In the last chapter, I told the terrifying story of Sherry West and her fatal encounter with attackers. In chapter four I told the story of Amber, the high school girl with the positive pregnancy test. The structure of these stories draws people in. They want to find out what happens. Perhaps you still want to know (I never finished either story). Oftentimes telling a story as your attention-getting device, but not finishing it, sets up a kind of tension you can relieve at the end of your message. Once you have reminded your audience what you have told them, you can reveal the end of the story, bringing your audience back to the beginning and creating a sense of psychological unity.

The attention-getting device will likely take up a third or more of your introduction. The other five parts often consist of no more than a sentence or two each.

2. Reveal your topic

As soon as you gain your listeners' attention, let them know what you plan to speak about by generally *revealing the topic* of your presentation. In the startling statement or statistics example I used above, I reveal in the final sentence my topic of abortion. Had I used the Burke quotation, the connection seems less clear, so I need to tie the two together, maybe like this: "Edmund Burke spoke about fighting against government tyranny, but citizens also can conspire to do evil by cloaking it in virtue. The existence of abortion—the intentional killing of unborn human beings in the womb—has been sold to Americans as a 'right,' and if good people won't rise up, we, like our unborn neighbors, will get swallowed up in that struggle."

Even in Amber's story, the congregation knows only that she's pregnant. I have to create the link to the topic: "Thousands of young women like Amber, anxious and scared, are desperately seeking answers to their untimely pregnancies, every single day in America. And for more than 25 percent of them, the answer they choose is to end the life of their child through abortion."

3. Show the topic's importance

Speakers should assume that once the audience hears the topic, some audience members will think, *so what*? You need to answer the "so what" question by providing a *significance statement*.

In a sentence or two, explain why people should listen to what you have to say. You might comment on the depth and breadth of abortion: "Every day across the United States, abortion kills nearly 2,500 unborn children." You can explain the impact of your topic through analogies. Find out the number of students at your area high school—maybe it's 250—and put a picture in the minds of your listeners: "Imagine the effect on our community if a tragedy struck our high school and all of the students instantly perished. Abortion kills *ten times* that number every day." Your significance statement should make people understand the importance of your presentation.

4. Use a goodwill statement

In some presentations, you don't need a *goodwill statement* in the introduction because your message won't trouble many people. If a youth pastor speaks on the perseverance of Job, he probably won't bother soothing the potentially ruffled feathers of those students who don't feel especially beset by troubles. But the subject of abortion requires goodwill statements.

When speaking at a church, I often say something such as, "I know abortion is an emotionally difficult subject. Statistically, it's very likely that some people in this room either have had an abortion, helped someone to get an abortion, or know someone who's had an abortion. Much of what I will say may be difficult to hear, but I want to assure you that I have no desire to rip open old wounds or judge anyone. I want to tell the truth to help people avoid a terrible mistake, but also to declare to those who may have already had, or been involved in, an abortion, that there is forgiveness, healing, and restoration through Jesus Christ." If I were speaking at a secular university, I might remove the overtly Christian appeal at the end; but if I had an opportunity to speak later to troubled students one-on-one, I certainly would talk about forgiveness, if at all possible.

If you're a pastor or a long-time teacher and you fall into the statistic of church leaders who rarely or never have spoken about abortion, I am about to ask you to do something both hard and humbling. Confess to your congregation that you have neglected teaching about this topic. Tell them you're sorry for this neglect, because not speaking about abortion may have given them the impression that abortion is unimportant or that it's so bad it makes redemption impossible. Ask for forgiveness and make it clear that you intend to speak out now and in the future to protect fellow image-bearers: babies, as well as mothers and fathers. By making such a difficult confession, you will free many in your congregation and they will see you as human, fallible and humble, but also courageous and determined. Goodwill statements and confessions can give congregants the strength they need to work through their own "sins of the past."

5. Describe your expertise—why should they believe you?

The next optional element, a *credibility statement,* typically explains in a sentence or two why anyone should listen to you on this subject. If you're a pastor or lay leader, I certainly hope that you've earned a share of credibility in the minds and hearts of your people, based on what they know of your character. In other words, they don't think you'd deliberately lie to them.

But few church leaders have particular expertise in the area of bioethics (although if you do, this would be a great time to reveal it). As long as it's true, you could say, "Many of you don't know that in addition to my seminary degree, I hold a minor in bioethics from Johns Hopkins University." Alternately (and probably more honestly), you could simply state, "In preparing for this message today, I read a half-dozen books on both sides of the abortion issue, and I'm eager to share what I discovered."

Even if you lack the credentials to make a great credibility statement in your introduction, you can still build credibility throughout your message by incorporating good quality evidence and reasoning. The more solidly you build your case, the more likely people in your small group or congregation will recognize you've done your homework and think, *Wow, you really know your stuff!* In other words, "I believe and trust you."

6. Show where you're going

In the final part of your introduction you *preview your main points*. In a single, declarative sentence, you reveal the major points of your message in the order you intend to deliver them.

I recommend structuring the body of your presentation first, and then stringing your main points into that preview. "This morning, I want to explain the case for abortion as argued by abortion-choice advocates, evaluate those claims to see if they're true, talk about the nature of the being in a woman's body from the moment of conception, and come to some conclusions about how this knowledge should affect the way we think and act."

Previews make up one of the most important structural aspects of any presentation. A preview helps your audience to anticipate what's coming, track with your arguments as you make them, and gives them a sense of closure. By laying out all of your points in advance, the audience can relax in the knowledge that *you know* when you're going to be done. If you've ever endured a speaker who's "concluded" three or more times, you know the problem.

Finally, by telling your audience what you are about to tell them, you fulfill the first of three requirements of great speakers: "tell 'em what you're gonna tell 'em; tell 'em; then tell 'em what you told 'em." In other words, you prepare their minds. People can do what you tell them to do only if they can remember what you've said.

Keep It Together

Have you ever taught someone how to drive a car with a manual transmission? It takes a while for newbie drivers to get the hang of a stick shift and a clutch. If the car doesn't completely stall, it jerks along from gear to gear. Instead of that smooth shift you hear when an experienced driver sits behind the wheel, you must endure the sound of gears groaning and grinding.

Hearing a message without transitions feels like that. The speaker lurches from one point to another, damaging or even losing the cohesion of the message. A speaker who knows how to use transitions, by contrast, is like the experienced driver who knows when to push the clutch in and let it out to move the car through its gears and create a smooth, seamless experience.

Effective speakers use the structural tools of *transitions* to move their audience from point to point in their presentations. Transitions reinforce what has just been said and preview what's to come. If I were using the motivated sequence to craft a presentation, immediately after I finished establishing the Need, I'd move to the Satisfaction section. A simple transition will help my audience know where I am in my presentation and enable them to follow along.

A simple model for transitions works like this: "Now that we've finished with X, let's move on to Y," or in this case, "Now that you understand how bad abortion is, let's look at some solutions." If in one of my introductory courses you volunteered to present early, and you used this transition, I would say, "That's great!" Your transition accomplishes precisely what you want it to do. As you gain experience, your transitions will become more sophisticated: "Abortion is destroying our nation and our community, but we have ways to work together to save the lives of unborn children and empower men and women to make life-affirming decisions." This second transition still reflects the model—review and preview—but it's better integrated and more artistic than the first one.

Place transitions between each of your main points. You don't need one before the first main point, because you can simply pause at the end of your preview of main points in the introduction and then move into the body of the message. You also don't need a transition after your last major point, because the first part of your conclusion will take over the job of the transition.

End Well

I can't tell you how many speech students I've heard finish the last major point of their speech, stop, and then say, "That's it!" If you have to announce the end of your presentation, you haven't done it right.

Speakers who end their speech with "Thank you" exemplify another pet peeve of mine. If you've done your job, the audience will thank *you*—often signaling their appreciation with applause. If you present a developed conclusion, no one will need to wonder if you're finished. Good conclusions consist of two parts: a *wrap-up* and a *concluding device*.

The *wrap-up* serves as a review in the same way your preview of main points served to let people know what's coming. But while the preview consists of a single sentence, your wrap-up can contain multiple sentences. If the preview is the "tell 'em what you're gonna tell 'em" part of your speech, and the body is the "tell 'em" part, then the wrap-up is where you "tell 'em what you told 'em."

At the end of a motivated sequence speech, you might say, "This morning we've looked at the problem of abortion, some solutions, and how you can get involved." Once again, in my basic course, I'd call that an excellent start. But a better wrap-up will incorporate details of the main points of your presentation to reinforce what you just said: "It's a terrible thing to look at the destruction created by abortion. How it's killed more than 60 million children and scarred countless other people. But even though our culture makes abortion seem unstoppable, we have ways to speak up and act to rescue babies, moms, and dads—all created in the image of God. By signing up for our advocate training, by generously donating to XYZ Pregnancy Help center, by volunteering to counsel and pray, we can make an impact for life right here in our community."

Then pause. You're about to head into your *concluding device*.

A concluding device enables you to end your message in a clean, powerful way. Just like attention-getters, you have many ways to end your presentation well.

You may choose to signal the end of your speech, not so much by what you say as by how you say it: "And if we're all willing to do our part by loving others, speaking out and rescuing, we can replace our culture of death . . . with a culture of life." Draw out the sentence, pause at the ellipsis, and deliver the final clause. Everyone will recognize that you've ended your presentation.

Quotations can add punch to the end of your presentation. You could say, "We need to act. As Dr. Mildred Jefferson—the first black woman to graduate and the first woman ever to graduate in surgery from Harvard Medical School—told us, 'The fight for the right to life is not the cause of a special few, but the cause of every man, woman and child who cares not only about his or her own family, but the whole family of man.'"[190]

Stories not only provide a good way to begin a presentation, they also give you a great way to end it. Either find a story that neatly encapsulates your core message, or begin a story as your introductory attention-getting device and end it as your concluding device. You could begin with the story of Amber—afraid, crying, clutching the slip of paper that confirmed her pregnancy. At the end of your message, after the wrap-up, you might say, "When Amber left the pregnancy center that day, she had a lot to think about. Later, she returned. As she walked through the center door, you could see that she'd been crying. Again, her mascara ran down her face—but this time, her tears were tears of joy. She walked through the door, smiling, her hand cradling the sling over her shoulder, protecting a special bundle. She couldn't wait to introduce us to Anna, her 6-pound, 4-ounce baby girl."

"Why Can't I Just Read Some Messages?"

After a long pro-life apologetics class or a speaker training session, participants often ask me, "So, instead of all this theory and organizational structure, why don't you just give us good pro-life presentations to read?"

It's a fair question. Here's my response.

I don't want to turn people into "speech givers;" I want to turn them into powerful speakers and advocates. All speakers know that the effectiveness of a presentation depends on its context and the people who make up the audience. Contexts and audiences change. Therefore, we must constantly modify our presentations in order to address those changing contexts and appeal to those individual audiences.

Even if I handed you a presentation that knocked it out of the park ten years ago in Detroit, it may not be the message your audience needs to hear today in Nashville or San Diego. Many of the arguments may remain, but the supporting materials—the evidence, testimony, statistics, and reasoning—would need updating. Good presentations must adapt to their audiences.

Speakers don't need to be handed speeches. Instead, they need to develop public-speaking skill sets. These last three chapters have equipped you with the structural skills you need to make a good start toward transforming the minds and engaging the wills of your listeners.

Maximize Your Ability to Advocate

This book cannot provide everything you need to maximize your abilities as an advocate. Joining Toastmasters or taking a good speech class (it should require a minimum of seven speeches or you're wasting your time) at a local community college can help you develop as a speaker.

As I write, it appears as if I will teach a pro-life oriented speech course as part of the Applied Bioethics program at a midwestern Christian university beginning in the summer of 2021. If you can spare two weeks during the summer, you can take these college-transferable classes. There you can deepen your understanding of pro-life apologetics, theology, and communication. I also offer a complete pro-life speaking course with an online practice environment that interested people in your church can take together. You can find out about either of these options at SpeakerForLife.com.

Even if you never had the time to take additional training, if you will simply master the structure outlined in these three chapters, you will become a well-organized advocate. Just getting well-organized will make you more effective than many other glib, but otherwise scattered, speakers. And while coaching can certainly improve your delivery, your own conviction and sincerity will win over many.

Speaking up and speaking out against abortion will protect Christians and those in the world against abortion advocacy. Speaking up about the plight of unborn children and engaging the will of others to join the battle will result in additional voices and more hands to do the work needed to give women and men the resources they need to make life-affirming decisions.

While advocacy should certainly start in the church, it shouldn't end there. Take the time, learn the skills, continue to read and study, and become a Contender—both inside and outside the church. The lives of little children, created in God's image, are counting on your voice to intervene on their behalf.

Still, speaking up is only part of the battle. In the next few chapters, we will tackle the other half of the Contenders strategy: Rescue.

Chapter 14

Equipping the Church for Rescue

Imagine a church whose members effectively resist the pull of abortion-choice advocacy. They know these lies of the Enemy and how to refute them. It never occurs to them to go to an abortion clinic, and it would be unthinkable for them to send someone else there.

People still sin in this church; it's not a perfect place. But these Christians not only know the truth, they also realize that their church freely offers forgiveness toward the broken, including its own members. If a couple falls into sexual sin and conceives a child, that child will not be marked, excluded, or implicated for the sin of the parents. The church will embrace and love that baby. It will encourage the parents to seek counsel, receive forgiveness, healing, and a better way forward through parenting or adoption. Those who've experienced abortion, and who now grieve, find grace. The church partners with a pregnancy help center or clinic specializing in giving women and men the medical, physical, emotional, and spiritual support they need. And the church welcomes and disciples all of them as fellow scarred travelers on the road of life, through a dark and dying world, looking forward to their final redemption.

What a beautiful church! But it will never come about by accident.

Abortion has become such an effective tool in the hands of the Enemy—killing some image-bearers of God, damaging others—that you can expect opposition, arriving first in the form of procrastination. Remember, the longer people know without doing, the more faint their knowledge becomes . . . until their desire to act fades away.

Rescue Begins with Training, a Team, and a Plan

Imparting knowledge and strengthening the will requires action. The sooner, the better. It starts with a church-wide strategy to instruct and equip Christians, followed by partnerships with PHCs. By teaching and doing, we protect believers, create unified, life-affirming campuses, reach out to our communities, and change the world.

Not just the pastor

Inoculating the church against abortion advocacy requires a team. Planned Parenthood targets even elementary school kids. Our culture challenges biblical doctrines regarding sexuality and offers abortion as the appropriate response to an untimely pregnancy, regularly using political activists, educators, and attractive entertainers. No pastor can handle all of this alone. Creating a cultural consciousness that permeates the church requires involvement by ministry staff and interested Christians at every level.

When I began teaching in the Applied Bioethics program, most of our initial students were ministry professionals, many of whom worked in PHCs. Before the training, few of them could make a coherent, organized, and effective case for life (though they certainly could by the time they finished). Your staff has a heart for Jesus and genuinely wants to see the church become resistant to abortion advocacy; but to become effective, they need training. Having them read this book would make an excellent start.

Any influencer in your church can join, get the training, and make contributions. The longer they remain on the team, the more valuable they become. They'll get a lot of practice!

Not just once

A knowledgeable team has value only if you have a plan for moving that knowledge out of their heads and into the minds and hearts of your people. That requires a prolonged campaign of persuasion.

Think about your local high school. Every year, at each level, students repeat the same curriculum. In math, it might be algebra 1, algebra 2, geometry, trigonometry, and calculus. To move to the next level, students must master the earlier material. Why does the school have to repeat the classes every year? Because each year the school gets new students who don't know.

Sound familiar?

Every year our congregations change. Our kids advance a grade, some church members leave and new people come, sometimes arriving with ideas informed by an abortion-choice culture. Without a plan to teach a biblical worldview regarding sexuality and abortion, disaster can ensue. Jill Chandler, executive director at the Women's Pregnancy Center explains: "Many young women facing unexpected pregnancy check the box marked 'Christian' on our intake forms, yet they consider abortion and experience pressure to abort from Christian family members and friends."[191] If pastors, teachers, and other influencers don't diligently and regularly teach a life ethic throughout our congregations, before long before abortion-choice claims find their way in and wreak havoc.

Fortunately, many topics that make up a biblical pro-life worldview don't require a semester-length curriculum. Some can be taught in a single lesson, but nevertheless need frequent repetition to sink in.

Elementary school-aged children can learn about God's plan for marriage and fetal development. (While discussion of marriage lies outside the scope of this book, recognize that LGBTQ+ advocates and organizations are propagandizing young children in libraries and schools.) You can teach children that God is the Giver of life. He values everyone, including those not yet born. Elementary-school children love holding the models of unborn babies at various stages in their development, or seeing beautiful photographs and videos of babies in utero. Later in life, when someone tries to tell them that the "thing" in a woman's body after conception is just "potential life," a "blob of tissue" or a "clump of cells," your kids can confidently respond, "From the very first day of my life, even when I was just a single cell, I was already me. Through all of the changes, I stayed me. God loves me now and loved me then. We should take care of everybody, no matter if they are inside or outside of their mommy's body."

Students in grades 6-8 need a deeper understanding of life in the womb. With parental permission and gender-segregated classes, basic discussions can begin about how babies come to be. Some are created according to

God's design in marriage. Some people get caught up in sin, however, and conceive children outside of that bond. Teach students that all babies are innocent, regardless of the circumstances of their conception. All babies deserve support and protection.

As students mature, teach them God's plan for healthy sexuality. Let them hear the arguments the secular world puts forward to support its emphasis on casual, consequence-less sex. Teachers must prepare to refute those claims and offer a better way.

"Just say no" provides an insufficient response to a secular worldview that portrays marriage as boring and passionless, sexual desirability as the ultimate status symbol, and hook-up culture as exciting. Students need to learn and come to believe that marriage, though sometimes challenging, is worth it, and that the lifestyle the entertainment media sells is a lie. Don't shy away from admitting that sex outside of marriage, like every sin, is often fun.[192] God designed sex to be exciting. Even in sin, the thrill remains. But outside the context of marriage, sin's pleasures quickly fade. Teach your students that the hook-up culture the media depicts doesn't last and can lead to pain, sexually-transmitted infections, emotional insecurity, and incredible heartbreak. Those most invested in promoting a sexually promiscuous worldview also plan to profit from it. This includes not only people in the media, but also abortion clinics. Teach your students to recognize the kind of organizations that tempt people to kill unborn children in order to cover up guilt and shame.

Imagine how you would fare if you only heard important instructions once, perhaps years before you ever had to act on them. And if you failed to remember, if you didn't take the required steps, there would be devastating consequences. Would that make you nervous? We study for exams, repeating the information over and over to make it easy to recall when tested. Never fear repetition; it's a safeguard.

By high school and throughout college, students become the direct targets of the abortion-choice worldview. Teenagers get bombarded with advertisements, television shows, movies, radio programs, websites, and podcasts, all of which advocate, directly or indirectly, the benefits of unbridled sexuality (so long as it's, you know, "safe"). Parents can attempt to shelter their teens from this content, but if their children have contact with other teens—even other teens at church—they will encounter this alluring but unbiblical and ultimately damaging view of sex.

We should show them how Hollywood operates. By casting attractive actors, using flattering lighting, a romantic score, and a plot line that makes virtue appear as if it stands in the way of true fulfillment, Hollywood can make sin look attractive and compelling. It also doesn't hurt if Hollywood ignores morals, replacing them with moralizing characters depicted as killjoys or hypocrites. While movies and television are fiction, the emotions they elicit feel real. Pulling back the curtain to show how Hollywood manipulates teens' feelings can provide an excellent antidote.

Teach high school and college students the beauty of sex as God designed it, and the physical, emotional, and spiritual damage that can result from (here's that word) fornication. They need to know that an entire industry has sprung up to facilitate the hiding of guilt and shame, trying to eliminate the consequences should a sexual act result in the creation (as designed) of another, distinct, whole human being.

Help these students become very familiar with what fetal development looks like, with the different types of abortion, and how each type of abortion is performed. Teachers can show web pages of abortion-promoting sites that describe abortions as "safe," using "gentle suction," and then expose these lies. Abortion is an act of violence that kills an innocent human being. Argument by argument, students will hear all the claims of abortion-choice supporters and advocates. Refute each of those claims in turn, using science, moral philosophy, and Scripture.

Don't shrink from tests. Often, we think we're "training" our students when really we're just exposing them to information. How hard would you have worked in your classes to master material, if you never had tests to hold you accountable? Through quizzes, role playing, and debate (staff can play the abortion-choice advocate) students can learn to defend their positions.

Your students need this information *early*. Don't wait until Sanctity of Human Life month in January. Secular colleges from coast to coast sponsor a Sex Week; many college Sex Weeks have their own Facebook Page. Rachel Minkovitz, writing as a contributor for *Her College* about the upcoming Sex Week at Bates College in Maine, describes the event:

> There's a full calendar of programmed activities, including an a capella concert, cookie decorating, lectures and discussions about myriad topics like anal sex, feminism and faking orgasms, and bi/pansexuality, and sex trivia and karaoke. Be on the lookout for these events in the Bates Today emails, and I'll see you cats around campus![193]

And where there's Sex Week, expect to see Planned Parenthood. At the University of California at Irvine, Planned Parenthood had a two-day presence in 2020, described as follows: "Thursday, February 13th and 14th Tabling on Student Center Terrace, #3 & 4 with Planned Parenthood—sexual health games, activities, and resources (free Heart and ONE condoms and condom case)."[194] Planned Parenthood co-sponsors many of these events.

We're in a war. We shouldn't send untrained, unequipped students into a brutal conflict with real casualties, including both dead and wounded. Abortionists really do want to kill the children conceived by your students. They'll make forceful arguments and lavish promises. They'll expose to ridicule and harsh criticism those students who voice a biblically-grounded view of sexuality. Ohio State's Sex Week featured a workshop titled "Don't Have Sex, Because You'll Get Pregnant and Die: Ohio Sex Ed"—mocking the sexual education program for K-12 in Ohio that focuses on abstinence.[195] If we intend to save physical lives and keep our people and others from damage, we must confront abortion-choice arguments head-on, and regularly. Anything less will leave our students unprotected, easy prey for the ungodly.

More than students need to hear these messages. Many adults grew up in churches that ignored this battle, and, unfortunately, some of them became its walking wounded. They never learned about the sanctity of life, the reality and evil of abortion, or the toll abortion has taken on women and men, both inside and outside of the church. We need to fill that gap. Also, the subsequent call for confession and repentance—so that people can find forgiveness, healing, and restoration—must come regularly from the pulpit, addressed each time the Scripture passage under consideration touches on a related subject.

Despite the pulpit's powerful platform, we must support it with messages in Sunday School, youth and college groups, and small group fellowships. We should offer an annual series of messages on human sexuality that includes discussions about abortion. If your church has a "new believers" class, or a church membership class, make sure its section on biblical sexuality teaches about sexuality, abortion, and post-abortion healing.

Not just words

Words alone will never create a pro-life worldview among your congregants. No matter how much you talk, words will never make your church a safe place for women and men to come and talk about, or deal with, an untimely pregnancy. And if you *only* talk, few people who have abortion in their past will see your church as a place where they can find welcome, support, and healing.

To your words, add visible actions. Speaking about abortion and the value of all human life, coupled with welcoming and discipling people with untimely pregnancies, sends the message that the culture of this church reflects its teaching. Fortunately, most churches have a local PHC nearby. Unfortunately, the ties between the two have sometimes frayed to non-existence. Many years ago, I spoke with a director outside of Atlanta who told me she had 600 churches in her service area, but received regular financial support from only twelve—that's two percent. Other PHCs have robust relationships with area churches, which needs to become the norm. If church and PHCs strike up a real partnership, then the dream of a compelling, life-affirming worldview can become a reality.

What You Don't Know About Pregnancy Help Centers and Clinics

I surveyed more than 150 PHC directors in 2020. I asked them about the *one thing* they wished church pastors and Christians knew about their work. Although I wish space allowed me to print all of their responses, I have quoted some and summarized the rest below. You might expect directors of non-profit organizations to say they wished pastors knew they needed more financial support, but only three directors out of more than 150 even mentioned money.

Many directors wanted to dispel a common misconception about what they do. Lisanne Boling, CEO of The Care Center, represents many of their voices:

> Most pastors who are marginally, if at all, involved in the work of our Center, see us as providing pregnancy tests and ultrasounds and then handing out diapers. Though these are a few of our "services," that is an oversimplification and trivialization of what we do ... our mission goes well beyond meeting a physical need and seeks to meet an emotional and spiritual need as well. We are the Light and Truth of Christ to our clients (many of whom would never enter a church building).[196]

These PHCs help save the lives of thousands of children every month. Real life-and-death decisions get made inside their walls daily.

Directors and staff alike rejoice when clients decide to abandon their intention to abort their children. Staff work tirelessly to support that decision for life by counseling, transporting clients to doctor appointments, stocking boutiques so pregnant moms have baby and maternity clothes, holding Bible studies, and a host of other services. Clinics also try to intervene early, offering sexually-transmitted infection (STI) tests, and while waiting for results, talking with clients about making healthier choices. That way, these same people won't need to return for a pregnancy test. They work with clients who've had abortions, offering counseling, prayer, and Bible study to guide them toward healing. These same staff members cry and grieve when, despite their best efforts, some clients leave the center determined to abort their children. Monumental spiritual battles take place there every day.

Christians and clergy need to see PHCs as extensions of the local church—they lead many of their clients to Jesus and provide initial discipling. But, they desperately need the church to welcome, minister to, and disciple these clients.

Although the church may not realize it, many clients at PHCs attend a local church. Some of these clients have used abortion as a way to try to cover up shame and guilt. Dana Schwiethale, executive director at Loving Choices Pregnancy Centers of Northwest Arkansas, says she wishes "pastors knew the importance of talking about abortion in church. So many girls we meet with are in a church, but don't have anyone they feel they can reach out to, so they feel abortion is their only option, so they will not be judged."[197]

Other clients have been pressured to have abortions by Christian family members and friends. Quite a few sexually active clients come to the center for STI testing. Jill Chandler wants Christians to understand, "Being pregnant is not a sin. A baby is always a blessing given by our Creator. Sadly, many women would rather endure the ongoing pain of a secret abortion than face the fallout of embarrassment and shame from their church family."[198]

As a result, center directors, over and over again, implored pastors and Christians to speak up. This was the most frequent response of all the directors surveyed. Judy Rouse, executive director of The Life Center, doesn't mince words: "I would ask the question, 'Why have many pastors stopped talking about abortion from the pulpit? Why has the function of running a church taken precedence over the fact that 1 out of 4 women in the congregation may have had an abortion?"[199] Valerie Millsapps, executive director of the Pregnancy Resource Center in Maryville, Tennessee, says, "I wish pastors that don't know about abortion and the emotional trauma that affects those who choose abortion would have the courage to look behind the curtain of the abortion industry. Once they do, they no longer have an option but to speak up and speak out often."[200]

These directors didn't limit their calls for speaking out to the pulpit. *All* Christians must speak out. Directors want Christians to learn the truth about abortion and fearlessly talk about it. Unfortunately, too many Christians adopt the culture's values. As a result, most Christians are in denial about just how many of their fellow believers have had abortions. Breanne Hunt, executive director at Lifeline Pregnancy Help Clinic, explains the urgency: "Each day if you choose to say and do nothing, thousands of unborn babies will pay the ultimate price for you to be comfortable in keeping quiet. We may not all be able to do something extravagant, but everyone can do something!"[201] Linda Brown, Executive Director at LaVie Pregnancy Care Center, sums up the problem:

The body of Christ has been complicit in the advancement of abortion through our complacency. I know it's hard to hear, but it's true. I was guilty of it for years. We cannot say we value life and do nothing to defend it. Can you even imagine the difference God's people would make for eternity if every believer engaged in the battle for life? This matter is in our hands! Rise up![202]

Directors told me that when PHC clients do come to church, they often feel unwelcome and judged. I recall a conversation with an executive director who told me that she went to an area pastor to see if he would disciple some of her clients. He told her, "I don't think that pregnant, unwed teenagers would be a good fit at our church." I spoke to a group of pastors the next day, recounted the story, and said that if that if they think that way, they need to look for another job. The church is *precisely* the place where people who have stumbled need to come to gain strength.

How Much PHC Directors and Staff Appreciate Their Pastors and Churches

Much of my survey research provides a wake-up call for the church. But I also asked directors how their pastors or churches helped to equip them for ministry. Many admitted that they would not be running a PHC if not for the influence of godly pastors and supportive churches. Angela Bennett, CEO of SCV Pregnancy Center, told how her pastor led by example:

> One night he told me about the tiny church that he once led. During snowstorms, no one showed up for church, but he did. He was ready to serve. It didn't matter if anyone came or not. He was where God wanted him to be, ready to do what God called him to. The rest was up to God. I have served as the CEO for a pro-life pregnancy medical ministry for 19 years. During difficult times, and there have been many, I show up, ready to serve. That's what God asks of me. The rest is up to Him.[203]

Some directors said that they couldn't list all the ways they felt supported, but that it started with the pastor, who made his excitement for their PHC contagious. I read of pastors who came to the center and counseled with the dads, taught directors how to disciple others by discipling them, and offered simple acts, such as praising the ministry on their Facebook page.

Many directors echoed what Brent DeSaye, executive director of the Community Pregnancy Center, wrote: "It is those pastors and laypeople who have taught the Word and stayed true to it, not bending to the influences of this fallen world, that have best equipped, encouraged and strengthened me for this battle for lives."[204] Bob Foust, involved in pregnancy help center ministry for more than thirty-five years, says directors also appreciate their pastors' prayers: "Brother Al (as everyone calls him) prayed for me and our center by name from the pulpit at least once a month. He also would greet me and say 'Bob, I pray for you because hell knows your address.' He understands the mission of pregnancy centers."[205]

Directors expressed gratitude for their home churches and affiliate churches, both of whom made their clients welcome, provided behind-the-scenes support, cooked for new moms, made blankets, and tangibly demonstrated their love. Directors mentioned small-group leaders because of their regular prayer for the ministry, and how they encouraged other members to support the center. Churches of all sizes received acclaim. Some directors expressed their gratitude for small churches, some of which launched their ministries, with everyone in the fellowship giving and active. Vikki Parker, executive director of Options Pregnancy Center, captured that sentiment:

> When going to war in the enemy's camp to take back a baby and mother's life—it's some of the hardest wars I have fought—I had a church family as well as a Pastor behind me 100%. I don't know that I would have made it had it not been for him and this church. He led and the church followed. I am forever grateful. He didn't just teach me how to fight; he and the church fought with me.[206]

Partnering for Rescue

PHCs are locations for ministry. As the church equips its people to serve, the center has a place for everyone to practice service. Centers and clinics have much to offer.

Connie Wyatt says she and her staff at Wise Choices Pregnancy Resource Center will help meet the needs of the church: "We have ways to give to and help the church, train the church, equip the church, and speak *life* to the church. We desire to partner with them to get the word to their congregations."[207] Erin Rogers, executive director of the Bakersfield Pregnancy Center, adds, "We are the people reaching the individuals who need churches like yours. When you support us with your time, people, or funds, you are giving us an opportunity to funnel our clients directly to your church. Let me speak at your church, participate in Missions conferences, come be a host of a baby shower, give us information about events at your church and we can share them with our clients."[208]

PHCs have a place for anyone who will serve. Jana Pinson, executive director of Pregnancy Center of Coastal Bend, explained, "Everyone in the church—every Christian—has a role to play in a pregnancy center. If you can pray, fold, talk, use the phone, file folders, mentor parents, mop, counsel, mail, sort or anything else, you can support life in your community!"[209] Others added that if you can prepare a newsletter, put on a baby shower, lead a Bible study, help with an event or a baby bottle campaign, swing a hammer, do plumbing, or landscaping—whatever skills you possess—they're both needed and welcome. Consider a short list of ways to serve:

Counselors (and not only women)

Not everyone has a gift to counsel women experiencing an untimely pregnancy, but some do. You don't need a master's degree in social work to become an effective counselor or client advocate. You need only a teachable spirit, a willingness to work, and availability.

Each year as I keynote PHC banquets, I hear countless client testimonies about how they were transformed by their interactions with counselors. I always say, "Just think. If you volunteer to be a client advocate now, next year, that could be you she's talking about." The same is true for you.

And not just women! Many centers have men's programs and have great need for godly men to act as mentors to the young men who accompany women to the PHC. If your center doesn't have a men's program, get together with the director and men in your church and spearhead one.

Tech support

Because they have more than enough to do running PHCs, many directors lack high-end technical skills in computer systems management. They need help connecting and securing hardware and installing and integrating a wide array of software programs. Most PHCs need both technical help and center staff software training.

Event coordination

Virtually all PHCs put on several community outreach and fundraising events each year. They need people who know how to do logistics, coordinate other volunteers, or volunteers to participate in the events once planned. That could be you.

Social media help

We no longer live in an era where an ad in the yellow pages is sufficient. If you're young enough, you might wonder what I mean by "yellow pages." Young people communicate over a wide array of platforms, and no sooner do PHC staff become aware of one, than a half-dozen others pop up. They need help learning how to use the channels preferred by their prospective donors, clients, and allies.

If you confine your social media presence to occasional posts on Facebook, this isn't your position. But if you regularly use Whatsapp, Instagram, SnapChat, Google Hangout, Spike, Zoom, TikTok, or whatever other communication or social media platforms appear by the time this book goes to press, you can volunteer those services.

Transportation

If you have a car and some time, you can provide transportation. Aborting a baby takes only one trip to the abortion clinic. Interacting with the services of a PHC—counseling sessions, ultrasounds, Earn While You Learn programs hosted at the center, doctor visits, and Bible studies—requires transportation that some clients can't access. Check with the center to see if you can help.

Giving

At certain times of life, some people can't do direct volunteer ministry. But everyone can volunteer indirectly. When you give financially to the work of a center, you fund staff who can then get its work done. The fruit of your work transforms into their work. PHCs always welcome one-time gifts, but ongoing monthly support provides the financial lifeblood of a center. Pray about how much you can give monthly; then do it.

Take it a step further. Call the local PHC and find out what kind of items they routinely need, and then make it a point to help provide those things. Most centers need pregnancy tests, STI tests, ultrasound machine upgrades, as well as diapers, baby wipes and other baby hygiene products, maternity and baby clothes. Every Christmas, my family reaches out to our center's director and asks if any clients need Christmas presents for themselves, their newborns, or their other children. We get a list, shop, and then drop off the gifts.

Other support

If you can pray, you can communicate. If you can communicate, you can send a card. Like so many in intensive ministry positions, PHC directors and staff sometimes feel overwhelmed and alone. Send them a card filled with words of encouragement from your family, small group, or church. Describe how you pray for them and ask for their prayer requests. Get on the center's mailing list and keep up on events there. Make the region's PHC, *your* PHC. (You can locate your local PHC at Optionline.org.)

The activities just listed give only a few examples of ways Christians in the church can become a part of the work of an area PHC. Not everyone can become a counselor, but both men and women can help by lending their skill sets, sometimes without ever setting foot in the center. If you don't see your skill set mentioned in this list, reach out to your area PHC director and see how your skills can help them contend for life. Make the call!

What Every Congregant Should Know About Their PHC

"Stunned and disappointed" summed up my reaction when my survey of students at a large evangelical university on the West Coast showed that fewer than seven percent would refer a friend with an untimely pregnancy to a PHC. A shocking 53 percent didn't know where to send them, and 42 percent would send them to Planned Parenthood.

Regularly getting out information about the local PHC can save lives.

Everyone at your church should know, at minimum, the name and location of the local PHC. We hope that few will need it for themselves, but some will, and still others will refer their friends experiencing untimely pregnancies (or who know someone else who is).

I encourage PHCs to come up with what kids call "swag" or "merch"— branded items that high school and college students can use. Maybe it's a pop socket for their phone, stickers for their bumper or guitar case, pins for their backpack, or a branded air freshener for their car. All of these should include contact information or a way for students to download an app. Maybe youth pastors will go "old school" and have students repeat the name and location of their center, over and over. If pastors and influencers will follow a campaign of persuasion, their other congregants will learn by repetition. Whatever the method, make sure they know.

In addition to name and location, make people aware of the many services offered by their PHC. Most centers provide counseling and physical and spiritual support, but some have added limited ultrasound and other medical resources. Others have moved toward full-blown medical clinic status.

To find out what services your local center or clinic provides to clients, arrange a tour for all leaders and other interested church members. Sandra Franke, executive director at the Pregnancy Help Center of the Concho Valley, spoke for the welcoming attitude of her fellow directors: "Come in and see the center." When people do, "they get it."[210]

What Happens Next?

Once the church builds a team and adopts and implements a teaching plan that reaches all ages with a biblical pro-life worldview, they're ready to act. You don't have to wait until everyone knows everything before beginning to partner with a PHC. The centers will help with training.

If a church will do this, then perspectives will change about more than abortion. Congregations will have a clearer view of human frailty and sin, get equipped with strategies to stand strong in the face of temptation, and learn to love, forgive, and restore their fellow image-bearers. In doing so, they will become a testimony to the world.

This strategy does not come without difficulties, of course. Some of those difficulties simply make up part of our messy, complicated lives. Others arise from the tension of interacting with worldviews in opposition to our own. We'll discuss both over the final two chapters, but you will also see how—by adopting this strategy, by building Contenders—we will extend the ministry of the church out into the world.

Chapter 15

Contending in the Midst of Hard Choices

"Wouldn't it be great if every time people in your congregation sinned, some corresponding physical, visible manifestation would follow them around for, say, four months?"

I've asked this question to countless ministry professionals over the years at training sessions. "Just think, as you stand at the doorway to greet parishioners as they exit, you wouldn't have to wonder about the state of your flock. Jim would walk up to you with a bright, green cloud over his head."

"Peace be with you, Jim. Still struggling with envy, I see."

"Yeah, pastor, I'm trying hard to shake it, but I saw a guy at work with a Rolex and, *bam*, the cloud turned bright green again. I'll try to tone it down before next Sunday. Sorry."

Ministry leaders laugh, some say, "that cloud would make counseling a lot easier," but others suddenly become solemn. They think long and hard. They, too, are part of the congregation. *Their* sins would become manifest. *All* of them.

Suddenly, it doesn't seem like such a good idea, after all.

A Quick Word About Invisible Sins

Few sins carry physical manifestations. A lifetime of alcohol or drug abuse can lead to liver failure or other physical problems, but usually it takes a very long time for any visible symptoms to show. Most sins remain cloaked. People prone to anger and violence, for example, may have elevated blood pressure, but it doesn't tend to "show."

For that reason, most sins go completely undetected by other people. We disguise them well. We mask our pride as "confidence" or "assertiveness." We attribute our greed to a "good work ethic." Maybe we routinely eat more than we should and falsely attribute our weight gain to hormonal imbalances. Scripture urges us to confess our sins, in part because many kinds of sin are so easy to hide—and hiding them damages us both spiritually and relationally.

Sexual sin fits into that category.

Pornography plagues our nation. Decades ago, people who wanted to view pornography had to drive to a seedy part of town and slip into an X-rated theater, hoping no one saw them. The advent of the internet makes consumption of porn a virtually private affair, and it can cause immense damage to marriages. Statistics tell me that more than a few reading this book probably have struggled against this kind of "invisible" sexual sin.

A 2016 study by the Barna Group found that 81% of male teens and young men seek out pornography, and 67% do so monthly. Over half of female teens and young women have sought it out, and 33% do so monthly. If you wonder if all of that porn usage affects the pulpit, Barna also found that 57% of pastors and 64% of youth pastors "admit they have struggled with porn, either currently or in the past," with 21% of youth pastors and 14% of pastors willing to admit to researchers that they currently struggle with it.[211]

I don't reveal these statistics to shame Christians and clergy. Most of them feel consumed with guilt and are laboring to find a way out. Instead, I want to show that forms of sexual sin run rampant both in the world and in the church. The Apostle Paul warned Timothy, a pastor, to "flee youthful lusts," because Paul knew that even in the first century (as in all centuries) humans feel a strong temptation to sin sexually.[212] Today, however, these sins can exist mostly hidden, and, as a result, people "get away with it"—at least, regarding public shame. This makes me wonder how some Christian people, clergy included, could ever look down their noses at a pregnant, unwed woman.

I sense that they feel free to do so because *that* woman has a physical manifestation indicating that, at least a few months ago, she engaged in sex outside of marriage. Unlike many men and women who make plans to sin in order to reduce consequences (and therefore sin freely and undetected), perhaps this young woman and her boyfriend got caught up in a moment. Maybe they had intercourse just one time. For many who judge such women, the hypocrisy staggers the imagination. I would worry less about the pregnant girl and more about pride of the self-righteous—often the more lasting, damaging, and even damning sin. There but by the grace of God go many of us.

I don't argue that we should wink at sexual sin. We shouldn't. But the statistics show that we should take the log out of our own eyes before we attempt to take the speck out of anyone else's. Some churches and Christian schools have excellent policies and procedures to deal with sexual sin and unwed pregnancies on their campuses, but others do not.

A judgmental, punish-prone culture might keep a campus looking pristine—no pregnant women to see here!—but in many cases, policies designed to encourage holiness end up driving young men and women to compound their sin.

But What About Discipline?

The Scripture has a lot to say about people caught up in sin. When the religious leaders of Jesus' day caught a woman in the act of adultery (did they set a trap?), they dragged her before the Lord and awaited His verdict.[213] He told them, "he who is without sin should cast the first stone." You know the story: one by one, silently, every man slinked away.

If any sinner in the Scriptures felt sorrowful only because she got caught (at least at first), it was likely this woman. The verb "caught" in these verses appears in the perfect tense, thus referencing her present character.[214] She hadn't had much time to consider the moral dimensions of her crime. Angry men seized her, forced her out of someone's house, and placed her directly before Jesus, who did two things. He declared his refusal to condemn her, and He told her to "sin no more." The encounter fascinates me because here was the one Man who had *no* sin. He had every right to cast stones. Instead, He offered forgiveness.

The Survey

In 2020 I randomly selected two Christian high schools from each state in the U.S. and evaluated their honor codes. What did they say about young women who became pregnant while enrolled, or about young men found to have impregnated a young woman?[215] I felt motivated to do this research by the story of Maddi Runkles, a student at Heritage Academy in Maryland.

After what Maddi describes as "a deliberate failure to adhere to a pledge of chastity I signed at my school," she discovered she was pregnant.[216] Maddi was a model student with a 4.0 G.P.A. and student leadership positions. She confessed to her error in 2017 and didn't try to sugarcoat it. She determined to give birth to her child.

Initially, the school board intended to bar her from campus, strip her of all of her leadership roles, and deny her the ability to attend school events or her own graduation. The board eventually compromised and let her remain in class and attend school functions, but remained adamant in its refusal to allow her to walk at graduation. Maddi went public about the controversy, with her father's support. The resulting media attention caused a number of Christian leaders to consider both Maddie's transgression and the appropriateness of the school's response.

Heritage Academy administrator, David R. Hobbs, wrote in defense of the school's decision. Hobbs tried to clarify that Runkles was being disciplined, "not because she's pregnant, but because she was immoral."[217] Maddie Runkles already felt frightened and heartbroken. She told *ABC News*: "I wanted to go have an abortion because I was scared to death what people would think of me. My reputation, I thought it would be ruined."[218] Maddie knew the school would disapprove. Instead, she told her parents and chose to keep her baby.

Heritage Academy does not stand alone. Compared to some other Christian high schools, the school was downright accommodating. Many honor codes I surveyed either remain silent on what happens when students become pregnant or impregnate others, or opt for vague policies. As of this writing, several schools in my research had harsher policies. I include their names because they make their policies public, and I hope that they (and similar schools outside of my research sample) will rethink their approach.

In a one-sentence policy, Abbeville Christian Academy in Alabama dismisses any students discovered to be pregnant.[219] Christian Unified Schools in California defines "Immorality" as "pre-marital or homosexual sex" and the punishment is expulsion—the same punishment as possession or use of explosives or a weapon, or using or selling drugs—with no second chances (as it offers for other offenses, such as fighting, hazing, the possession or use of pornography, or theft).[220] New Creation Christian Academy in Georgia requires the male or female student to immediately notify administrators if they discover they are "prospective parents," upon which they will be denied access to classes and forbidden to participate in any school-sponsored activities.[221] "Maternity or paternity" is a "Level III" offense at Hamilton Christian Academy in Louisiana, resulting in "immediate referral to the Board for removal from school."[222] Dayton Christian School in Ohio classifies "sexual immorality" as a Level III offense, and implies that such behavior results in "5 or more [disciplinary] points." Accumulate 10 points and the punishment is detention—unless the student gives birth and chooses to parent. Then the penalty is dismissal.[223] And Kirk Academy in Mississippi "has a policy against pregnancy or marriage of students." Students who can be categorized as "are or have been pregnant," or a "known father of born or unborn children" will "not be permitted to remain in school or complete any further work or enroll." Additionally, such students "will be prohibited from receiving any awards or honors of any kind from Kirk Academy."[224]

"Two men went up into the temple to pray, one a Pharisee and the other a tax collector. The Pharisee stood and was praying this to himself: 'God, I thank You that I am not like other people: swindlers, unjust, adulterers, or even like this tax collector. I fast twice a week; I pay tithes of all that I get.' But the tax collector, standing some distance away, was even unwilling to lift up his eyes to heaven, but was beating his breast, saying, 'God, be merciful to me, the sinner!' I tell you, this man went to his house justified rather than the other; for everyone who exalts himself will be humbled, but he who humbles himself will be exalted." Luke 18:10-14

Imagine that you attend one of these schools. What message do such rules convey about the educational institution's ideas regarding grace and forgiveness following confession and repentance? How do you suppose a sixteen-year-old girl who becomes pregnant while attending such a school would respond? What might she do if she got pressure from her boyfriend, a senior on a scholarship who didn't want his name revealed? Or from her parents who don't want to endure her expulsion and the attendant shaming?

Maddi Runkles strongly considered abortion as a quick fix to all such problems. Maddi chose bravely; many students do not.

Such policies drive many girls to the abortion clinic. When she returns to school, perhaps students think she seems a little sad. Maybe she blames it on her breakup with her boyfriend. She holds the secret tight, because confession will most certainly *not* lead to forgiveness, healing, and restoration. Instead, it will lead to shame, humiliation, and expulsion. It may take years before she tells anyone, if ever. Young men often become the forgotten victims of abortion. What may have seemed like an "easy way out" will weigh increasingly heavily on them, especially if they pressured the young woman to abort.

This is not the way.

If we want students to learn to be gracious and merciful, they must have objects of grace and mercy in their midst. I have asked pastors, "When pregnant girls meet with you in your office for the first time, how do they behave?" The pastors tell me that these young women (and young men who sometimes accompany them) already feel ashamed and saddened that they've let down their parents, their leaders, their friends, and God. Then I ask, "How many of you have ever had a pregnant teenage girl come to you with haughty eyes saying, 'Yes, I had sex with my boyfriend, and I'm gonna have sex with him again, and I'm gonna tell all the girls in my youth group to get busy and have sex with their boyfriends.'" Answer? None.

(Now, should you ever happen to find a young woman or a young man with a brash, aggressive attitude toward sex in your youth group, then, yes, they'd have to go. Even then, I believe that godly leadership would still pursue such teens, hoping to lead them to Jesus, even if they couldn't yet take part in youth activities.)

Some schools fear that treating a pregnant teenager like other students would encourage sexual sin among the rest of the student body. I have two responses.

First, surely administrators cannot believe that, absent a pregnant teen in their midst, students would live in a world free from the allure of sexual sin? The media does not portray unwed pregnancy as the sensual side of sex. The media go out of their way to hide it. If anything, students will see that their pregnant classmate:

- likely lost her boyfriend
- has no husband
- will have a child at a very young age
- can't play soccer or run track
- might have to excuse herself because of morning sickness
- is easily tired
- once the baby comes, might fall back a semester or two because she has obligations to her newborn.

Anyone with eyes to see will take special note of all these significant challenges. I will assume the pregnant student repents of her behavior, so her classmates will have the opportunity to rally around her for her life-affirming decision. Should they throw her a baby shower? Why not? If other girls consider a baby shower so attractive that they would choose to endure an untimely pregnancy in order to get one, they have other issues far more significant than being around a pregnant teen.

Second, these policies are grossly unfair. Initially, they're unfair because often the father of the child does not attend the school and so lies beyond the reach of administrators. Even if he is a fellow student, if the girl refuses to identify the father, he remains free. *His* abdomen won't expand; no one will know. But it's unfair as well because it may take only a single lapse of judgment for a teenage student to lose everything she has worked for. At the same time, the research cited above shows that many pastors and youth pastors also fall into these kinds of sins, as do the vast majority of teens at most schools. Nobody gets pregnant while watching abusive pornography. It's easy to hide.

One could argue that the boy or girl with a single lapse of judgment— or perhaps a rebellious period in his or her life, followed by heartfelt repentance—is in a better position than an unrepentant pornography abuser or a serial fornicator who had the "good sense" to make sure his girlfriend took birth control pills. And probably he also had the number of Planned Parenthood safely stored on his cell phone.

The girl who chooses life *will* be found out—she can't hide the child growing in her womb—and, in the cases of schools such as the ones I identify above, she will be punished, shamed, and humiliated. The woman caught in adultery got a better deal. Students who have sex, but never get pregnant or who abort their children, also continue to roam free because they had more skill at covering up their own, similar sins.

A Better Model

Fortunately, a substantial number of schools have found a way to balance godly discipline with forgiveness, healing, and restoration. Christian Heritage School in Connecticut begins its discussion of student pregnancy with the following context:

> Children are gifts from God, so we want to be clear in our dealing with pregnant students that we are not confusing the immoral act with the value of the child (Psalm 119:13; Psalm 127:3-4). We believe in the sanctity of life for both mother and child. Therefore, our Christian community is called to offer genuine support to those students who are facing the prospect of pregnancy and parenthood at such a young age.[225]

Christian Heritage does require both the mother and the father (assuming he is a student) to complete their semester through at-home instruction until the birth of the child. Afterward, students can petition to return to regular classes. They will receive appropriate support and counsel. The students can select a faculty or staff member to serve as their advocate at the school and will meet with this adult for mentoring. Such a clearly superior approach creates a life-affirming environment, without excusing sin. The policy plainly states that if students refuse to go through the reconciliation program the school has offered, they will be dismissed. Both sides give.

Calvin Christian School in California, in its section on serious public sins, explains one mission of the school: "Christian Schools are institutions for sinners, redeemed, but nevertheless sinners. Policies regarding certain public serious indiscretions such as, but not limited to, premarital sexual activity, alcohol and drug use, and others need to be addressed. The policies and administration of the policies should reflect discipline and love."[226]

In its subsection regarding student pregnancy, Calvin Christian School states that "student fathers and student mothers may be considered for continued education."[227] Unlike the majority of policies evaluated, Calvin Christian declares that the students may choose marriage and remain enrolled at the school. It imposes conditions regarding pursuit of extra-curricular activities, but frames them less as punishments than as a reorientation toward upcoming parental responsibilities. It offers counseling and support, involving parts of the students' own communities: parents, pastors, and teachers.

As I never had a son or daughter attend any of these schools, I have no way of knowing how well or faithfully these institutions implement their policies. Still, these last two schools can serve as models for policies that should be in place in every Christian school. Without ignoring sin, these policies are designed to draw involved students down a path of repentance and reconciliation, along the way supporting the students and their children. When younger students see an older student, perhaps with her baby, and they ask about it, students will be able to say, "That's what we do here. Our school is quick to forgive when we admit we've sinned, and we support life, just like Jesus."

When Single Congregants Become Pregnant

Imagine two scenarios. In the first, Molly is a regular, enthusiastic church member. Twenty-three years old, she has faithfully attended church, attends a young singles group, and has many friends. She has been well-discipled and enjoys sharing her faith with others.

One Wednesday night, Molly brings her new friend, Maggie. They became friends eight months before, ever since they met at the gym. Over time, Molly slowly shared the gospel, and five months ago, Maggie became a new believer. Now, Maggie is seeking Christian fellowship, more like-minded friends, and deeper discipleship. Molly introduces Maggie to the singles pastor, Sean, who immediately notices that Maggie is pregnant. She wears no wedding ring, and confirms that she is single.

How should Sean interact with Maggie? What about other members of the group?

Now change the scenario. Everything remains the same, except there's no Maggie. Molly comes in tears and confesses to Sean that she and her boyfriend made a mistake, and she is pregnant.

Both women confess faith in Jesus. Both women became pregnant out of wedlock. If we don't treat Maggie essentially the same way we'd treat Molly, then we become guilty of showing partiality. When new people come to church, even with some evident sin in their lives, we welcome them. But if we have known the person for some time, we feel strongly tempted to judge. While we see the new person as an opportunity to minister, we tend to see the familiar believer as a failure (and as a bad reflection on the church).

If this situation typifies our churches, no wonder we so rarely see pregnant, unwed young women there. Youth pastors speak about chastity and saving sex for marriage because they know that a sensuality-worshiping culture tempts their students, and some of those students become its victims. But if, like Maddi Runkles, our young people believe that confession of sexual sin that resulted in pregnancy will bring them humiliation and censure, they will quit coming—or worse, they will abort their children in secret. They certainly will not speak to fellow church members.

The research on women who have had abortions is damning.

Care Net in 2015 commissioned a study that discovered 37 percent of American women attended a Christian church once a month or more when they had their first abortion.[228] Over 25 percent attended weekly or more. About 65 percent believe that church members judge single, pregnant women. Nearly 60 percent of post-abortive women either expected or actually received condemning or judgmental reactions from the local church. The more often women attended church, the more likely they expressed fear of a negative reaction. As they considered the possibility of getting an abortion, only 16 percent of regular attenders said they talked to anyone at the church. Of those who said the church influenced them, less than 20 percent of regular attenders received from the church any information about alternatives to abortion, and 10 percent said someone at the church either referred her to an abortion clinic, drove her to her abortion appointment, or paid for her abortion. Some 57 percent considered it unsafe to talk to a pastor about her abortion. And nearly half of post-abortive women believe that "pastors' teaching on forgiveness doesn't seem to apply to terminated pregnancies."

These statistics may represent the way some pregnant, unwed women perceive the church, but those numbers describe only the past. We can change those perceptions in the future if we change the way we message and act in church.

While we must call abortion what it is and continue to speak out against sexual immorality, at the heart of our churches we must offer robust messaging on forgiveness and reconciliation. Christians can communicate compassion by doing a few, simple things that show we care.

Church to PHC

Christian leaders at area churches should offer visible ministry, on their campuses, to single moms. Congregations and the community will quickly see that the church supports, rather than condemns, women who have chosen to work through the complexities and difficulties of being a single mom.

Give your people the information they need to help themselves and others. Heartbeat International operates Option Line, a clearinghouse of pregnancy help center locations and other information. Option Line offers a 24/7 staffed hotline at 1-800-712-4357, and on its website *(www.optionline.org)* visitors can also chat or communicate by text messaging. Print the name, phone number, and location of all the pregnancy help centers in your immediate area in your church bulletin, on your website, and in other outward-facing communication channels.

Offer to host speakers and teachers from your area PHCs. Inviting speakers not only demonstrates support of the center's work, but enables the people at your church to get to know and interact with staff. If they, or someone they know, needs the services the PHC offers, seeing a friendly face now will help in decision-making later. People go to those they trust. Planned Parenthood has a $500M taxpayer-funded promotion machine. We must overcome it by putting our center or clinic staff directly in front of our people, with support from church leaders and influencers.

Be open about fundraising support for PHCs, explaining who they are, what they do, and why they are worthy of funding. Hold baby bottle campaigns. And encourage members to use their skills to volunteer and pray.

Welcoming PHC Clients

As you saw in the last chapter, PHC directors need partnerships with local churches so that their young clients, both women and men, can be effectively discipled. While PHCs will evangelize and offer Bible studies, they know that they cannot substitute for the local church. These spiritually curious clients, some of them new believers and others just ungrounded, need a place to land and learn.

Unsure about how to take that first step? Contact Embrace Grace (*www.embracegrace.com*)—it provides everything you need to create an Embrace Grace group at your church to support women with untimely pregnancies, incorporating them into the life of the Body of Christ. It offers curriculum, tools, and on-going training to support a successful launch and continued care.

When discipleship classes, small groups, and congregations welcome clients, it silences the voices telling pregnant, single women to expect judgment from the church. Their experience, and later their testimony to others, will show exactly the opposite. You'll watch these attenders become members who will grow and thrive in their faith and become witnesses to others, both inside and outside the church.

What Contenders Can Expect

First, *expect internal backlash*. Pregnant women often anticipate judgment and condemnation from Christians, because some Christians *are* self-righteous and judgmental. Nothing much has changed over the centuries. Matthew 9:10-13 records a scene replayed in various church contexts for millennia:

> Then it happened that as Jesus was reclining at the table in the house, behold, many tax collectors and sinners came and were dining with

Jesus and His disciples. When the Pharisees saw this, they said to His disciples, "Why is your Teacher eating with the tax collectors and sinners?" But when Jesus heard this, He said, "It is not those who are healthy who need a physician, but those who are sick. But go and learn what this means: 'I DESIRE COMPASSION, AND NOT SACRIFICE,' for I did not come to call the righteous, but sinners."

When Jesus ate and drank with "sinners," those considered the "righteous" of His day criticized. When the church sides with repentant sinners, offering them forgiveness and fellowship, some at your church, sitting in self-righteous judgment, will have these sins of their own exposed. Solid teaching from the pulpit, clear messaging from other leaders and influencers, and healthy discipleship programs will bring healing. Still, some in your congregation may take offense and leave. Be ready.

Second, *expect brokenness*. When Contenders speak openly about sexual sin and abortion, inviting confession and repentance, brokenness will follow. I challenged pastors in a training session in Florida to speak on abortion from the pulpit, offering apologies if they had not preached on it before. I told them to speak with compassion. One pastor took me at my word. At the end of his sermon, he offered an altar call, telling anyone who had ever "had an abortion, helped someone to obtain an abortion, or who knew someone who had experienced abortion" to come forward. The pews virtually emptied and people knelt and wept together over mistakes made and lives scarred and lost. Brokenness always precedes revival.

Third, *expect hospitality*. Of all of the spiritual gifts, hospitality often gets short shrift (along with helps). PHCs sometimes encounter women who get kicked out of their homes by boyfriends, spouses, or parents if they refuse to abort the baby they carry. These women need a safe, welcoming, and loving environment. If that appeals to you, consider starting, spearheading at your church, or participating in a maternity home, or serving as a host home for such young women.

When you read "maternity home," perhaps an image emerges in your mind from a film out of the 1940s. A run-down tenement sits on the outskirts of town. Women stream in from other parts of the state, waiting to give birth to children who get snatched away from the arms of their unworthy mothers. Chastened, the women return home, hoping they can escape the shame of being "a fallen woman."

Nope. Not even close.

You might find a modern maternity home in a neighborhood like yours. They welcome women who choose to parent, whether through single motherhood or adoption. Mary Peterson, of the National Maternity Housing Coalition, explains that more than 400 housing options exist throughout the U.S. alone. House parents—a married couple who model the biblical family for the mothers—staff many maternity homes.[229] Other staffing options include "live-in," which may be empty nesters or single women who provide help and guidance, and a shift staff home, which provides a caseworker in the daytime and someone who answers the phone in the evening.

Some of the mothers seeking a place to land have been kicked out of their homes. Others have more complicated situations involving domestic violence, unemployment, or substance abuse. Each kind of situation requires a different kind of maternity home environment. Some homes continue to provide care for six to nine months after the woman gives birth, while others offer support for years after birth.

You don't have to create a maternity home from scratch or on your own. You can contact Heartbeat International and select its "housing" option, or connect with the National Maternity Housing Coalition to get more information. Both provide manuals and checklists, active social media groups for help and advice, and consultation available either virtually or in person.

If you become aware of someone you know who is experiencing an untimely pregnancy, you can serve as a host home. Becoming a host home is not for everyone, nor for every season in life—and not every PHC offers a host home program. But if they do, and you have a spare room and resources, have taken training so that everyone knows what to expect, and don't have circumstances or limitations that would make hosting a pregnant woman exceedingly difficult, then consider it. My wife and I can attest that we received much more from our experience than we gave.

Fourth, *expect more ministry*. PHCs always need volunteers. Too often, people think "volunteer" means "counselor." But as you saw in the "wish list" in the last chapter, everyone can have a role to play. Many in the church don't perceive that their skill set lends itself to ministry, often because they have a too-limited view of what constitutes "ministry." Once a year, many PHCs have a "volunteer appreciation" party. Everyone, from the person who cleans up and files, to the ultrasound tech, to the counselor, all get recognized for their service and receive a small token from the director. Your connection with the center can encourage others to believe that they, too, can make a difference. In this way, the Body of Christ moves from the walls of the church into the world. When that happens, the world changes.

Fifth, *expect spiritual battle.* I already told you of the titanic spiritual battles that occur inside PHCs daily as they fight for the lives of God's image bearers. If you or your church commits to take part in this war, you will face opposition. As abortion-choice supporters and advocates recognize that the days of legal abortion may be numbered, some will become increasingly strident and aggressive. The Enemy will rouse himself—a sure sign that you are doing something important for the Kingdom.

Undeterred

Don't allow any of these battles to deter you. Rejoice when someone slanders you for obeying Christ. And know that our position likely will get worse before it gets better. In the next chapter, I'll show how the battle will shift after the overturn of *Roe v. Wade*. Some people honestly think that event will mark the end of abortion as an issue.

They couldn't possibly be more mistaken.

Chapter 16

Don't Wait for a Post-*Roe* World

A consensus continues to build that *Roe v. Wade* inevitably will be overturned. From a legal perspective, the ruling is fatally flawed. The U.S. Supreme Court created a constitutional right to abortion out of the "penumbras"—literally "the shadows"—emanating out of the Constitution. But from a political perspective, some continue to believe the court will soon have a conservative-originalist majority sufficient to overturn the landmark decision. However, the 2020 decision in the Supreme Court case—*Bostock v. Clayton County, Georgia*—should give optimistic pro-lifers pause.[230]

Bostock officially redefined "sex" in Title VII of the Civil Rights Act to include "sexual orientation," turning sexual desires into a protected class. It looked like another example of the Supreme Court legislating from the bench, instead of looking at the clear meaning of laws as passed by Congress. Does the Supreme Court have the courage to overturn *Roe* in the midst of a fractious culture? Only time will tell.

Unfortunately, too many people in the United States labor under the illusion that overturning *Roe v. Wade* will bring a sudden end to abortion in the United States. It won't. In fact, nothing could be further from the truth. Worse, the persistent belief that this single court decision holds the key to ending abortion has caused too many Christians to focus exclusively on politics, leaving crucial work undone or underfunded.

Don't get me wrong. Overturning *Roe* would represent a gigantic step toward protecting the lives of unborn children. We should work to make sure that officeholders who share a belief in the sanctity of human life and the depravity of abortion fill the White House, the House of Representatives, and the Senate.

In this final chapter, let's consider what happens if the court overturns *Roe*, what needs to happen both now and then, and why we absolutely, positively should not wait until abortion becomes illegal before we work to make it unthinkable—because we can do that *right* now.

Everything Changes, Nothing Changes

Abortion-choice advocates already have begun to prepare for the overturn of *Roe v. Wade*. And even if the court does not overturn *Roe* outright, a mounting number of restrictions on abortion may amount to the same thing in many states.

But overturning *Roe* will not end legal abortion in the U.S.

Should the Supreme Court choose to overturn *Roe v. Wade,* abortion will cease to be a federal issue and abortion policy will return to the states, where it stood before *Roe.* A single, focused battle will fragment into fifty individual conflicts.

Ten states have prepared for the eventual overturn either by leaving on the books their pre-*Roe* laws or court cases.[231] Seven other states have passed "trigger laws"—making abortion illegal—which will take effect immediately following such a Supreme Court decision. Another two have legislated abortion restrictions currently enjoined by court order, but which would likely become law in the case of overturn. And two additional states have expressed an intent to restrict abortion to the post-*Roe* legal maximum. In these twenty-one states, abortion would either become illegal outright, or it would be limited to instances where pregnancy threatened a woman's life, resulted from cases of rape or incest, or in which fetal abnormalities were deemed lethal to the baby.

Anticipating *Roe's* demise, abortion-choice advocates have not remained idle. Both Washington, D.C. and Oregon have enshrined into law the legality of abortion throughout pregnancy. According to the Guttmacher Institute, eleven other states have codified *Roe* prior to viability.[232] However, many of these identified states, particularly New York, actually permit abortion throughout pregnancy, relying on the slippery "health" exception to grease the skids. Remember that any kind of "health" can be invoked to justify late-term abortions. Vermont, Rhode Island, and Illinois adopted similar legislation in 2019.

I understand the temptation to think that the states making abortion illegal immediately would not require pro-life attention, so pro-life advocates could zero in on battleground states instead. But abortion-choice advocates do not intend to surrender any states at all. They already have begun to strategize their way back to full legality for abortion in all states.

Abortion-Choice Strategies for a Post-*Roe* Nation

In her book *Pro,* Katha Pollitt evaluates a host of potential compromises with pro-life advocates and legislation.[233] She supposes give-and-take might occur around several possibilities:

- reasons for having the abortion
- compromises on gestational age
- by geography (where some states would have legal abortions, while others would not)
- ban abortion but ameliorate poverty
- set limits on abortion to imitate Western Europe (which has a variety of gestational-age bans)
- emphasize adoption

Pollitt rejects each area of compromise in turn. For her, only *Roe* will do—for everyone.

In *Handbook for a Post-Roe America*, Robin Marty, unwilling merely to sit back and observe the current state of political uproar, takes about 300 pages to outline the strategy abortion-choice advocates must take in order to maintain the availability of abortion regardless of its legal status. She complains that since rich, privileged people can always access abortion, fairness dictates that everyone should be able to do the same. And she laments that "most of America is a spotted wasteland where pregnant people live over a hundred miles from care." By "care" she means "abortion clinics," and she labels such areas bereft of killing centers as "abortion deserts."[234]

Stockpiling

Marty's handbook calls for the stockpiling of emergency contraception and setting up a "personal emergency abortion fund" so that her readers can afford the cost of the abortion and the expense of travel to abortion states.[235] Personal physicians will be vetted to ensure they have affirming attitudes toward LGBTQ patients, will help anyone get an abortion, and not report aborters even when abortion becomes illegal. Doctors who fail to pass the litmus test must be avoided.[236]

Organize Politically

Abortion-choice advocates offer two different public strategies to deal with legalization. In states where abortion continues to be legal, Marty suggests several approaches:

- killing "trigger laws"
- codifying *Roe* into state law
- offering sample legislative language
- lobbying to allow people other than doctors to legally perform abortions.[237]

In states where abortion becomes illegal, Marty demonstrates abortion-choice advocates' willingness to cynically leverage hard cases to get to abortion on demand: "Pressuring your legislators to ensure that at a minimum victims of sexual assault will still have access to abortion care…is not just a reasonable action that reflects the majority's beliefs on abortion. *It also offers a clear incremental step toward repealing abortion bans as a whole* down the road, and it exposes just how radical the Right's position has become" (emphasis added).[238]

Abortion-choice advocates seek to get people to focus on the circumstances of conception and completely ignore the human being targeted by abortion. In doing so, they assume that those who capitulate thereby devalue the life of the unborn child in one situation—so why not others? Much of her handbook gives contact information for abortion-choice advocacy organizations.

Create Pregnancy Centers That Offer Abortion

I found Marty's argument for "All-Options Pregnancy Centers" truly schizophrenic. She wants to create pro-life pregnancy centers that also offer abortions.[239] As of this writing, only two such centers exist, one in Indiana and one in the San Francisco Bay area. With the exception of condoms, the wish list of items she says such centers need could have been copied and pasted from any PHC website. She wants the appearance of a life-affirming center—it's good public relations—but she lacks a life-affirming commitment. Nowhere in her description of these centers, except in wish list items such as "baby blanket" where she can't avoid the term "baby," does she ever mention the nature or inherent value of human beings in the womb. Unborn children, to Marty, have value only if the women carrying them say they do.

It will never work.

Most pregnant women will never seek care for their unborn child at a place where, right down the hall, the same center staff intentionally and actively kill children of an identical gestational age. As Kirk Walden, national pro-life strategist and speaker, points out, "while the Planned Parenthoods spend millions on lobbyists, public relations experts and more, the abortion industry can never communicate a message of hope. Never. Pregnancy help centers can, and will."[240]

Funding

Immediately after Marty suggests the expansion of such abortion-choice pregnancy centers, she cuts to the chase and instructs her readers to fund abortions directly through the National Network of Abortion Funds. She compares funding abortions to Christian tithing.[241] Like a good fundraiser, she asks her readers for one-time gifts, monthly donations, in-kind donations, and the donation of miles and points. She also calls for volunteers for transportation, host homes, translation services, and to help minors obtain a judicial bypass so they can avoid parental consent and notification laws.[242] Marty wants to create an Underground Railroad, except at the end of this line waits not human freedom, but human extermination. Her transportation volunteers will take their clients to death camps.

Abort Anyway

The remainder of Marty's handbook discusses "self-managed" abortions, international associations that provide RU-486 through the mail, and other methods that women in a post-*Roe* world might employ to abort their children. She shows how to construct homemade menstrual extraction and vacuum aspiration devices, describes how to use them privately, and shows how to employ drugs at any gestational age to trigger what would appear to be a "miscarriage." And while she notes that all of this outside of a doctor's office is illegal in most states, she not only makes the information available, but spends an entire chapter explaining how her readers can avoid detection by the authorities, as well as infiltration by pro-life advocates.

In other words, in a post-*Roe* world, where the state recognizes the humanity and personhood of human beings in the womb and protects them by law, Marty advocates ignoring the law. Many pro-life advocates avoid using the legal term "murder" when referring to abortion because of the technical and legal nature of that word. But in a post-*Roe* world where no legal distinctions remain between pre- and post-born children, Marty advocates murder in its fullest legal sense.

Other Threats Remain

Assuming *Roe* gets overturned and abortions become illegal through legislation, other threats to the sanctity of life will remain. Euthanasia proponents will continue to press their agendas. While arguments for abortion also argue for involuntary euthanasia, as Gary Atkinson demonstrated, other arguments independent of abortion rationale will arise. Chinks in the armor of pro-life sentiment will be exploited wherever found. The end game of all of these maneuvers is to legalize euthanasia and get abortion thrown in with it.

Pressure likely will come from Europe, where euthanasia already thrives (as weeds thrive). Once the authorities in power devalue human life to the point where some humans can dehumanize and kill other humans at one stage of life, before long we will have to fight the same battles on behalf of humans at other stages of life (or for humans with certain "unwanted" or "burdensome" attributes).

We must create a culture that understands the truth about human life, values it properly, and protects it in law.

A Word About Voting

We can help people see abortion as unthinkable even before it becomes illegal. That said, if we ever want to see a change in the law, we need to see a change in the hearts of lawmakers. If lawmakers will not change heart, then we have to change lawmakers. That means, wherever possible, to limit our votes only to those committed to life from conception to grave.

"But won't that make me a single-issue voter?"

Please. You're already a single-issue voter. Let me explain.

Imagine a candidate in your district who stood right with you on every single issue. (Hard to imagine, I know, but hang in there.) The candidate agrees with you about guns, free speech, immigration policy, welfare policy, road and hospital construction, and with your commitments on monetary and foreign policy. I mean, this candidate ticks every last one of your boxes. One week before the election, the candidate, overwhelmed by the outpouring of support, steps up to the microphone at a pre-election rally and says:

"Ladies and gentlemen, I am so humbled by your support. I am grateful beyond belief for all of the hours you have put in making calls, walking districts, and soliciting donations. I feel that over the last few months, we have become more than a political movement; we have become friends— family, even. That is why, in addition to all of the great work I intend to do to fully establish the freedoms we have all come to expect, I finally feel comfortable enough to tell you that I intend to use the bully pulpit of my new office to extend that freedom to minors. To advocate on behalf of NAMBLA, The North American Man-Boy Love Association, to make sure that everyone can experience sexual freedom, no matter their age."

If you're unaware—and I hope you are—NAMBLA is a real organization dedicated to normalizing homosexual pedophilia.

I doubt I have to imagine your response.

Congratulations. You're a single-issue voter. Everyone is. All voters prioritize issues, and some legislative agendas are a bridge too far, even if you have widespread agreement about everything else.

Given what we know about what abortion is, what it does, and how it dehumanizes, degrades, and kills innocent people, why wouldn't that qualify as a watershed issue? Had I used a reinstitution of slavery instead of pedophilia in the example above, you would have the same reaction. Some acts are too horrible to contemplate, compromise, or countenance. Abortion is precisely that kind of issue.

Don't let anyone put you off about voting for pro-life candidates by attempting to slander you about being a "single-issue voter." Talk with them at length, push hard enough with increasingly vile and immoral policy positions, and you'll reveal that they, too, are single-issue voters.

We Know What to Do

Daily we must remind ourselves that we don't have to wait.

We don't need a president to issue an executive order, a legislature to pass a law, or a court to render a ruling from on high to help a woman or couple in our community to make a life-affirming decision today. Nothing in *Roe v. Wade* or the law requires anyone to have an abortion. We have only mindsets to change, arguments to defeat, and circumstances to overcome.

We can all do that *right now*. To be authentically pro-life, as my friend John Ensor once explained at a meeting, "is to speak up and to rescue."

A church-wide strategy must always begin with prayer. We need to pray for wisdom, discernment, strength, resolve, and perseverance.

We have a strategy. Unmask abortion, speak out from our pulpits, teach the truth about the sanctity of human life throughout the church in every venue, class, and group. When we do, we create Contenders who will take that pro-life advocacy out into the world. Contenders will convince those in the mushy middle, both inside the church and out, by exposing and defeating the shifting claims of abortion-choice advocates. Then we can start encouraging our newly-convinced listeners to exercise pro-life convictions in their everyday life by voting, speaking up, and rescuing through the work of pregnancy help centers.

Contenders in the church will empower more Christians to communicate the scientific, moral, and biblical rationale for pro-life convictions, and exhort those believers to act. Through the actions of the church, we can strengthen and extend the national network of PHCs using the three-pronged strategy of prayer, volunteering, and giving.

We Must Act

In his book *The Wall*, Kirk Walden compares the building of an impervious barrier protecting men, women, and their unborn children from the evil of abortion to Nehemiah's rebuilding of the ancient protective wall around Jerusalem. He explains that if only twenty percent of all families that currently claim to be pro-life—but who aren't currently giving—affirmed their conviction by donating as little as $8.33 a month to their area PHC, our nation's frontline warriors who save the lives of unborn children every day would see their budgets swell by *one billion dollars*.[243] They would use that money to retrofit and expand pregnancy help centers, blanket our communities with a message of hope, and turn PHCs into the very first place people think of sending anyone who comes to them with an untimely pregnancy.

But strategy doesn't *do*. Planning only *thinks*.

We must act.

We must give of our time and our talents. We must give of our resources. We must engage our wills.

We're not playing an academic or philosophical game here. The actual lives of fellow image-bearers of God are at stake. Being a Contender means loving our neighbors as ourselves—including those in the womb.

Pick Up the Gauntlet

The abortion industry, through its advocates and practitioners, has thrown down the gauntlet.

Pick it up.

You have the knowledge you need. Now engage your will to do God's will. Rise up with a group, and if no one will rise up with you, stand alone. Your courage will inspire others to believe that they, too, can make a difference. Open your mouth for the voiceless. Rescue.

Be a Contender.

In Israel stands a wall of remembrance. On it appear the names of people who risked themselves to save those Jews who, during World War II, found themselves herded to slaughter by the Nazis. Oskar Schindler's name appears on that wall.

Do you remember the movie *Schindler's List*? At war's end (and the end of the film), we see Schindler filled with self-doubt. Had he done enough? Couldn't he have done more? This sort of agonizing self-reflection comes only at the end of a great conflict.

History has rendered its verdict. Schindler, a man who began the war as an opportunist, ended as a hero. He saved the lives of more than 1,200 Jews.

One day, the battle over abortion will come to an end, either because the church rose with one voice to stop it or at the return of Jesus, for He will not abide it. I know that God also loves memorials, for the Old Testament is filled with them.

I believe that one day, another wall will rise, either here or in heaven. On that wall of remembrance will appear the names of those who stood up—

gave of their time, their treasures, and their talents—who *Contended* for the lives of their unborn neighbors.

Only one question remains. On the day that wall goes up, will your name be on it?

Notes

1   Joe Maxwell & Steve Hall, "Still-Silent Shepherds," WORLD Magazine, January 10, 2014.

2   Story used with permission from both Jon DeLange and Mary.

3   Randy Alcorn, *ProLife Answers to ProChoice Arguments*, (Sisters, OR: Multnomah Publishers, 1992).

4   Christopher Kaczor, *The Ethics of Abortion. Women's Rights, Human Life, and the Question of Justice* (New York: Routledge, 2011).

5   Francis J. Beckwith, *Defending Life: A Moral and Legal Case Against Abortion Choice* (New York: Cambridge University Press, 2007) 95.

6   C.S. Lewis, *The Screwtape Letters*, (New York: The Macmillan Company, 1948), 39-40.

7   "A New Ethic for Medicine and Society.," *California Medicine: The Western Journal of Medicine*, (September 1970): 68.

8   Ibid., 67.

9   Ibid., 67.

10 Ibid., 67.

11 Some have argued that child sacrifice to Molech did not actually occur among the Israelites. Rather, children were "passed through the flame" in the same way you pass your finger quickly through a lighted candle. Proponents of this view see the rite as a kind of baptism, passing children from the Israelite deity to the pagan deity. This view, however, is completely unsubstantiated. Recent archeological evidence, to the contrary, has uncovered mass graves of incinerated children in known sacrificial sites. Additionally, the biblical evidence is conclusive; some verses do not denote merely "passing," but clearly identify burning a child in sacrifice as the mode of idol worship: for example, Deut. 12:31, 2 Kings 16:3, and Jer. 19:5. The descriptions in this section relied on the following sources: George Rawlinson, *History of Phoenicia*, Longmans Green and Co., 1889, accessed through The Guttenburg Project, https://www.gutenberg.org/files/2331/2331-h/2331-h.htm#link2HCH0011; Patricia Smith, "Infants Sacrificed? The Tale Teeth Tell," *Biblical Archaeology Review* 40:4 (July/August 2014) https://www.baslibrary.org/biblical-archaeology-review/40/4/11; Caleb Strom, "Was Moloch really Ba'al, the Ancient God Who Demanded Child Sacrifice?" *Ancient Origins*, February 10, 2019, https://www.ancient-origins.net/myths-legends-asia/identity-moloch-0011457; and

"Ancient Carthaginians really did sacrifice their children," *University of Oxford News and Events*, January 23, 2014, http://www.ox.ac.uk/news/2014-01-23-ancient-carthaginians-really-did-sacrifice-their-children

12   Mary Elizabeth Williams, "So what if abortion ends life?" Salon, January 23, 2013, https://www.salon.com/test/2013/01/23/so_what_if_abortion_ends_life/

13   1 Jn. 5:19,21.

14   The full text of the speech can be found in the library database at Texas Christian University, https://lib.tcu.edu/staff/bellinger/abortion/Ragsdale.htm.

15   "The Very Reverend Katherine Hancock Ragsdale Named President and CEO of NAF" *National Abortion Federation*, October 30, 2019, https://prochoice.org/reverend-katherine-hancock-ragsdale-named-president-ceo-naf/.

16   "Family Planning – A Special and Urgent Concern" *Planned Parenthood Gulf Coast, Inc.* Accessed February 7, 2020. https://www.plannedparenthood.org/planned-parenthood-gulf-coast/mlk-acceptance-speech

17   Alveda C. King, "Dr. Martin Luther King and the Civil Rights of the Unborn," *Priests for Life*, https://www.civilrightsfortheunborn.org/martin-luther-king-unborn.htm.

18   "Planned Parenthood Statement Regarding Martin Luther King Jr. Day," *Planned Parenthood*, January 30, 2014, https://www.plannedparenthood.org/about-us/newsroom/press-releases/planned-parenthood-statement-regarding-martin-luther-king-jr-day.

19   Emma Green, "A Pastor's Case for the Morality of Abortion," *The Atlantic*, May 26, 2019, https://www.theatlantic.com/politics/archive/2019/05/progressive-christians-abortion-jes-kast/590293/.

20   Terry Williams, "Blessing the Corners," *Ohio Religious Coalition for Reproductive Choice*, October 8, 2019, https://www.ohiorcrc.org/blog/2019/10/8/blessing-the-corners, accessed February 5, 2020.

21   "Faith Leaders From Across Country To Host Blessing Ceremony For Abortion Clinic Providers And Staff" Religious Coalition for Reproductive Choice, press release, May 19, 2020, https://rcrc.org/rcrc-hosts-national-virtual-blessing-for-abortion-clinic-providers-and-staff/, accessed May 30, 2020.

22   Carol Kuruvilla, "Interfaith Clergy Gather to Bless Texas Abortion Clinic and Staff," *Huffington Post*, July 10, 2019, https://www.huffpost.com/entry/austin-abortion-clinic-blessing_n_5d24efe8e4b07e698c42007e?guccounter=1&slideshow=true&fbclid=IwAR0OzigrkuHlW3sQMMN4NmRd6zgGR03Q63AJWY3Im0PkURiicl0YTGJ89nw. Accessed September 3, 2019.

23   Ibid.

24   "Planned Parenthood Clergy Advocacy Board Releases Response to Smear Campaign," *Planned Parenthood*, July 20, 2015, https://www.plannedparenthood.org/about-us/newsroom/press-releases/planned-parenthood-clergy-advocacy-board-releases-response-to-smear-campaign. Accessed February 3, 2020..

25   Ibid.

26   Letter from Margaret Sanger to Dr. C.G. Gamble, December 10, 1939. https://libex.smith.edu/omeka/files/original/d6358bc3053c93183295bf2df1c0c931.pdf. Accessed February 9, 2020.

27 Ibid.

28 "Birth Control or Race Control? Sanger and the Negro Project," *The Margaret Sanger Papers Project*, Newsletter 28, (Fall 2001), https://www.nyu.edu/projects/sanger/articles/bc_or_race_control.php. Accessed January 10, 2020.

29 I'd like to note that the word "conservative" regarding a church or a theological stance has become a problem for the same reason that churches and theological stances should reject the terms "liberal" or "progressive." The terms are too closely tied to politics. I'd like to see churches that currently describe themselves as "conservative" adopt "orthodox" instead, as it is more accurate and descriptive.

30 Heather Clark, "Study Reveals Most American Pastors Silent on Social Issues Despite Biblical Beliefs," *Christian News Network*, August 12, 2014, https://christiannews.net/2014/08/12/study-reveals-most-american-pastors-silent-on-current-issues-despite-biblical-beliefs/.

31 George Barna, "Pastors of Conservative Churches Say They Won't Preach What the Bible Says about the Issues," *George Barna*, July 13, 2016. http://www.georgebarna.com/research-flow/2016/7/20/pastors-of-conservative-churches-say-they-wont-preach-what-the-bible-says-about-the-issues, Accessed February 12, 2020.

32 "Pastors Face Communication Challenges in a Divided Culture," *Barna Group*, January 29, 2019. https://www.barna.com/research/pastors speaking out/. Accessed February 8, 2020

33 Louise Radnofsky and Ian Lovett, "Trump Signs Religious Rights Order," *The Wall Street Journal*, May 5, 2017, A3.

34 Josh Sanburn, "Houston's Pastors Outraged After City Subpoenas Sermons Over Transgender Bill," *Time*, October 17, 2014, https://time.com/3514166/houston-pastors-sermons-subpoenaed/.

35 Michael Barajas, "Why Didn't the City Think Subpoenaing a Bunch of Pastors Might be a Big Deal?" *Houston Press*, October 17, 2014, https://www.houstonpress.com/news/why-didnt-the-city-think-subpoenaing-a-bunch-of-pastors-might-be-a-big-deal-6731686.

36 Samuel Smith, "Georgia Demands Pastor Surrender Sermons After Filing Federal Religious Discrimination Claim," *The Christian Post*, October 26, 2016, https://www.christianpost.com/news/georgia-demands-pastor-surrender-sermons-after-filing-federal-religious-discrimination-claim.html.

37 Barna, "Pastors of Conservative Churches," 2016.

38 As of the date of this writing, we are negotiating with a major Christian university to offer this program, beginning the summer semester of 2021.

39 Jenna Jerman, Rachel K. Jones, and Tsuyoshi Onda, "Characteristics of U.S. Abortion Patients in 2014 and Changes Since 2008," Guttmacher Institute, May 2016, https://www.guttmacher.org/sites/default/files/report_pdf/characteristics-us-abortion-patients-2014.pdf Accessed February 4, 2020.

40 Col. 4:6.

41 Gen. 1:28.

42 Gen. 30:22-23 records the joy of Rachel when she discovers she is finally pregnant.

43   Ps. 127:3.

44   Ps. 139:13-16.

45   Ps. 139:14.

46   Luke 1:39-45.

47   Ex. 20:13.

48   Yifat Monnickendam, "The Exposed Child: Transplanting Roman Law into Late Antique Jewish and Christian Legal Discourse," *American Journal of Legal History*, 59.1 (March 2019): 30. https://academic.oup.com/ajlh/article/59/1/1/5310000.

49   Rom. 3:19-27.

50   Mark 12:38-40.

51   James 2:1-7.

52   I Jn. 5:21.

53   Michael R. Strain, "Beto O'Rourke's Bad Idea to Punish Conservative Churches," *Bloomberg. com*, October 16, 2019. https://www.bloomberg.com/opinion/articles/2019-10-16/beto-o-rourke-s-bid-to-end-tax-exemptions-for-churches.

54   Matt. 10:34-36.

55   2 Tim. 3:16-17.

56   Rachel Jones, Henna Jerman, and Meghan Ingerick, "Which Abortion Patients Have Had a Prior Abortion? Findings from the 2014 U.S. Abortion Patient Survey," *Journal of Women's Health*, 27:1 (January 2018): 58-63.

57   Proverbs 30:20.

58   1 Cor. 6:9-11.

59   Alyssa Wooden. "Why are we having less sex today than ever before?" *The Johns Hopkins News-Letter*, February 14, 2019. https://www.jhunewsletter.com/article/2019/02/why-are-we-having-less-sex-today-than-ever-before.

60   Rachel Goldstein and Bonnie Harper-Feisher, "Adolescent Oral Sex and Condom Use: How Much Should We Worry and What Can We Do?" *Journal of Adolescent Health*, 62 (2018): 363.

61   Lisa Cannon Green, "Women Distrust Church on Abortion," *Lifeway Research*, November 23, 2015. https://lifewayresearch.com/2015/11/23/women-distrust-church-on-abortion.

62   These numbers add up to more than 100% because some students included two or more answers.

63   Green, "Women Distrust Church on Abortion."

64   To get an idea about how targeted Planned Parenthood has been, look at the "brand book" created for them by the marketing firm FireBelly: https://www.firebellydesign.com/work/planned-parenthood

65   Meghan Graham, "Planned Parenthood Launches Roo, A Sexual Health Chatbot for Teens," *Ad Age*, January 24, 2019, https://adage.com/article/agency-news/planned-parenthood-launches-roo-a-sexual-health-chatbot-teens/316365,

66   Phil. 3:1.

67   2 Pet. 1:12-13, 15.

68   Jennifer Kabbany, "University launches first-ever online abortion class." *The College Fix*, October 9, 2014, https://www.thecollegefix.com/university-launches-first-ever-online-abortion-course/.

69   You can find more information about Deeper Still retreats at https://www.godeeperstill.org.

70   Francis Schaeffer, *How Should We Then Live. in The Complete Works of Francis Schaeffer*, Vol. 5, (Westchester, IL: Crossway Books, 1982), 84

71   C.S. Lewis, *The Abolition of Man*. (New York: MacMillan, 1947), 16-17.

72   For a complete rundown of this theory, see Leon Festinger, *A Theory of Cognitive Dissonance*, (Stanford, CA: Stanford University Press, 1957). Cognitive Dissonance Theory was popular in the 1960s and 70s, then declined by the early 1980s, only to reemerge, reinvigorated, in the 1990s and beyond.

73   Francis J. Beckwith, *Defending Life: A Moral and Legal Case Against Abortion Choice* (New York: Cambridge University Press, 2007), xii.

74   Scott Klusendorf, "All We Did Was Survive: The State of the Pro-Life Movement Under President Trump," *DesiringGod*, January 20, 2019, https://www.desiringgod.org/articles/all-we-did-was-survive.

75   "What happens during an in-clinic abortion?" *Planned Parenthood Federation of America*, 2020, https://www.plannedparenthood.org/learn/abortion/in-clinic-abortion-procedures/what-happens-during-an-in-clinic-abortion. Accessed February 4, 2020.

76   "Facts About In-Clinic Uterine Aspiration" *Michigan Medicine*, http://www.med.umich.edu/1libr/Gyn/ObgynClinic/Facts_About_MVA_Uterine_Aspiration.pdf Last revised January 2019. Accessed February 4, 2020.

77   Many medical organizations refer to aspiration and D&E abortions as "surgical;" here are a few: UC San Francisco's Health Page, https://www.ucsfhealth.org/treatments/surgical-abortion-first-trimester. Accessed April 10, 2020; Planned Parenthood's "In Clinic" abortion page advises that both of these procedures are "also called surgical abortions." https://www.plannedparenthood.org/learn/abortion/in-clinic-abortion-procedures. Accessed April 10, 2020. And UCLA Health identifies D&E abortions as "surgical abortions." https://www.uclahealth.org/obgyn/surgical-abortion-second-trimester. Accessed April 10, 2020.

78   *Planned Parenthood Center for Choice v. Greg Abbott*, April 9, 2020. https://assets.documentcloud.org/documents/6834373/4-9-20-PP-v-Texas-Second-TRO.pdf.

79   Dilation and Evacuation (D&E)," *Healthwise*, 2020, https://www.uwhealth.org/health/topic/surgicaldetail/abortion-dilation-and-evacuation-d&e-for/tw2462.html Current as of May 24, 2019. Accessed February 4, 2020.

80   Mark L. Rienze, "Gosnell's Crimes Not Uncommon: Column," *USA Today*, May 14, 2013, https://www.usatoday.com/story/opinion/2013/05/14/gosnell-abortion-murder-infanticide-column/2158421/.

81   John Stonestreet and David Carlson, "The Born Alive Protection Act Voted Down, Again," *Breakpoint*, February 27, 2020, https://www.breakpoint.org/the-born-alive-protection-act-voted-down-again/.

82   Caroline Kelly, "Two abortion restriction bills that forced tough votes for vulnerable senators fail in the Senate," *CNN.com*, February 26, 2020, https://www.cnn.com/2020/02/25/politics/senate-abortion-vote/index.html.

83   Keith L. Moore, T.V.N Persaud, and Mark G. Torchia, *The Developing Human: Clinically Oriented Embryology*, 11th Ed. (Philadelphia, PA: Elsevier, 2020), 11.

84   "A New Ethic," 68.

85   "The Gift of Life," Health Education Service, N.Y. State Department of Health, 1951. For photo images of this booklet, including the back stamp showing it was distributed by *Planned Parenthood Federation of America*, please visit https://speakerforlife.com/resources/.

86   "Plan Your Children for Health and Happiness," *Planned Parenthood Federation of America*, no date. Multiple versions of this pamphlet exist, but the wording among them is virtually identical. The one from which I quote here is an original in my possession. While it does have an address on the back for Planned Parenthood, it does not include a zip code. That would date this particular pamphlet before 1963, the date the zip code was mandated in the U.S. Photographs of this pamphlet can be found at https://speakerforlife.com/resources/.

87   Ibid.

88   Camille Paglia, "Fresh Blood for the Vampire," *Salon*, September 10, 2008, https://www.salon.com/2008/09/10/palin_10/.

89   David Boonin, *A Defense of Abortion* (Cambridge, NY: Cambridge University Press, 2003), xiv.

90   Christopher Kaczor, *The Ethics of Abortion*.

91   Katha Pollitt, *Pro: Reclaiming Abortion Rights* (New York: Picador, 2014), 68.

92   Ibid, 69.

93   David Boonin, *A Defense of Abortion*.

94   See Christopher Kaczor, *The Ethics of Abortion: Women's Rights, Human Life, and the Question of Justice* (New York, NY: Routledge, 2011); also Francis J. Beckwith, *Defending Life: A Moral and Legal Case Against Abortion Choice* (Cambridge, MA: Cambridge University Press, 2007); Stephen Napier, *Uncertain Bioethics: Moral Risk and Human Dignity* (New York: Routledge, 2020)—all three present compelling challenges to Boonin's arguments.

95   Stephen D. Schwarz, *The Moral Question of Abortion* (Chicago, IL: Loyola University Press, 1990), 15-16.

96   Pollitt, 69.

97   Amy Littlefield, "The Day I Learned Aborted Fetuses Aren't People," *Rewire News*, October 19, 2015, https://rewire.news/article/2015/10/19/day-learned-aborted-fetuses-arent-people/

98   See Boonin, Pollitt, or Michael Toolley, "Abortion and Infanticide," *Philosophy and Public Affairs*, 2:1 (Autumn 1972): 37-65.

99   Boonin, 83.

100 Andrew J. Peach, "A Natural Response to Boonin," *International Philosophical Quarterly*, 45.3, (September 2005): 359.

101 Ashley May, "Mom pleads with doctor to resuscitate baby delivered at 21 weeks. 'Miracle' daughter is now a healthy toddler," *USA Today*, November 14, 2017. https://www.usatoday.com/story/news/nation-now/2017/11/14/mom-delivers-earliest-premature-baby-ever-and-chooses-resuscitate-miracle-aughter-now-healthy-toddle/861386001/. Accessed April 13, 2020.

102 https://www.drhern.com/. Accessed April 26, 2020.

103 Susan Soesbe, *Bringing Mom Home: How Two Sisters Moved Their Mother Out of Assisted Living to Care For Her Under One Amazingly Large Roof* (Rend Press, 2018.

104 Schwarz, 17.

105 Not many books have been written exclusively on the propensity of humans to dehumanize others. For a scholarly view, see David Livingstone Smith, *Less Than Human: Why We Demean, Enslave, and Exterminate Others* (New York, NY: St. Martins Press, 2011). Unfortunately, Smith does not include unborn human beings in his analysis of dehumanization, but his approach to the overall topic is worthwhile.

106 Kaczor, 143.

107 "Induced Abortion in the United States," *Guttmacher Institute*, September 2019, https://www.guttmacher.org/fact-sheet/induced-abortion-united-states. Accessed April 1, 2020.

108 Kaczor, 17.

109 Schwarz, 147.

110 Ibid.

111 Robert T. Mueller, "When Male Rape Victims Are Accountable for Child Support," *Psychology Today*, February 21, 2019, https://www.psychologytoday.com/us/blog/talking-about-trauma/201902/when-male-rape-victims-are-accountable-child-support.

112 Neil Postman, *Amusing Ourselves to Death* (New York: Penguin Books, 1985), 99-100.

113 Paul Sims and Jill Foster, "The mother who risked everything to have her ectopic baby," *The Daily Mail*, June 26, 2011, https://www.dailymail.co.uk/health/article-2008476/The-mother-risked-ectopic-baby.html.

114 *Doe .v Bolton*, 1973.

115 Judith Jarvis Thomson, "A Defense of Abortion," Philosophy & Public Affairs, 1.1 (Fall 1971) transcript accessed at University of Colorado, Boulder's website: https://spot.colorado.edu/~heathwoo/Phil160,Fall02/thomson.htm.

116 Thomson's argument has been through a number of amendments and versions, and it's not the goal of this book to address them all. Those interested in a detailed refutation of all of Thomson's work can find it in Christopher Kaczor's book *The Ethics of Abortion* in Chapter 7, "Is it Wrong to Abort A Person?" and, from a slightly different perspective in Francis J. Beckwith's book *Defending Life*, also in Chapter 7, "Does It Really Matter Whether the Unborn Is a Moral Subject? The Case from Bodily Rights."

117 Kaczor, 166.

118 Thomson, n.p.

119 Kaczor, 173.

120   Ashley McGuire, "Cultivating a Pro-Adoption Culture," *Institute for Family Studies*, June 17, 2019. https://ifstudies.org/blog/cultivating-a-pro-adoption-culture.

121   Ruth Graham, "Choosing Life with Down Syndrome," *Slate*, May 31, 2018, https://slate.com/human-interest/2018/05/how-down-syndrome-is-redefining-the-abortion-debate.html.

122   Heidi L. Lindh, Robin Steele, Jane Page-Steiner, and Alan E. Donnenfeld, "Characteristics and perspectives of families waiting to adopt a child with Down syndrome," *Genetics in Medicine*, (May 2007) https://www.nature.com/articles/gim200741

123   See Anna Higgins, "Sex-Selection Abortion: The Real War on Women," *Charlotte Lozier Institute: American Reports Series*, Issue 11, April 2016, https://s27589.pcdn.co/wp-content/uploads/2016/04/Higgins-Sex-Selective-Abortion-paper_April12_FINAL_April122016_-1.pdf

124   "Banning Abortions in Cases of Race or Sex Selection or Fetal Anomaly," *The Guttmacher Institute*, January 2020, https://www.guttmacher.org/evidence-you-can-use/banning-abortions-cases-race-or-sex-selection-or-fetal-anomaly.

125   "Population Bomb" Fandom, *Captain Planet and the Planeteers Wiki*, https://captainplanet.fandom.com/wiki/Population_Bomb, accessed May 1, 2020.

126   Jacqueline Kasun, *The War Against Population: The Economics and Ideology of World Population Control* (San Francisco, CA: Ignatius Press, 1999).

127   Emiko Jozuka, Jessie Yeung, and Jake Kwon, "Japan's birth rate hits another record low in 2019," *CNN*, December 29, 2019, https://www.cnn.com/2019/12/25/asia/japan-birthrate-hnk-intl/index.html.

128   See Gilda Sedgh 2012 "Induced Abortion Incidence and Trends Worldwide From 1995 to 2008," *The Lancet* 379 (2012): 625-632; Gilda Sedgh, "Abortion Incidence Between 1990 and 2014: Global, Regional, and Subregional Levels and Trends." *The Lancet* 388 (2016): 258-267; and Susheela Singh, Lisa Remez, Gilda Sedgh, Lorraine Kwok, and Tsuyoshi Onda, "Abortion Worldwide 2017: Uneven Progress and Unequal Access," *Guttmacher Institute*, 2018, https://www.guttmacher.org/report/abortion-worldwide-2017.

129   Michael J. New, "How the Legal Status of Abortion Impacts Abortion Rates," *Charlotte Lozier Institute*, May 23, 2018. https://lozierinstitute.org/how-the-legal-status-of-abortion-impacts-abortion-rates/7.

130   Phillip B. Levine and Douglas Staiger, "Abortion Policy and Fertility Outcomes: The Eastern European Experience," *Journal of Law and Economics* (April 2004): 238, 240, https://www.dartmouth.edu/~dstaiger/Papers/2004/LevineStaiger%20JLE%202004.pdf.

131   Ibid, 236.

132   Phillip B. Levine, Douglas Staiger, Thomas J. Kane, and David J. Zimmerman, "*Roe v. Wade* and American Fertility," *The National Bureau of Economic Research*, Working Paper No. 5615 (June 1996): 15, https://www.nber.org/papers/w5615.pdf

133   Theodore Joyce, Robert Kaestner, and Silvie Coleman, "*Changes in Abortions and Births and the Texas Parental Notification Law*," New England Journal of Medicine (March 9, 2006), https://www.nejm.org/doi/full/10.1056/nejmsa054047

134   Patt Morrison, "The coat hanger, symbol of dangerous, pre-Roe abortions, is back," *Los Angeles Times*, March 25, 2014, https://www.latimes.com/opinion/la-xpm-2014-mar-25-la-ol-the-coat-hanger-symbol-of-dangerous-preroe-abortions-is-back-20140324-story.html.

135   Bernard Nathanson, *Aborting America* (New York: Doubleday, 1979), 193.

136   Bernard Nathanson, *The Abortion Papers: Inside the Abortion Mentality* (New York: Frederick Fell Publishers, 1983), 41-42.

137   Ibid., 42.

138   Mary Calderone, "Illegal Abortion as a Public Health Problem," *American Journal of Public Health*, 50.7 (July 1960): 949. https://www.ncbi.nlm.nih.gov/pmc/articles/PMC1373382/pdf/amjphnation00308-0022.pdf

139   DA Grimes, ME Kafrissen, K.R. O'Reilly, and NJ Binkin, "Fatal hemorrhage from legal abortion in the United States," *Surgery, Gynecology, and Obstetrics*, 157:5 (November 1983): 461-466. https://www.ncbi.nlm.nih.gov/pubmed/6314567.

140   Bill Clinton, "Abortion Rights and Medical Research Orders," transcript at *C-SPAN*.org, January 22, 1993. https://www.c-span.org/video/?37335-1/abortion-rights-medical-research-orders

141   Caitlin Flanagan, "Losing the Rare in 'Safe, Legal and Rare,'" *The Atlantic*, December 6, 2019. https://www.theatlantic.com/ideas/archive/2019/12/the-brilliance-of-safe-legal-and-rare/603151/

142   See Marie Sollis, "Tulsi Gabbard's Stance on Abortion Stuck in the '90s," Vice, October 16, 2019. https://www.vice.com/en_us/article/43k5db/tulsi-gabbards-stance-on-abortion-is-stuck-in-the-90s; Mallory McMaster, "The Only 'Extreme' Abortion Position is One Taking Away Access to Health Care," *Rewire.News*, October 18, 2019. https://rewire.news/article/2019/10/18/the-only-extreme-abortion-position-is-one-taking-away-access-to-health-care/; and Christina Cauterucci, "Abortion Might Finally Be a Winning Issue for Democrats," Slate, November 27, 2019, https://slate.com/news-and-politics/2019/11/democrats-are-unabashedly-supporting-abortion-rights-voters-are-too.html

143   Eliana Dockterman, "Leana Wen Wants to Have a More Nuanced Conversation About Abortion," *Time*, October 17, 2019. https://time.com/5703575/leana-wen-abortion-safe-legal-rare/.

144   Constance Grady, "Michelle Williams used her Golden Globes speech to celebrate a woman's right to choose," *Vox*, January 5, 2020. https://www.vox.com/culture/2020/1/5/21051186/watch-michelle-williams-golden-globes-2020-acceptance-speech-abortion-rights-choice.

145   The Busy Philipps' rally speech is embedded into a *Faithwire* YouTube episode, March 5, 2020, beginning at 35 seconds in: https://www.youtube.com/watch?v=cg3oqIi8xoY.

146   Christina Capatides. "Busy Philipps testifies before Congress on abortion and threats to Americans' reproductive rights," *CBS News*, June 4, 2019, https://www.cbsnews.com/news/busy-philipps-testifies-before-congress-on-abortion-threats-to-americans-reproductive-rights/.

147   *Shout Your Abortion* homepage, https://shoutyourabortion.com/.

148   Heather Wood Rudolph, "Why I Filmed My Abortion," *Cosmopolitan*, May 3, 2014, https://www.cosmopolitan.com/politics/a6674/why-i-filmed-my-abortion/.

149 Ibid.

150 Jessica Valenti, "Free Abortions on Demand and Without Apology," *The Nation*, August 27, 2013, https://www.thenation.com/article/archive/free-abortions-demand-without-apology/.

151 Meghan Murphy, "Mary Lou Singleton: 'We need to go back to rallying for abortion on demand without apology,'" *Feminist Current*, September 8, 2017, https://www.feministcurrent.com/2017/09/08/mary-lou-singleton-need-go-back-rallying-abortion-demand-without-apology/.

152 Maria Sollis, "I Learned How to Do an Abortion on a Papaya," *Vice*, July 24, 2019, https://www.vice.com/en_us/article/3k334w/how-to-do-an-abortion-with-manual-vacuum-aspiration-papaya-workshop0.

153 Ibid.

154 Ibid.

155 Ibid.

156 "Governor Cuomo Directs One World Trade Center and Other Landmarks to be Lit in Pink to Celebrate Signing of the Reproductive Health Act," posted on Gov. Cuomo's official webpage, January 22, 2019, https://www.governor.ny.gov/news/governor-cuomo-directs-one-world-trade-center-and-other-landmarks-be-lit-pink-celebrate-signing.

157 Sarah Rankin, "Gov. Northam signs Virginia Reproductive Health Protection Act," *WHSV* News, April 10, 2020, https://www.whsv.com/content/news/Gov-Northam-signs-Virginia-Reproductive-Health-Protection-Act-569544401.html.

158 Susan Milligan, "Oregon Passes Law Protecting Abortion and Reproductive Rights," *U.S. News and World Report*, August 15, 2017, https://www.usnews.com/news/national-news/articles/2017-08-15/oregon-passes-law-protecting-abortion-and-reproductive-rights.

159 Ibid.

160 Paglia, "Fresh Blood for the Vampire."

161 Ibid.

162 "A New Ethic," 68.

163 Ibid.

164 Mary Elizabeth Williams, "So what if abortion ends life?" *Salon*, January 23, 2013, https://www.salon.com/test/2013/01/23/so_what_if_abortion_ends_life/

165 Paglia, "Fresh Blood for the Vampire."

166 Jerry Coyne, "Should one be allowed to euthanize severely deformed or doomed newborns?" *Why Evolution is True*, July 13, 2017, https://whyevolutionistrue.wordpress.com/2017/07/13/should-one-be-allowed-to-euthanize-severely-deformed-or-doomed-newborns/

167 lberto Giubilini and Francesca Minerva, "After-Birth Abortion: Why Should the Baby Live?" *Journal of Medical Ethics*, 39 (2013): 261-263.

168 Ibid., 262.

169 Ibid., 261.

170 Ibid., 262.

171 Ibid., 263.

172 Gary M. Atkinson, "The Morality of Abortion," *International Philosophical Quarterly*, 14.2 (September 1974): 353.

173 Ibid., 361.

174 Ibid., 361.

175 Ibid., 362.

176 Jose Pereira, "Legalizing euthanasia or assisted suicide: the illusion of safeguards and controls," *Current Oncology*, 18.2 (April 2011), https://www.ncbi.nlm.nih.gov/pmc/articles/PMC3070710/.

177 Raphael Cohen-Almagor, "First do no harm: intentionally shortening lives of patients without their explicit request in Belgium," *Journal of Medical Ethics*, 41 (2015): 625-629.

178 Andrea Peyser, "Terminally ill mom denied treatment coverage—but gets suicide drug approved," *New York Post*, October 24, 2016, https://nypost.com/2016/10/24/terminally-ill-mom-denied-treatment-coverage-but-gets-suicide-drugs-approved/.

179 Jennifer Rankin, "Netherlands euthanasia case: doctor 'acted with best intentions'" *The Guardian*, August 26, 2019, https://www.theguardian.com/world/2019/aug/26/doctor-on-trial-landmark-euthanasia-case-netherlands-dementia.

180 Prov. 8:17.

181 For the truly interested, the roots of Inoculation Theory can be found here: William E. McGuire and Demitrios Papageorgis, "The Relative Efficacy of Various Types of Prior Belief-Defense in Producing Immunity Against Persuasion," *Journal of Abnormal and Social Psychology*, 62 (1961):327-337, , and Demitrios Papageorgis and William E. McGuire, "The Generality of Immunity to Persuasion Produced by Pre-exposure to Weakened Counter Arguments," *Journal of Abnormal and Social Psychology*, 62 (1961):475-481.

182 C.S. Lewis, *The Screwtape Letters*, (New York: The Macmillan Company, 1950), 70.

183 1 Pet. 3:1

184 PMichael McKensie, "When Good Men Do Nothing: Reflections from a Modern-Day Bürgermeister," *The Silent Subject*, ed. Brad Stetson, West Port, CN: Praeger Publishers, 1996), 161.

185 Alan H. Monroe, *Monroe's Principles of Speech*, military ed., (Chicago: Scott, Foresman, 1943).

186 Tom Watkins, Nick Valencia, and Phil Gast, *CNN*, March 23, 2013, https://www.cnn.com/2013/03/22/us/georgia-baby-killed/index.html

187 Bob Greene, "The Duty to Bear Witness to Brutality," *The Wall Street Journal*, April 3, 2020, https://www.wsj.com/articles/the-duty-to-bear-witness-to-brutality-11585953404

188 Ibid.

189 Edmund Burke, *Thoughts on the Cause of the Present Discontent*s, Sixth Edition, (Dodsley, 1784), https://oll.libertyfund.org/titles/796#Burke_0005-01_336

190   Dave Andrusco, "Pro-Life Perspectives: 'Black Pro-Life Pioneers—Mildred Jefferson,'" *NRL News Today*, February 3, 2012, https://www.nationalrighttolifenews.org/2012/02/pro-life-perspectives-black-pro-life-pioneers-mildred-jefferson/.

191   Personal email correspondence in reply to survey, May 8, 202.

192   Hebrews 11:25 describes Moses choosing to suffer with his people rather than continuing to enjoy "the passing pleasures of sin." Proverbs 7:6-23 provides a valuable look at the progression of sexual sin. It doesn't hold back. It portrays flirting and seduction as exciting and hard to resist. But it doesn't skimp on the outcome. At many junctures, the young man has a chance to get away, but doesn't. The best advice is not to put yourself in a place to be tempted.

193   Rachel Minkovitz, "Sex Week 2018," *Her Campus*, March 3, 2018, https://www.hercampus.com/school/bates/sex-week-2018.

194   "Sex Week—Click Descriptions for Event Listings," UCI Center for Student Wellness & Health Promotion webpage, https://studentwellness.uci.edu/event/sex-week, accessed May 22, 2020.

195   "Sex Week at OSU," Department of Women's, Gender and Sexuality Studies webpage, https://wgss.osu.edu/events/sex-week-osu, accessed May 22, 2020.

196   Personal email correspondence in reply to survey, May 8, 2020.

197   Personal email correspondence in reply to survey, May 8, 2020.

198   Personal email correspondence in reply to survey, May 8, 2020.

199   Personal email correspondence in reply to survey, April 29, 2020.

200   Personal email correspondence in reply to survey, April 27, 2020.

201   Personal email correspondence in reply to survey, April 28, 2020.

202   Personal email correspondence in reply to survey, April 30, 2020.

203   Personal email correspondence in reply to survey, May19, 2020.

204   Personal email correspondence in reply to survey, May 20, 2020.

205   Personal email correspondence in reply to survey, May 19, 2020.

206   Personal email correspondence in reply to survey, May 19, 2020.

207   Personal email correspondence in reply to survey, May 7, 2020.

208   Personal email correspondence in reply to survey, May 7, 2020.

209   Personal email correspondence in reply to survey, April 29, 2020.

210   Personal email correspondence in reply to survey, May 7, 2020.

211   "The Porn Phenomenon," *Barna*, February 5, 2016, https://www.barna.com/the-porn-phenomenon/

212   2 Tim. 2:22.

213   Jn. 8:2-11.

214   David Guzik, "Study Guide for John 8," *Blue Letter Bible*, https://www.blueletterbible.org/Comm/guzik_david/StudyGuide2017-Jhn/Jhn-8.cfm

215   The information in the following student handbooks were current as of the time *Contenders* went to press. I began to look at Christian colleges and universities as well, but quickly discovered that since most of them receive Title IX funding from the federal government, they are prohibited from discriminating against people on account of, among other things, pregnancy. They have mission statements and "expectations," but few in the survey had any enforcement mechanismsm.

216   Madeline Runkles, "I got pregnant. I chose to keep my baby. And my Christian school humiliated me," *Chicago Tribune*, June 1, 2017, https://webcache.googleusercontent.com/search?q=cache:XSu84lfTQaAJ:https://www.chicagotribune.com/opinion/commentary/ct-pregnant-teen-christian-school-20170601-story.html+&cd=21&hl=en&ct=clnk&gl=us

217   Meg Storm, "Christian School Not Backing Down From Decision to Discipline Pregnant Student Who Broke School Policy," *Faithwire*, May 25, 2017, https://www.faithwire.com/2017/05/25/christian-school-not-backing-down-from-decision-to-discipline-pregnant-student-who-broke-school-policy/.

218   David Wright and Sally Hawkins, "A pregnant teen in a class by herself," *ABC News*, June 30, 2017, https://abcnews.go.com/US/pregnant-teen-class/story?id=48361156.

219   *Abbeville Christian Academy 2018-19 Student Handbook*, 19, https://drive.google.com/file/d/1mOriUosX_wG1sFJEkq2XXwclow3ALy4u/view, accessed May 27, 2020.

220   *Christian Jr./Sr. High School Student Handbook 2019-2020,* Christian Unified Schools http://www.christianunified.org/docs/default-source/jr-sr-high-school-documents/cjhschsstudent-handbook.pdf?sfvrsn=30, accessed May 27, 2020.

221   *New Creation Christian Academy 2019-2020 Parent-Student Handbook*, 29, http://www.nccacademy.net/editoruploads/files/Forms/2019/Student%20Handbook%202019-2020%20Shannon%20120219.pdf, accessed May 27, 202.

222   *Hamilton Christian School 2020-2021 Parent/Student Handbook,* 13-14, https://static1.squarespace.com/static/5e5d8497b57717596a59475b/t/5ec54e86b9ee044b80cd79c1/1589989001011/2020+-+2021+Parent-Student+Handbook.pdf, accessed May 27, 2020.

223   *Dayton Christian School Parent/Student Handbook 2019-2020*, 39, 41, https://30lx324b9sdj3re6rq3raiif-wpengine.netdna-ssl.com/wp-content/uploads/2020/03/2019-2020-Parent-Student-Handbook.pdf, accessed May 27,2020.

224   *Kirk Academy 2019-2020 Junior High and High School Handbook*, 35, https://www.kirkacademy.com/sites/default/files/ka_student_handbook_2019-2020.pdf, accessed May 27, 2020.

225   *Christian Heritage School 2019-2020 Upper School Handbook Grades 6-12*, 23, https://www.kingsmen.org/editoruploads/files/2019.2020/US%20%20Handbook%202019%20-%202020_11_12_19.pdf, accessed May 27, 2020.

226   *Calvin Christian School High School Handbook for Parents and Students 2017-2018*, 18, https://www.calvinchristianescondido.org/HIGH_SCHOOLHANDBOOK__immunization_update_October_2017.pdf, accessed May 27, 2020. This was the most recent handbook link available through the Parents Central part of the school's site, as of the date of access.

227   Ibid., 19.

228   All results in this paragraph are taken from "Study of Women who have had an Abortion and Their Views on Church," LifeWay Research, conducted May 6-13, 2015, http://lifewayresearch.com/wp-content/uploads/2015/11/Care-Net-Final-Presentation-Report-Revised.pdf, accessed January 15, 2020.

229   Personal interview and email exchange, June 17, 2020. For more information, contact the National Maternity Housing Coalition at www.natlhousingcoalition.org.

230   *Bostok v. Clayton County, Georgia, 2020.*

231   The figures are extrapolated from "Abortion Policy in the Absence of *Roe*," *Guttmacher Institute*, May 15, 2020, https://www.guttmacher.org/state-policy/explore/abortion-policy-absence-roe, accessed May 31, 2020.

232   Ibid.

233   Pollitt, 171-191.

234   Robin Marty, *Handbook for a Post-Roe America*, (New York: Seven Stories Press, 2019), 11.

235   Ibid., 31-41.

236   Ibid., 41-42.

237   Ibid., 42-45.

238   Ibid., 51.

239   Ibid., 64-66.

240   Kirk Walden, *The Wall*, (Nashville, TN: LifeTrends, 2013), 77.

241   Marty, 69.

242   Ibid., 70-73.

243   Walden., 9.

Scripture Index

Index

W

Y

About the Author

Dr. Marc Newman, president of Speaker for Life, galvanizes Christian leaders into advocates and champions for the unborn. Marc has trained thousands of speakers nationwide in communication skills and apologetics. Energetic and compelling on the platform, Marc keynotes banquets each year to raise millions of dollars for pregnancy help centers and clinics.

A former Director of Speech and Debate at the University of California, Irvine, he's been a professor at both Palomar College and Regent University, teaching public speaking, debate, and the persuasive power of popular culture. He's appeared on *Fox News* and in *Time* magazine for his insights into the meaning behind movies. Marc's new book, *Mistletoe Movies: How Hallmark Christmas Films Speak to the Longings in Your Heart*, will be available in late 2020.

Have Dr. Newman Speak At Your Next Event

Church · Event · Conference · Fundraising Banquet

To book Dr. Newman to speak or for more information about training, go to:

www.speakerforlife.com

Made in the USA
Monee, IL
24 November 2021

82740132R00154